IMAGES
of America

AFRICAN AMERICANS IN MERCER COUNTY

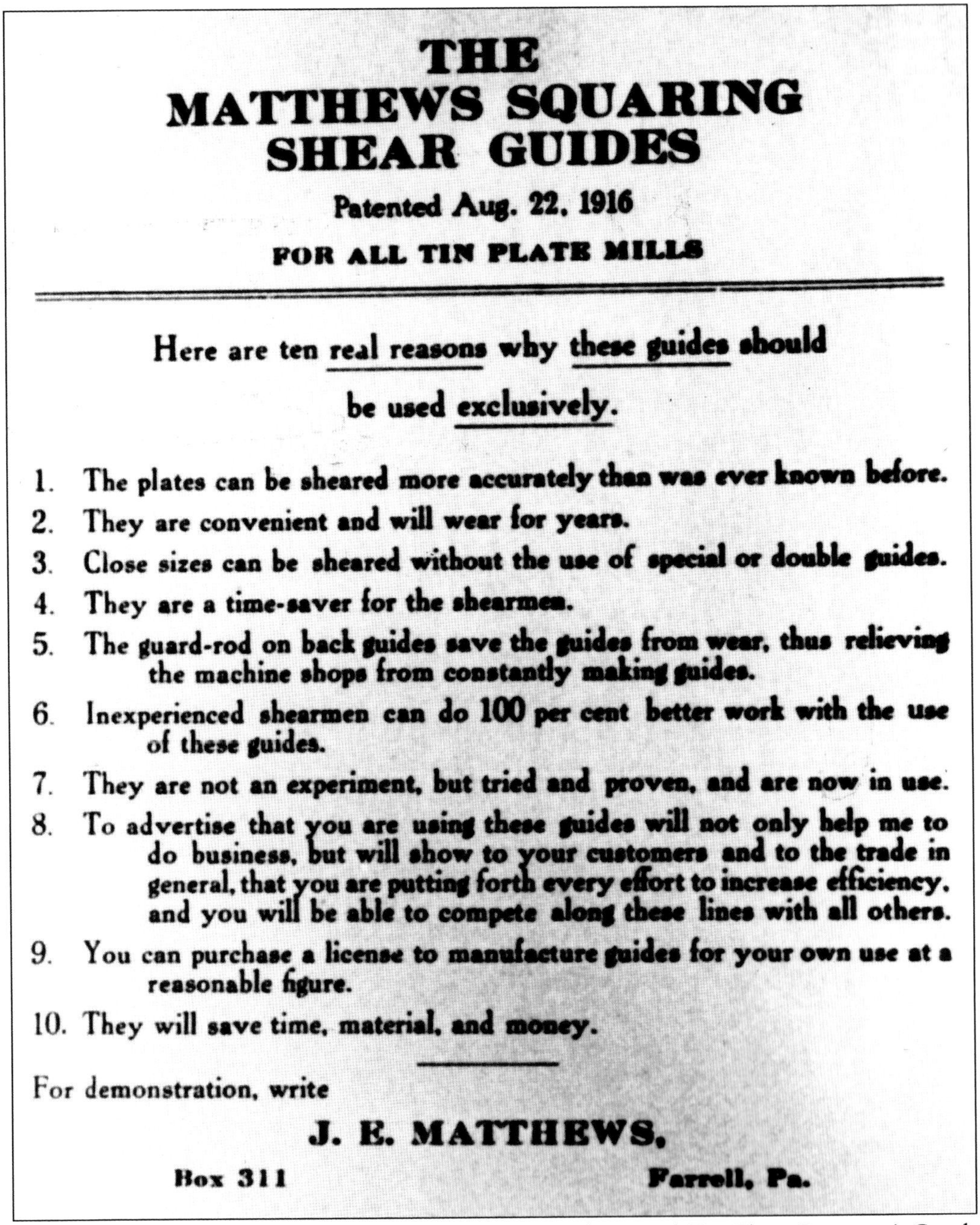

James Elmer Matthews, a shearman at the American Sheet and Tin Plate Company's South Sharon Works, invented a shear guide patented in 1916, recognized as "the work of a genius." This was followed by patents for several safety devices, including the padlock-guard (1919), sled brakes (1922), and bassinet cradle (1923).

On the cover: Please see page 67. (Courtesy of William Jarrett.)

IMAGES
of America

AFRICAN AMERICANS IN MERCER COUNTY

Roland Barksdale-Hall

ARCADIA
PUBLISHING

ISBN 978-0-7385-6501-9

Published by Arcadia Publishing
Charleston SC, Chicago IL, Portsmouth NH, San Francisco CA

Printed in the United States of America

Library of Congress Control Number: 2008942247

For all general information contact Arcadia Publishing at:
Telephone 843-853-2070
Fax 843-853-0044
E-mail sales@arcadiapublishing.com
For customer service and orders:
Toll-Free 1-888-313-2665

Visit us on the Internet at www.arcadiapublishing.com

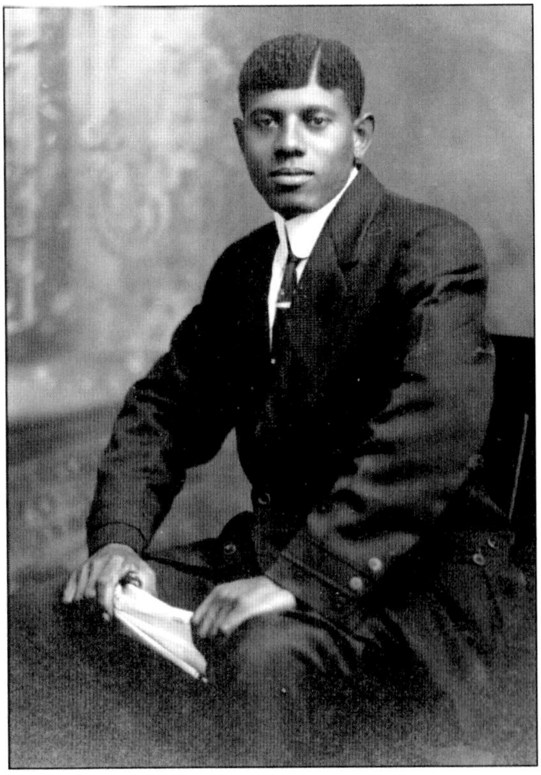

This book is dedicated to James Elmer Matthews (1886–1976), the first elected president of the Mercer County branch of the NAACP, inventor, and talented baseball player, and to future generations of Americans.

Contents

ACKNOWLEDGMENTS

It would be impossible to thank all the countless supporters who helped make this book possible. Please accept my humble appreciation to some who contributed to this endeavor, including Albemarle County Historical Society; Bethlehem Baptist Church; Black Men for Progress; Calumet Lodge No. 25, Prince Hall Affiliation; Cedar Avenue Church of God; Community Missionary Baptist Church; Friendship Baptist Church; Greater Morris Chapel African Methodist Episcopal Church; Greater Mount Zion Church of God in Christ; Mercer County Anti-Discrimination Committee; Mercer County Frontiers Club; Mercer County Historical Society; Mercer County branch of the NAACP; Miriam Chapter No. 47, Order of the Eastern Star, Prince Hall Affiliation; Msgr. Geno Monti School of Our Lady of Fatima; Ruth African Methodist Episcopal Zion Church; Second Baptist Church in Sharpsville; Second Baptist Missionary Church; Shenango Valley Urban League; Southwest Gardens Economic Development Corporation; Twin City Elks Lodge No. 187, Improved Benevolent and Protective Order of the World; Valley Baptist Church; Word Centered Fellowship Presbyterian Church; Veral Adair; Rev. Thomas Bolling; Dr. Dolores Bowles; Martha Cromartie; LaVerne Ellerbe; Tracy Hood; Renea Ingram; Toby Jackson; Bernice Jacoway; William Jarrett; Teresa Jefferson; Mary Floy Katzman; Donna Marie Lee; Dorothy Steverson Malloy; Bessie J. Martin; Shirley J. Matthews; Dr. Travis Mattox; Ethel McClain; Clara Mae Rucker McMillan; Samuel Moore Jr.; David Myers; Rev. Acquanetta Osborne; Russell C. Phillips; Joe C. Pulliam; Martha Richards; David Torrence; Robert "Ken" Torrence; Debbie Matthews Walters; John Whiteside; Shirley Matthews Williams; Milton Wilson; Thelma Wilson; Michael Wright; and Dr. Theodore L. Yarboro. All images, unless otherwise noted, are from the author's collection.

I would like to thank my editor at Arcadia Publishing, Erin L. Vosgien, for her expertise and ready response to inquiries. My mentors, Sara Dillard Austin, James Mendez Matthews, and Odell B. "June" Matthews Jr., shared waffles and countless stories.

Dr. Laurence Glasco, Dr. Joseph Rishel, and Patricia Powers provided the early guidance and encouragement that fostered my interest in local history. Colleagues at Penn State Shenango and Farrell Area School District gave a friendly boost at the right time, which led to this book.

Finally, to my precious wife, Drusilla, and children, Rillis, Drew, Vonita, and Imanuel-Tiefing, thank you for your love and patience not just with this endeavor but in this wonderful life.

INTRODUCTION

Beyond adversity, African Americans in Mercer County responded and adapted to changing times. The themes of struggle, renewal, and rebirth run throughout this book. Mercer County appeared to be a tranquil, pastoral, rural area in the 1830s, but there existed strong antislavery sentiments beneath the facade. Mercer County was along the Underground Railroad, which had stops in Pittsburgh, New Castle, and New Brighton, leading to Mercer and then into Venango County, Meadville, and Erie. More importantly, William Seibert's *The Underground Railroad from Slavery to Freedom* lists Richard Travis and Job Lawson as African American Underground Railroad operators. They worked in conjunction with both white and other African American abolitionists in Venango County, including James Lawson and James Kingsley. As found in the June 10, 1841, edition of the *Mercer Luminary*, one account told of an attempt to rescue a fugitive:

> Our community has been much excited for the last few days, in consequence of the forcible arrest and carrying off of a supposed fugitive slave.
>
> A week or ten days since, two men from Virginia, accompanied by two constables from Pittsburg [*sic*], passed through Mercer, in pursuit of three slaves, who had taken with them their master's carriage, a pair of horses, and some money. The carriage and horses, it appears, were left in the woods some distance from Pittsburgh. The pursuers proceeded to Erie; but the Slaves, as we learn, had got a start for Canada a few days previous. In the mean time information was lodged in town, that two runaway slaves were among the settlement of colored people in the north-east part of this county; and on the return of these pursuers from Erie, the intelligence was given to them by those with whom it was lodged. They then took the warrant, issued from Allegheny for those charged with the robbery mentioned above, to a justice of the Peace here, who endorsed it, without requiring the proof that he was empowered to do that it was genuine, and having got the high constable of the borough into their service and other facilities afforded them, they started out before day break on Sunday morning after their prey. One of these they found a short distance from the house at which he had been staying, gave chase, overtook him, beat him with clubs, and bound him fast.
>
> In the mean time, a number of colored people, having got wind of what was going on, hastened to the place for the purpose of rescuing the prisoner. This they would have done, but for the constable from Mercer, who was acquainted with them, and showed to them his legal warrant endorsed by the Justice of this place, threatening to prosecute them in case of interference, and also stating that he intended to lodge the man in the Mercer jail until a legal examination took place. Under these representations they desisted.

The posse hurried into town, (at a time when the great mass of the citizens were at church, and ignorant of the proceedings) waited but a few minutes to change horses, and drove off post haste for the South.

Thus has a man been arrested, bound, carried through our county, and hurried into slavery, without proof, without legal investigation, and without the benefit of such a hearing as he was entitled to by law.

Justice has been smothered—the feelings of the community outraged—and law set at defiance, by a band of hired ruffians, whose desire for reward has buried beneath it every dictate of humanity.

Whatever the laws require with respect to runaway slaves, however severe, should be obeyed by our officers. But we had hoped that none in Mercer county would go beyond what the law requires—much less those who are not officers—to aid in ferreting out and arresting the poor and oppressed slave, who has undergone toil and suffering to gain what is dear to every human being. But we have been mistaken. We rejoice to know, however, that there are but few; and that nine-tenths of our citizens look upon such conduct with abhorrence and indignation.

In a rural, colored settlement, Travis, Job Lawson, and their party created a safe harbor for fugitives. Until the 1850s, Liberia existed. Enactment of the revised Fugitive Slave Act (1850) hastened the departure to safe harbor in Ontario, Canada. In 1853, the Travis farm, home to Liberia, was sold. Liberia today is known as Stoneboro. The Liberia Cemetery, still in use, is all that remains visible from the once rural, colored settlement.

In the North and the South, free people of color were required to prove their freedom status. During the antebellum era, freedom was tenuous for them all; some were kidnapped and sold into slavery. In 1807, William Stewart (1759–1850), a free person of color, moved from North Carolina to Ohio. Free colored settlers carried a copy of their certificates of freedom. Dismayed by the revised Fugitive Slave Act, which restricted legal protection for fugitive slaves and free persons of color, he filed a certificate of freedom at the Mercer County Courthouse. During the 1840s, Stewart resided in Findley Township.

Dr. Charles D. Everette, a physician from Charlottesville, Virginia, was a slave owner. He was influenced by egalitarian thinking of founding fathers Thomas Jefferson and George Washington, as expressed in the Bill of Rights, which believed that everyone had the right to liberty. As a slave owner, that presented a problem. As early as 1840, Everette had made a preparation in his will to leave a magnanimous bequest for the relocation of his slaves. Initially Everette's plans involved resettlement in Africa, but they were altered to include migration to Pennsylvania. The search for a safe harbor in the United States, where former slaves might live as free people, was documented in legal records rich with genealogical content, as evidenced in court records and the *Laws of Pennsylvania of the Session of 1855*. The legal documents safeguarded their freedom.

In the bequest, Everette included more than $1,000 for each former slave. The former slaves used these monies to purchase family members who were still in slavery. These families settled in Indian Run. Edward Coles, son of Isaac Coles of Albemarle County, Virginia, freed 20 slaves that he inherited and in 1819 moved to Illinois, where two years later he became governor. A group of 61 former slaves—most from Everette's plantation—established the settlement of Pandenarium. The colored settlement at Pandenarium existed from 1855 into the late 1890s when economic opportunities attracted residents to neighboring towns and industrial centers. George Washington Lewis was one of the last survivors of the original colony to leave Pandenarium.

The influence of the Underground Railroad, antebellum settlements, and interracial cooperation likely fostered a progressive climate for later developments. The Erie Extension Canal opened doors to travel and contributed to the growth of towns located in the southwest corner of Mercer County, adjacent to Ohio. In addition to Sharpsville, the Shenango Valley was established on a floodplain that included Sharon, Hermitage, and the smaller neighboring communities of Farrell, Wheatland, West Middlesex, and Brookfield, Ohio. Remnants of the canal's locks are visible in Sharpsville. Well into the 20th century, Mercer County continued to attract progressive-minded people, as the doors opened for economic advancement in the communities of Farrell and Sharon. William Hunter Dammond, the first African American graduate of the University of Pittsburgh, was unable to locate employment as an engineer in Pittsburgh. He moved from Pittsburgh to Mercer County, where he located employment as a draftsman for the American Sheet and Tin Plate Company in Farrell. At the same time, other African Americans held semiskilled and skilled positions for the company. In 1918, American Sheet and Tin Plate Company's Farrell Works employed a remarkable "187 skilled and semi-skilled colored workers." They earned more money than the average mill worker in western Pennsylvania.

For African American migrants, adjustment to the North was not always smooth. Prior to 1908, the Shenango Valley's small African American population worshipped at the Ruth African Methodist Episcopal Zion Church of Sharon, the First Baptist Church of South Sharon, and South Sharon's Triumph Church of the New Age, but southern migrants found some African American churches "inhospitable." Earlier migrants from Little Washington organized Farrell's African Methodist Episcopal Church in order to provide proper "moral instruction" for "untrained and irresponsible" southern newcomers. Between 1908 and 1944, African American newcomers to the Shenango Valley organized 10 Baptist churches, 3 holiness churches, a Catholic church, a colored Methodist Episcopal church, and an African Methodist Episcopal church. Factors in the selection of a church included class, unfamiliar worship styles, and the desire for autonomy. As might be expected, this proliferation of churches, rather than minimizing factional strife, actually contributed to the fragmentation of the community.

Economic opportunity provided for the development of two 20th-century safe harbors. In 1916, African Americans from Sharon and Farrell mortgaged their homes, joined with African Americans from Pittsburgh, and purchased 116 acres for a sacred city on the hill, today known as the National Campground of the National Association of the Church of God. Around the same time in the secular world, African Americans were feeling the need to provide support and nurture for their children, and they created an organization known as the Twin City Elks Lodge of Pennsylvania, which became the largest Elks lodge in the state. Organized in 1914, the Twin City Elks Lodge of Farrell, with a membership that peaked at over 700, was recognized for almost 20 years as the largest Improved Benevolent and Protective Order of Elks of the World lodge in Pennsylvania. Reaching a cross section of African Americans in Farrell, it was a major unifying force in the community. In the aftermath of the great migration, a period of mass migration from the South to the North between 1916 and 1946, it was the only national secret society to increase its membership. This African American community agent, which accepted everyone regardless of class or position, was a safe harbor for southern migrants.

In Farrell and across the country, African American professionals "undertook to reconcile their personal interests with those of the working-class" through participation in Elks activities. The first two African American officeholders elected in Farrell were Elks. In 1928, Charles S. Butler and John Edmunds served as register assessor and constable, respectively. A semiskilled worker at the American Steel and Tin Plate Company's Farrell Works, Butler joined the Elks band, and by 1924, he was exalted ruler. A native of South Carolina, Edmunds also worked at the American Steel and Tin Plate Company and was an Elk; later he was hired as the first African American insurance man in the Shenango Valley. In 1930, Joseph Young, a charter member of Twin City Elks Lodge, succeeded Butler as the register assessor. Young had served as the lodge's treasurer from 1921 to 1926, and his wife, Cora, was a past daughter ruler and treasurer of the Elks' female auxiliary.

As early as 1915, political meetings were being held by "ethnic club committees of the Italian, Jewish, Colored and Croatian" communities for the purpose of endorsing candidates. Thirteen years later, elements from among the Croatian community encouraged Edmunds to run for office and supported his candidacy. Similarly, James Renshaw received support from African American Elks and also from Italian and Jewish voters. Since African Americans represented less than

12 percent of Farrell's total population in 1930, coalitions with ethnic whites were necessary in order to elect them to public office. African American councilman James Renshaw, a native of Alabama, served a term concurrent with Young's. While little is known about Renshaw, family members were in the local Elks. A sister-in-law, Minnie Renshaw, was also a past daughter ruler, Zylphia Temple's highest officer. The fact that three out of four of these African Americans elected to major public offices in Farrell were Elks is proof of the organization's high visibility in the borough. Even though ethnic whites saw African American Elks as leaders, it was their position in the larger community that determined their electability.

This period of judicious mixing soon ended, the result of plans by white ethnic businessmen to reclassify Farrell from a borough to a third-class city in 1931. Since African Americans in Farrell had not developed enterprises comparable to those of ethnic whites, their political influence diminished during the change. Joseph Franek, a Slovak businessman, was the first mayor of the new city. Prominent businessmen Michael Nevant, a Slovak, and Louis Levine, a Jew, were elected to the city council, which was now under the control of white ethnic business interests, with no representation from the African American community. The city of Farrell has its first African American and female mayor, Olive Brown McKeithan, 77 years later. In recent times, the implications of political empowerment, both on the local and national scene, await African Americans.

The opening ceremony of the Freedom Road Revisited Exhibition, cosponsored by the Mercer Anti-Discrimination Committee and the Mercer County Historical Society, was held at the specious rotunda of the courthouse and attracted various public officials. Comments about the exhibition ranged from "Did you see that?" to "I didn't know slavery was ever here." These were moving moments for sure. May readers, too, be moved by this humble presentation on the ongoing African American journey to freedom, as it is the story of all of America.

As James Elmer Matthews conveys in his poem "A Real American," written on October 27, 1917, a veil from the past shrouded the identity of the sons and daughters of slave ancestry.

> Colored Americans have hewed out the mountains and cut down the trees,
> Fought wars, tilled soil and prayed on their knees.
> They have dug shafts in the earth to mine coal and ore.
> They worked as slaves? Both North and South.
> Got freedom with the word "Negro" in their mouth.
> That word "Negro" enslaved his brain;
> Now that slave must be freed again.
> To make him free and free complete;
> Declare that word "Negro" obsolete.
> We are Americans.

Although their story peculiarly was America's, the struggle for full American citizenship along with accompanying responsibilities awaited. In the inauguration of the 44th president of the United States, Barack Hussein Obama, the full responsibility of American citizenship has come.

—Roland Barksdale-Hall

One

Liberia and Pandenarium
Passage to Safe Harbor

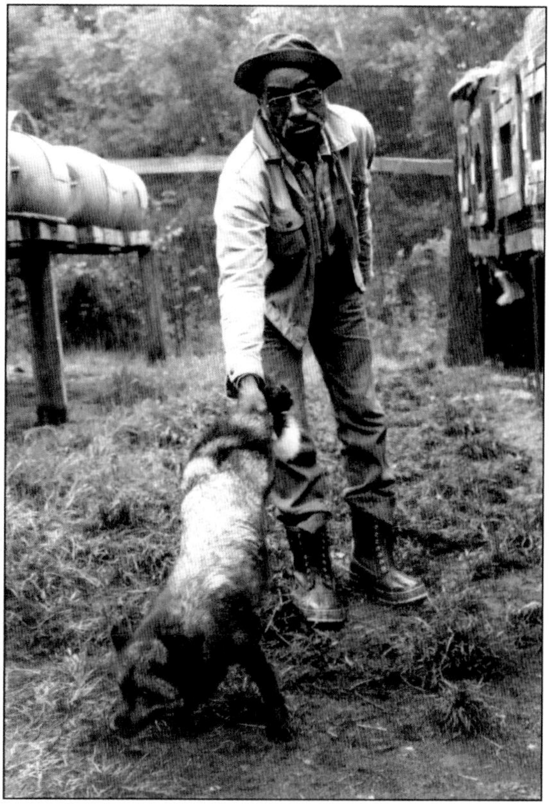

On the rolling hills, African American settlers farmed and hunted. The enterprising Adair brothers, featured in *Ebony* magazine, expanded upon southern rural traditions. James Adair Sr. enjoyed fur farming for two decades. Veral Adair built over 100 round cages (far left) for nesting boxes to breed foxes. Pictured here, Norce Adair grasps a silver fox by its hind legs on the Adair Brothers Fur farm in East Lackawannock in the 1980s. (Courtesy of Veral Adair.)

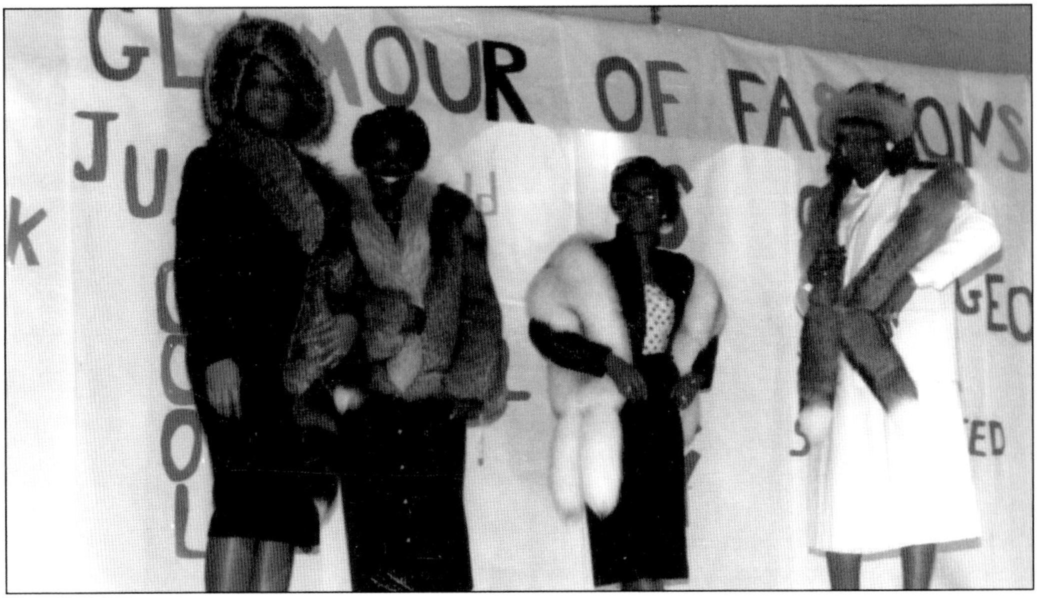

Adair Brothers Fur held glamorous style shows in Chicago and throughout Pennsylvania and Ohio. Veral Adair, a core maker, and James Adair Sr., a furnace operator, both workers at National Castings in Sharon, kicked off their steel-toe boots and dawned field boots. They teamed up with their brother Norce Adair to establish a farm in 1982 when local mills closed. Animals bred included silver fox, pearl fox, platinum fox, fishers, martins, and sables. (Courtesy of Veral Adair.)

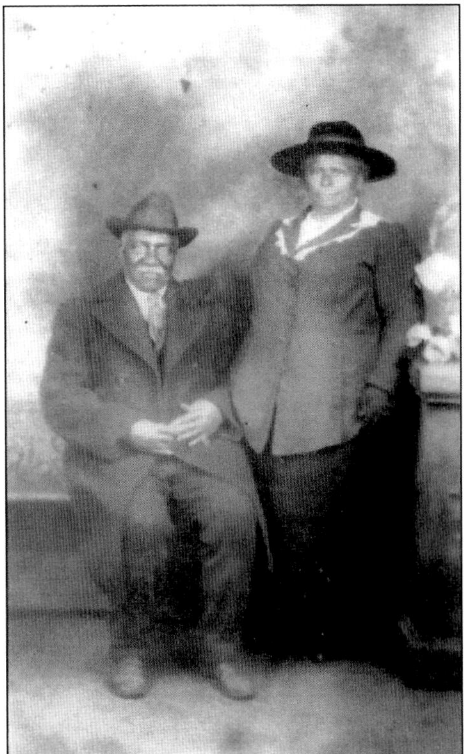

Adair Brothers Fur received numerous trophies, including the grand champion, at competitions in New York. At the dawn of the 20th century, Henry Pleasant Adair (1853–1926), a former slave, and Ellen Pruitt Adair (1858–1933) migrated from Talladega, Alabama, to Farrell. The couple began what became the large, enterprising Adair-James-Jarrett family in Mercer County. Descendants include James Adair Sr., Norce Adair, and Veral Adair. (Courtesy of William Jarrett.)

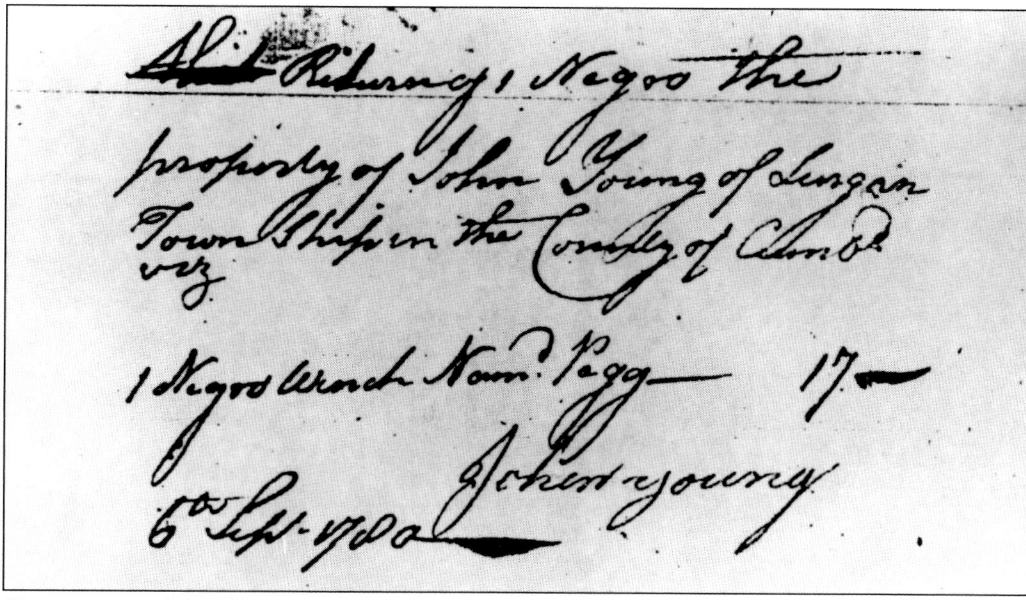

At Returns 1 Negro the property of John Young of Lurgan Town Ship in the County of Cumbd viz

1 Negro Wench Nam'd Pegg — 17 —

John Young
6th Sept 1780

Slavery existed locally on a small scale. In 1804, Margaret (Peggy) Johnston (1763–1854), accompanied by her master, moved from Cumberland County to Indian Run in Mercer County. At the same time, John Sheakley moved from Gettysburg to Mercer County with six slaves. In 1780, John Young Sr. registered a 17-year-old wench, "Peggy whose children became free at 28 as conditions of the Gradual Abolition of Slavery Act." (Courtesy of Pennsylvania State Archives.)

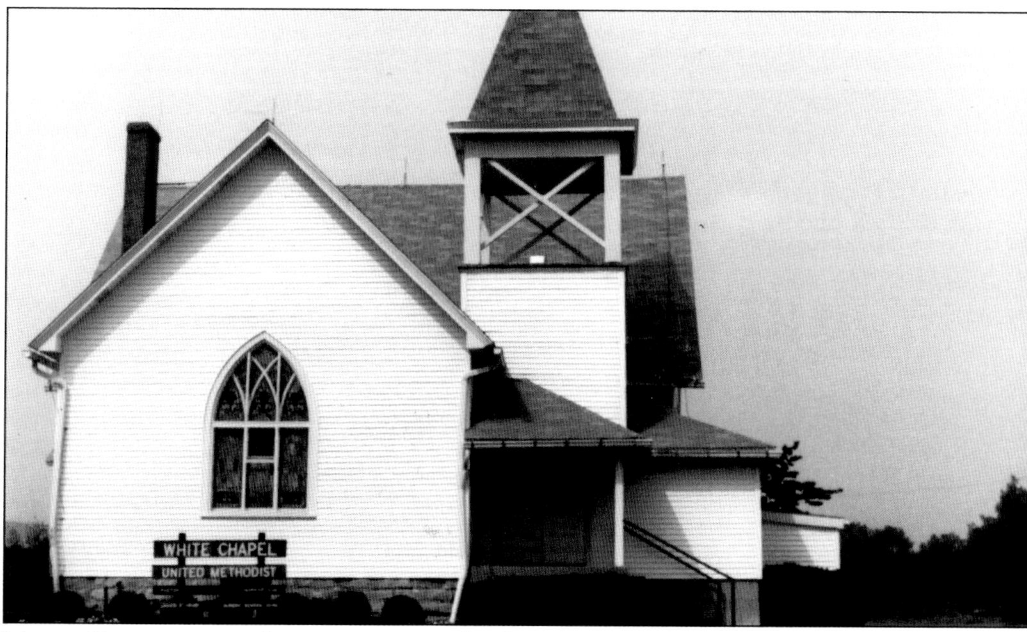

Mercer County acquired a reputation as a freedom stop. In 1835, the formation of an antislavery society at the Neshannock Presbyterian Church led to a split. Seven years later, due to deep religious sentiment, white Underground Railroad conductors John Young Jr. (1797–1880) and James Minick were joined by others to organize the White Chapel Church in Indian Run, known as a radical antislavery church. Shown is the current White Chapel Church, built in 1906.

$100 REWARD

Ran away from the subscriber, living near the Anacostia Bridge, on or about the 17th November, negro girl ELIZA. She calls herself Eliza Coursy. She is of the ordinary size, from 18 to 20 years old, of a chestnut or copper color. Eliza has some scars about her face, has been hired in Washington, and has acquaintances in Georgetown.

I will give fifty dollars if taken in the District or Maryland, and one hundred dollars if taken in any free State; but in either case she must be secured in jail so that I get her again.

JOHN. P. WARING.

Nov. 28, 1857.

H. Polkinhorn's Steam Job Printing Office, D street, bet. 6th & 7th sts., Washington, D. C.

According to Joseph Polk (1873–1970), Auntie Strange lost her fingers at the nub of one hand for a failed runaway attempt. Still, she struck out again, outwitted bloodhounds, and secreted herself in Liberia. Hundreds of enslaved individuals—many of whom came from upper South states—by some accounts ran away, sought refuge, and succeeded to live quasi-free in Liberia, a secluded African American settlement. Polk recalled during his childhood his mother kept a fire at night to keep away the prowling wolves. In the 1920s, he was employed as superintendent of an icehouse and remained on the land well into the 1960s. Polk was the last survivor from the colony known as Liberia, later known as Stoneboro. Polk descendants include Harvey L. Grannison, Joseph M. Grannison, and Samuel F. Grannison. (Courtesy of Mercer County Historical Society.)

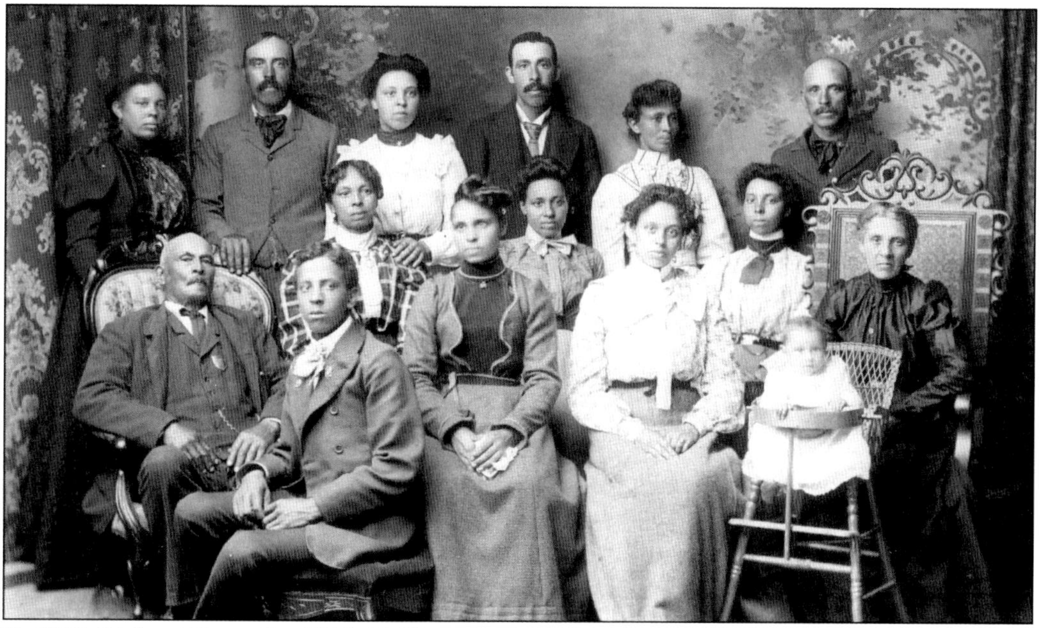

By 1820, Richard Travis Sr. (1745–1843) purchased over 100 acres for the development of Liberia. His resolve to select a name associated with liberty was courageous. Little is known about this Underground Railroad station except that there was a meetinghouse, suggesting a link between faith and a resolve to end slavery. Shown are descendants John Travis (1832–1912) and Louisa Travis (1835–1910) in Canada. (Courtesy of Buxton National Historic Site and Museum.)

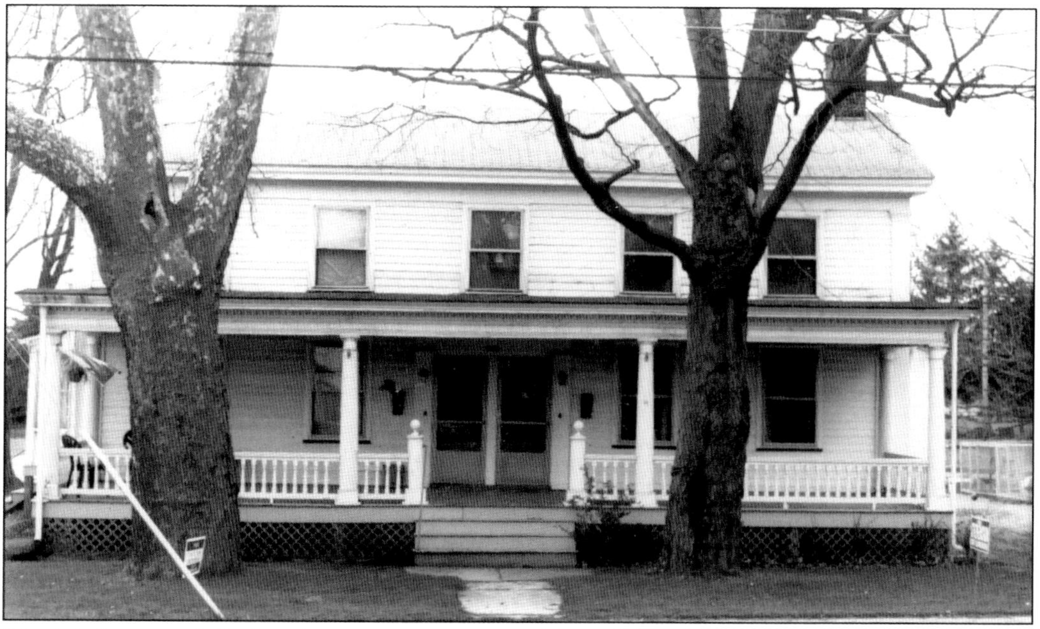

The Underground Railroad represents a successful model of interracial cooperation. African American conductors Richard Travis Jr. (born in 1819), James Lawson, and Job Lawson worked in a spirit of love and harmony with white abolitionist James Kilgore in Mercer on secret runaways to Liberia from Franklin, a station on the Underground Railroad. Shown is the Kilgore House at 246 South Erie Street in Mercer around 1995.

Mercer County Colored Troops Of The Civil War

NAME	RANK	COMPANY	REGIMENT
Allen, John	Unknown	Unknown	127
Anderson, Isaah	Private	B	43
Ford, William	Private	B	38
Garland, James H.	Private	A	127
Hall, Ebenezer, F.	Sergeant	Unknown	9
Lawson, Nathaniel	Corporal	B	43
Lewis, George	Private	K	127
Ramsey, George T.	Corporal	I	3
Richards, Crosby B.	Private	H	26
Roberts, Emery	Unknown	C	102
Roberts, Jacob	Private	H	6
Scott, Samuel	Private	A	8
Smith, G.	Unknown	D	45

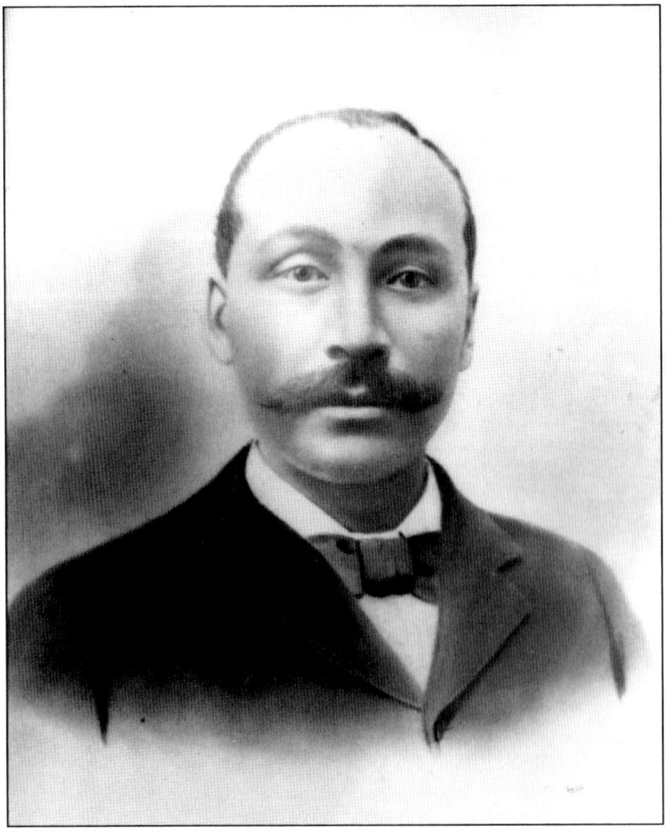

Isaah Anderson (*c.* 1832–1897) possessed the strength of Hercules. He was six feet four inches tall, weighed over 200 pounds, wore a size 14 shoe, and had large hands. His name became synonymous with great courage and strength. Others dared to challenge him in his prime. Anderson served alongside Nathaniel Lawson in Company B of the 43rd U.S. Colored (Infantry) Regiment and was interred in Liberia's burial ground with family, friends, and Civil War veteran Jacob Roberts. Pictured is Lawson, who was the son of Job Lawson, an Underground Railroad conductor, and grandson of Richard Travis Sr., founder of Liberia. (Courtesy of Josephine Lawson Gibbs.)

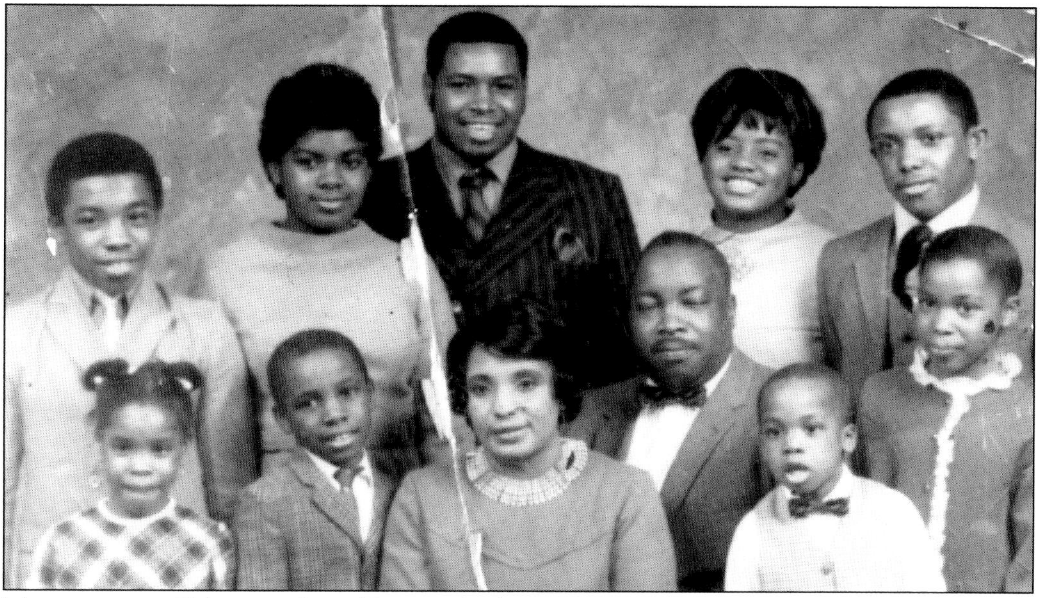

Many citizens of Liberia and neighboring Cool Spring in Mercer County fled to Canada in 1850 following the passage of the second Fugitive Slave Act. Citizens of Cool Spring included W. W. Devan, a Baptist pastor, and Dr. Abraham Whitfield, the first African American medical doctor in Mercer County during the 1840s. Pictured around 1968 are Benjamin and Josephine Lawson Gibbs and family, American descendants of Richard Travis and Job Lawson of Hermitage. (Courtesy of Josephine Lawson Gibbs.)

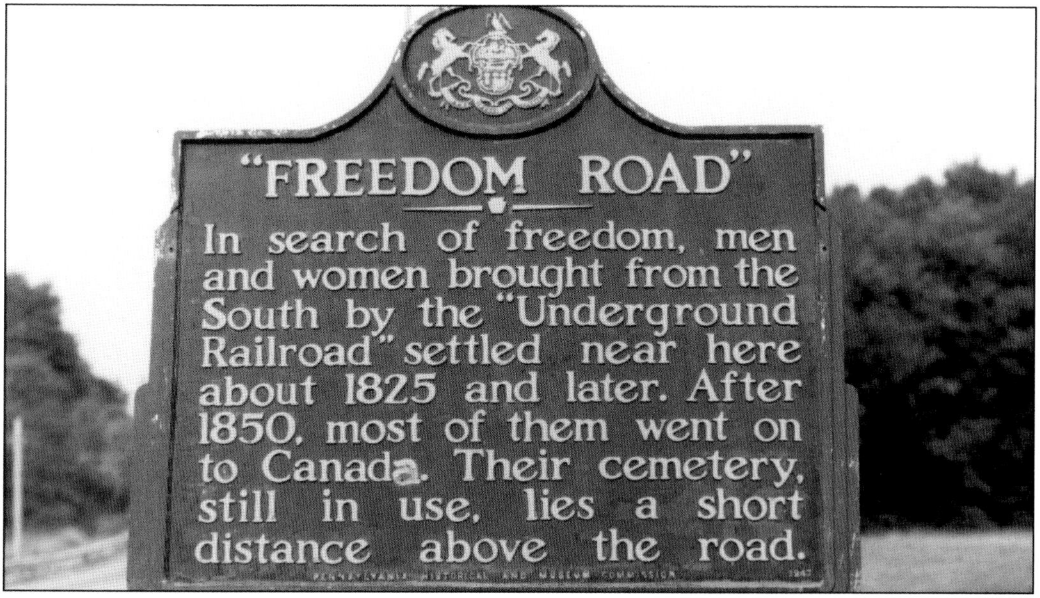

John Travis (1832–1912), born in Mercer County, moved to Canada in the 1850s and became a constable in Raleigh Township, Kent County, Ontario, Canada. Canadian descendants Dr. Brian Bowles and Dr. Dolores Bowles, a screenwriter, attended the integrated School Section (SS) No. 13 Raleigh School, which was renown for quality education and is now a national historic site. Today a Pennsylvania Historical and Museum Commission marker along Route 62 not far from the Liberia burial ground recalls Freedom Road. (Courtesy of Dr. Brian and Dr. Dolores Bowles.)

PAUL M. LAWSON

D-Philadelphia - 1961-1970 (House)

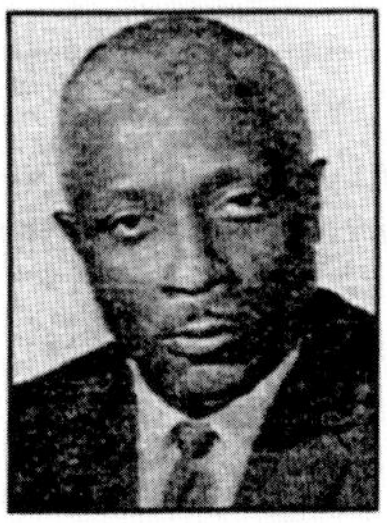

Paul M. Lawson, who was born in Franklin, Pa., on Jan. 29, 1914, represented the 23rd Legislative District of Philadelphia.

Lawson attended Hampton University and took extension courses at Rutgers, Cornell and Penn State universities, receiving an associate's degree from Penn State University.

Lawson served in the U.S. Navy as a machinist mate during World War II. He was chairman of the International Trustee Board of the United Auto Workers of America/AFL-CIO; and a member of the Veterans of Foreign Wars.

Paul Lawson, born in Franklin in 1914, served in the Pennsylvania House of Representatives during the civil rights era. Paul Lawson's biographical sketch and record of service appeared in *Black Legislators in Pennsylvania 1911–2001*. The Honorable Paul Lawson, a descendant of Richard Travis and Job Lawson, continues in the spirit of liberty. (Courtesy of Pennsylvania state representative Bill Robinson.)

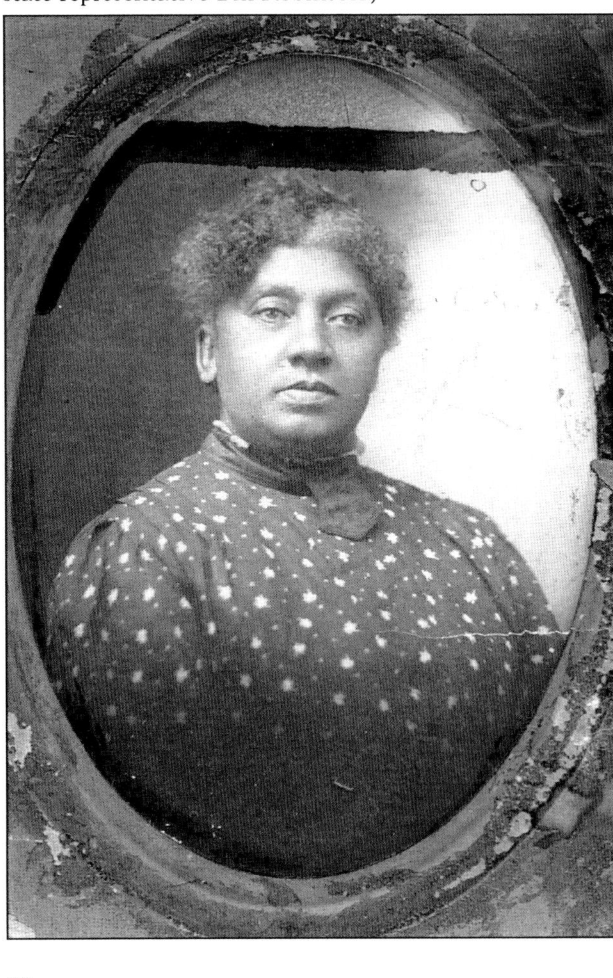

Unable to vote due to her race and sex, Matilda Matthews (1842–1938) cut material with scissors to support the campaign of Abraham Lincoln for president and participated in political advocacy. She migrated from Homestead to Hubbard, Ohio, then Brookfield, and settled in South Sharon. In 1917, Matthews served as the first chairperson for the Western Pennsylvania and Eastern Ohio Campground Association in West Middlesex. She is the mother of James Elmer Matthews, the first elected NAACP branch president. (Courtesy of Shirley Matthews Williams.)

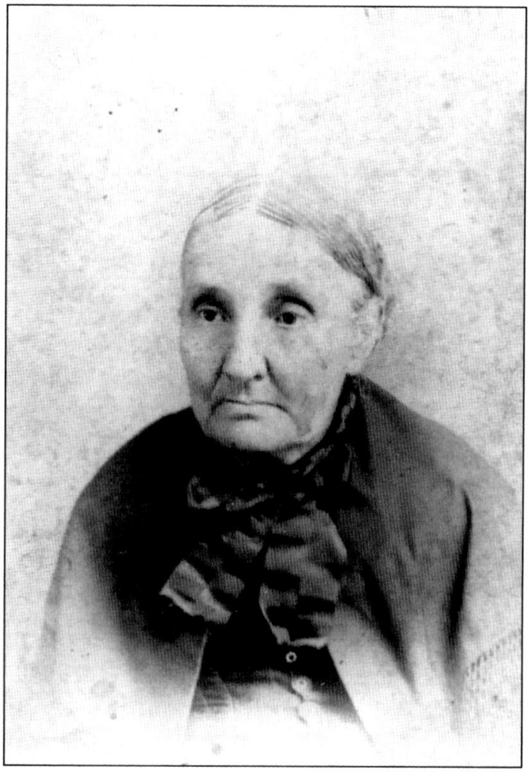

During the 1830s, Jesse Richards (1793–1885) married Mary Elizabeth Smith, a native of Allegheny County. In the North, the existence of interracial marriage predated the Civil War, although Smith's family disowned her when she crossed the color line. Richards received his freedom upon his master's death. Seen here is the couple, who lived in Stoneboro, formerly known as Liberia. They had 12 children.

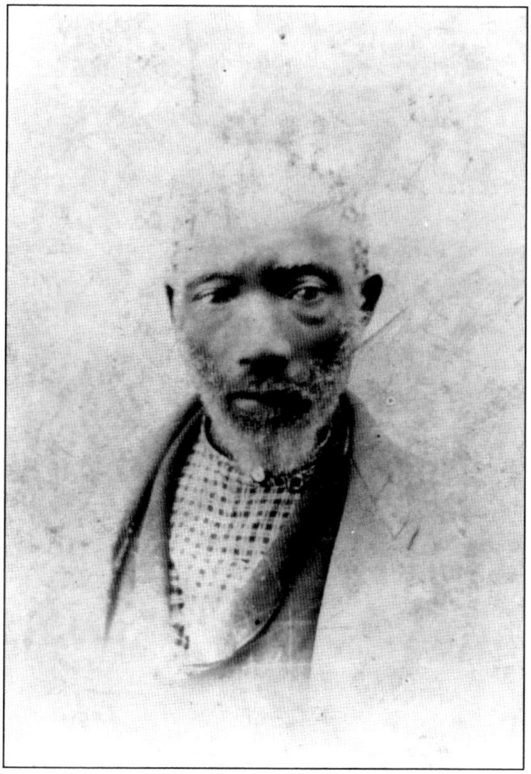

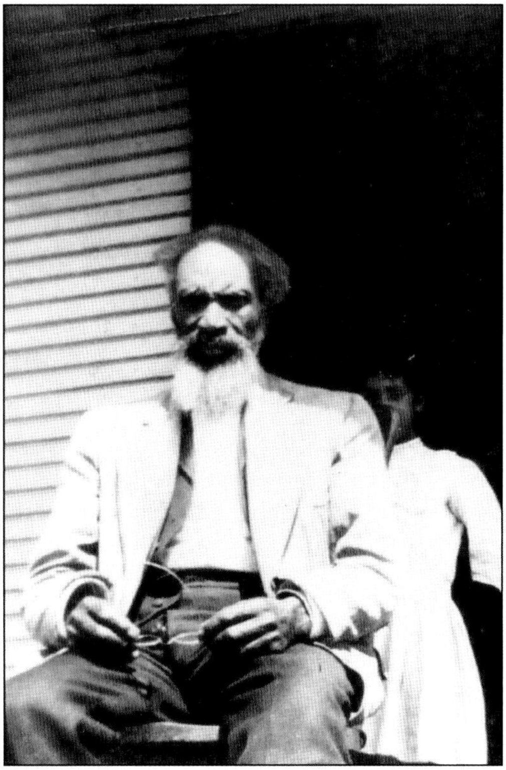

Shown are George Washington Lewis (*c.* 1836–1916) and Caroline Richards (1839–1902), daughter of Jesse and Mary Richards, around 1855. Lewis was a former slave freed by provision of Dr. Charles D. Everette's will. He served as a private in Company K of the 127th U.S. Colored Regiment, losing his hearing during the Civil War. They are buried in White Chapel Cemetery.

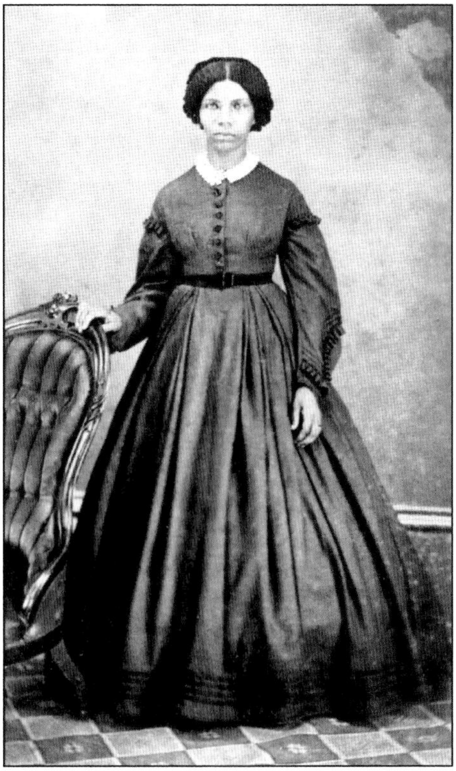

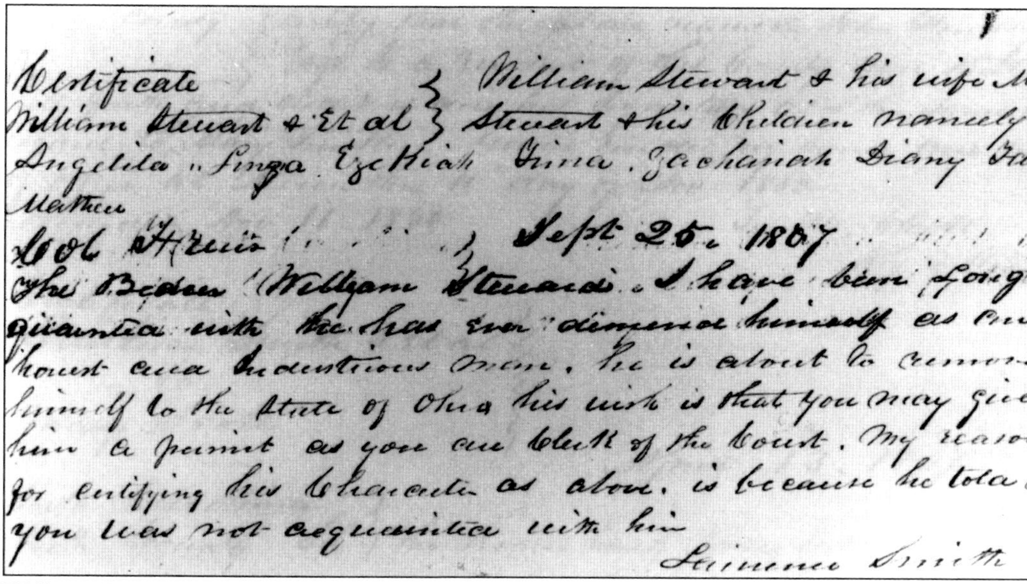

Certificate
William Stewart & Et al
William Stewart & his wife M[illegible] Stewart & his Children namely Angelida, Linza, Ezekiah, Irma, Zachariah, Diany, Fa[illegible] Matthew

Col. [illegible] Sept 25, 1807

The Bearer William Steward. I have been long acquainted with he has ever demeaned himself as an honest and industrious man, he is about to remove himself to the State of Ohio his wish is that you may give him a permit as you are Clerk of the Court. My reason for certifying his Character as above is because he told you was not acquainted with him

Lawrence Smith

William Stewart (1759–1850), a free person of color, moved from North Carolina to the Ohio Territory in search of freedom. He later moved to Findley Township in Mercer County, where, concerned about the erosion of legal protection for free persons of color, he filed a certificate of freedom at the Mercer County Courthouse to safeguard the liberty of his wife and children. (Courtesy of Mercer County Historical Society.)

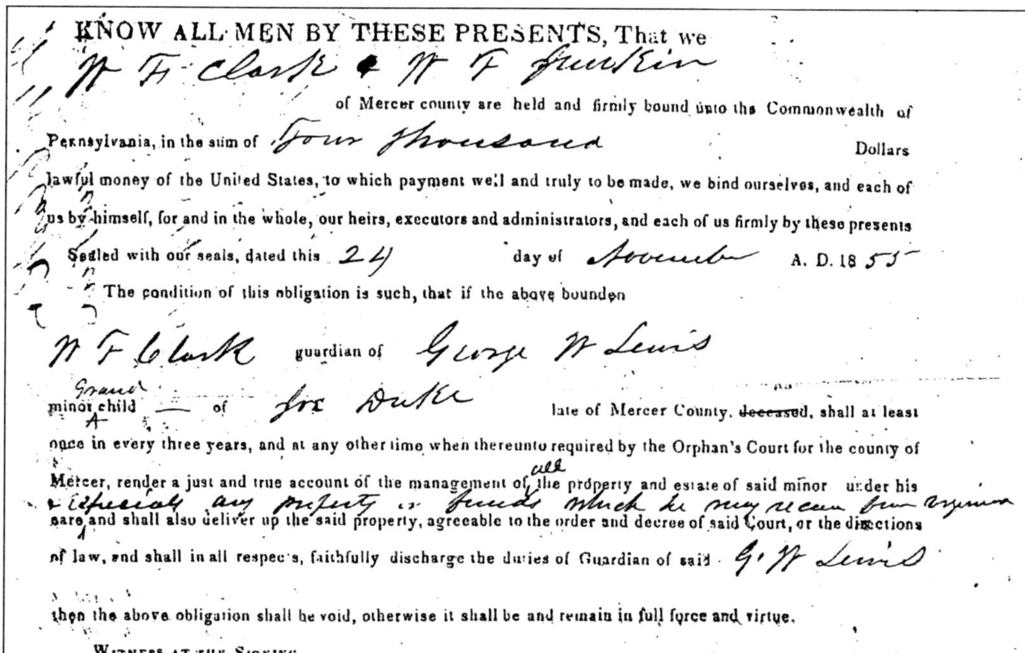

KNOW ALL MEN BY THESE PRESENTS, That we W F Clark & W F Junkin of Mercer county are held and firmly bound unto the Commonwealth of Pennsylvania, in the sum of Four thousand Dollars lawful money of the United States, to which payment well and truly to be made, we bind ourselves, and each of us by himself, for and in the whole, our heirs, executors and administrators, and each of us firmly by these presents Sealed with our seals, dated this 24 day of November A. D. 1855

The condition of this obligation is such, that if the above bounden W F Clark guardian of George W Lewis grand minor child of Joe Duke late of Mercer County, ~~deceased~~, shall at least once in every three years, and at any other time when thereunto required by the Orphan's Court for the county of Mercer, render a just and true account of the management of all the property and estate of said minor under his care & especially any property or funds which he may receive from Virginia and shall also deliver up the said property, agreeable to the order and decree of said Court, or the directions of law, and shall in all respects, faithfully discharge the duties of Guardian of said G W Lewis then the above obligation shall be void, otherwise it shall be and remain in full force and virtue.

WITNESS AT THE SIGNING.

Lewis, a grandson of Joseph Duke, witnessed slavery firsthand. As a slave, his uncle Windsor Duke had weighted pliers attached to his lip as a punishment and was maimed for life. Still, the large, extended Duke family was fortunate. Joseph Duke had 22 children. Seven of them accompanied him to Pandenarium, and three remained in slavery. Twelve already had died in slavery before Joseph Duke received his freedom. (Courtesy of Mercer County Courthouse.)

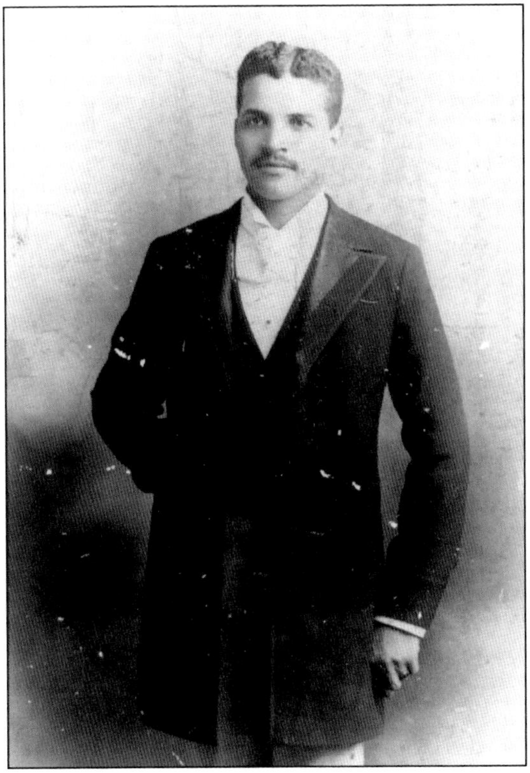

A few whites falsely accused Pandenarium citizens of stealing until they realized they had money. George Washington Lewis received $1,000 from Dr. Charles D. Everette's estate, which afforded three children a comfortable lifestyle. Emma Lewis (below) became a skilled seamstress. She was courted by Joseph Stoney, a chef at the Humes Hotel in Mercer. Shown to the left is a dapper Elmer Lewis, who met his bride-to-be, Lucy, at a formal dance. This photograph of Lewis was taken at the Branch Gallery in Emlenton in 1889.

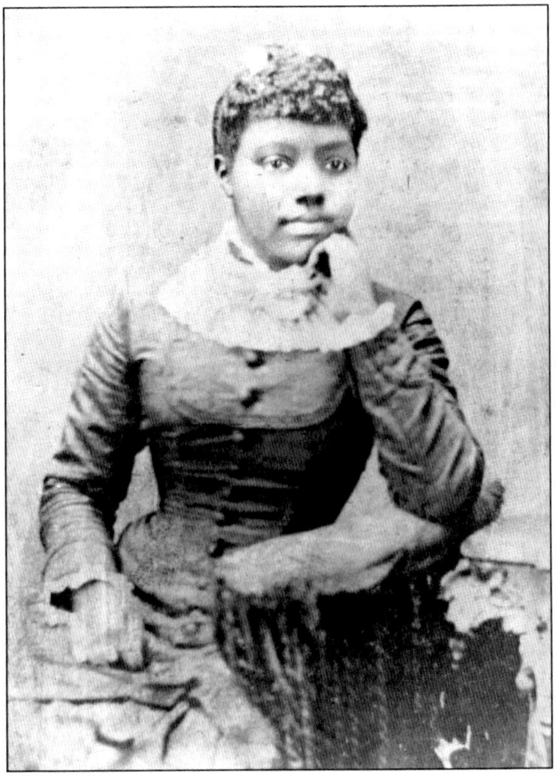

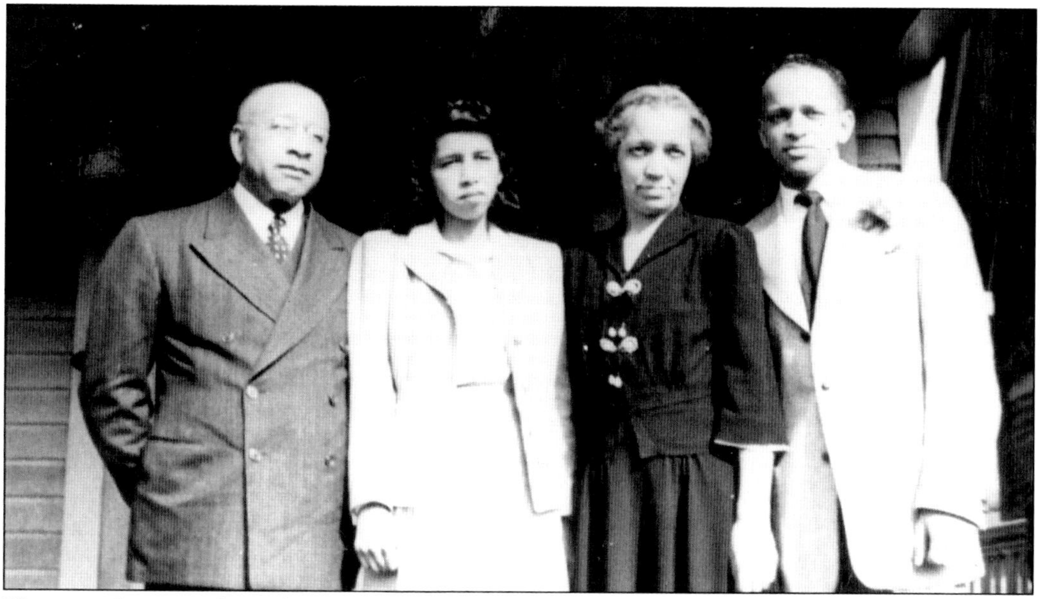

The significance of Pandenarium, viewed by some as "an experiment in freedom," can be best judged over several generations. Descendants of George Washington and Caroline Lewis include Florence Lewis Lawson, daughter of Elmer Lewis, who moved to Wellington, Ohio. Shown are, from left to right, Dr. William H. Lawson, an unidentified daughter, Florence Lewis Lawson, and son Dr. William E. Lawson in Detroit. An intelligentsia arose from the citizens of Pandenarium.

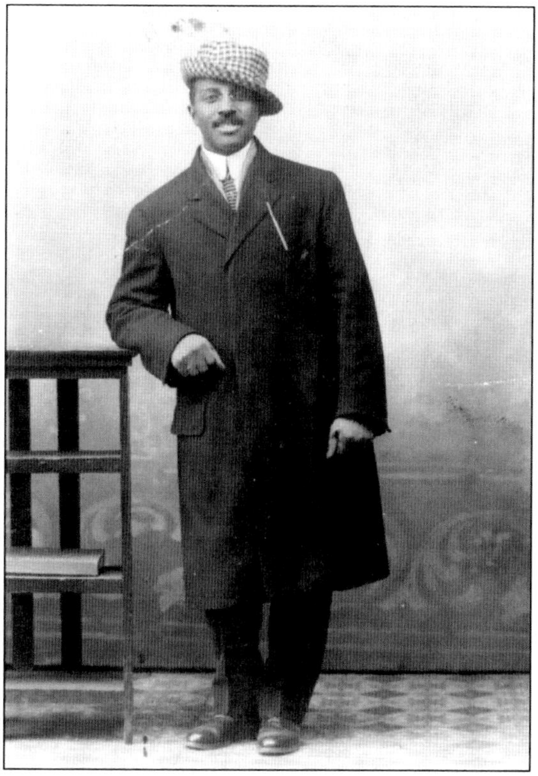

In 1894, Emma Stoney's dying wish was that her children be kept together. George Washington and Caroline Lewis raised three grandchildren, Ollie, Elizabeth, and Joseph Stoney, in Pandenarium. Pandenarium existed well into the 1890s when residents began to move to Sharon, Farrell, and elsewhere, as they sought employment. Pictured is Joseph Stoney Jr. before enlisting with his father, Joseph Stoney Sr., to serve in the Spanish-American War.

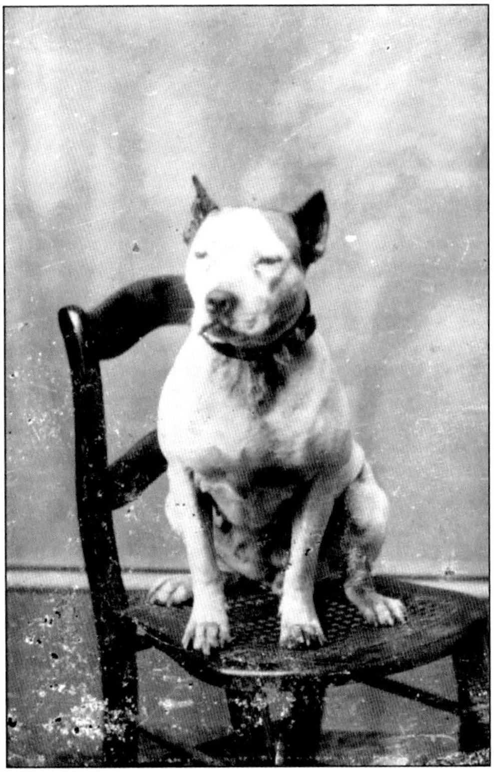

Mother Caroline Lewis's first impression of suitor Joseph Stoney, who hailed from Charleston, South Carolina, was that he was too much of a fast-talker and city-slick dresser for her liking. Fortunately her impression was not a lasting one. Shown are Joseph Stoney, chef, and Emma Stoney, seamstress, at their two-story white frame house in Stoneboro in the 1890s. Joseph bred pups from Granger, his pedigree bulldog, and sold them for $50.

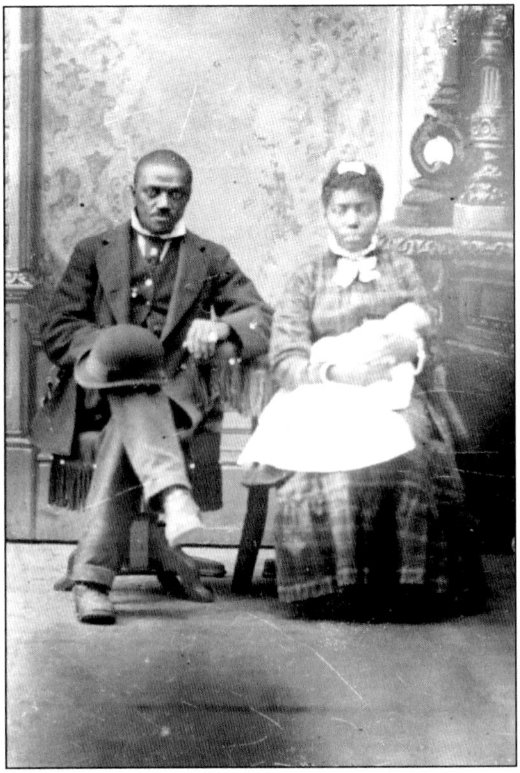

Two

WHEATFIELD AND SHARPSVILLE

RIVERSIDE CHURCHES AND COMMUNITIES

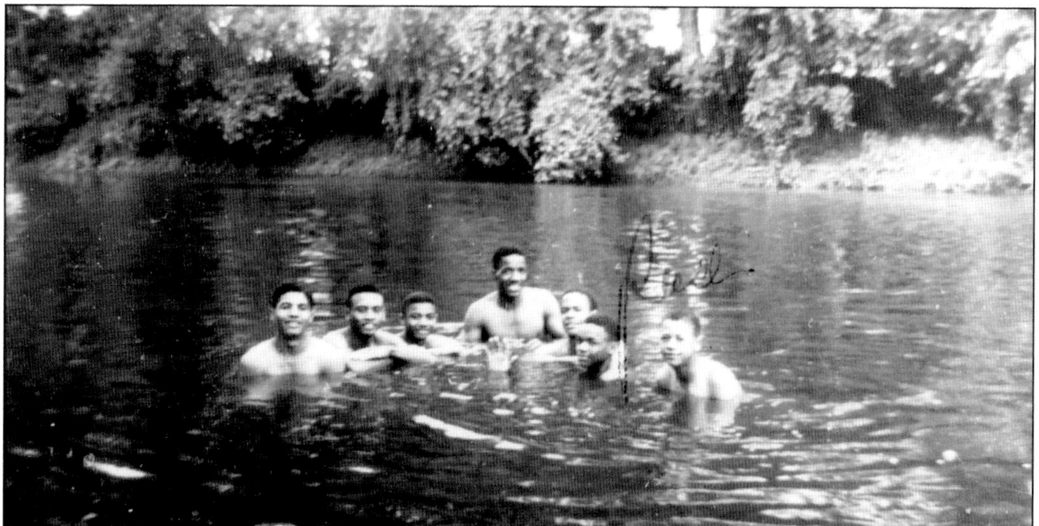

On the shore of the Shenango River, the settlement of Wheatfield, today known as Wheatland, was established. Settler Thomas Bronson bought 200 acres from John Thompson in 1807. Mothers frowned upon their boys swimming in these rivers. Still many ventured out only to receive a thrashing when their mothers saw their eyes red, hair kinky, and skin ashy. Campground workers are pictured in the same rivers near West Middlesex during the 1940s. (Courtesy of Shirley Matthews Williams.)

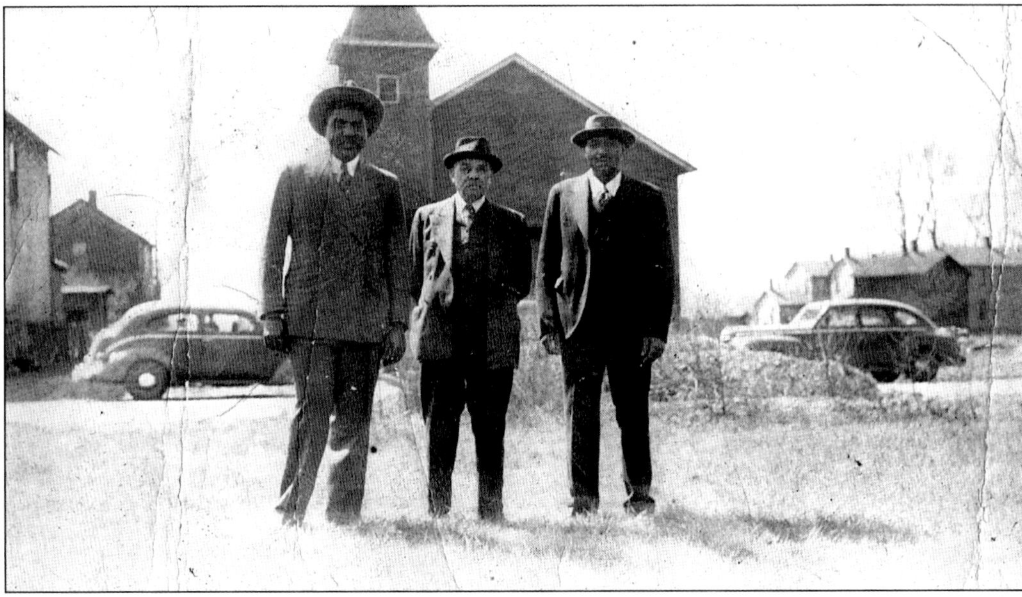

In the 1820s, Thomas Bronson moved to Jefferson Township and purchased 400 acres in what became known as Charlestown. Descendants reside in Charlestown on inherited land and also in Sharpsville. Shown in front of the first Valley Baptist Church at 122 Main Street in Wheatland are, from left to right, Robert Jones, Rev. Samuel Delane Jr. (1895–1957), and Dea. William Henderson Sr. in the 1940s when new converts were baptized at Rocky Springs in West Middlesex. (Courtesy of Donna Marie Lee.)

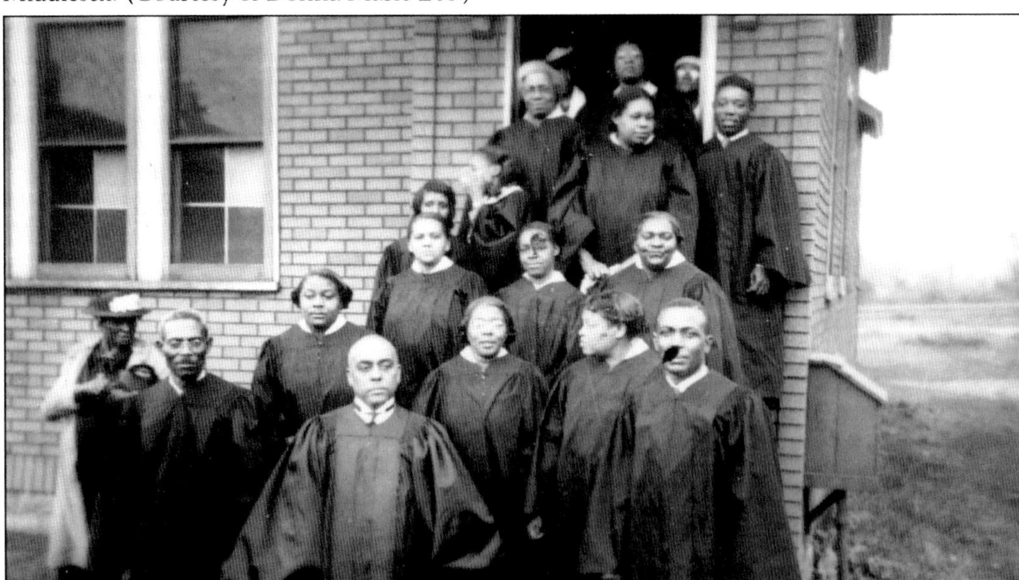

Wheatland flourished into the late 20th century. In 1912, Valley Baptist Church organized on the hill in Wheatland. During the pastorate of a Reverend Johnson, services were held in a former blacksmith shop. Choir members include Rev. Samuel Delane Jr., Dea. George Edward Borders, Natalie Green Borders, Thomas Lewis, Daisy Delane, Bessie Lewis, Laura Hosey, and Eunice Hosey. With a team of horses, Frank Bruce, a Wheatland businessman, excavated office buildings along Broadway Avenue.

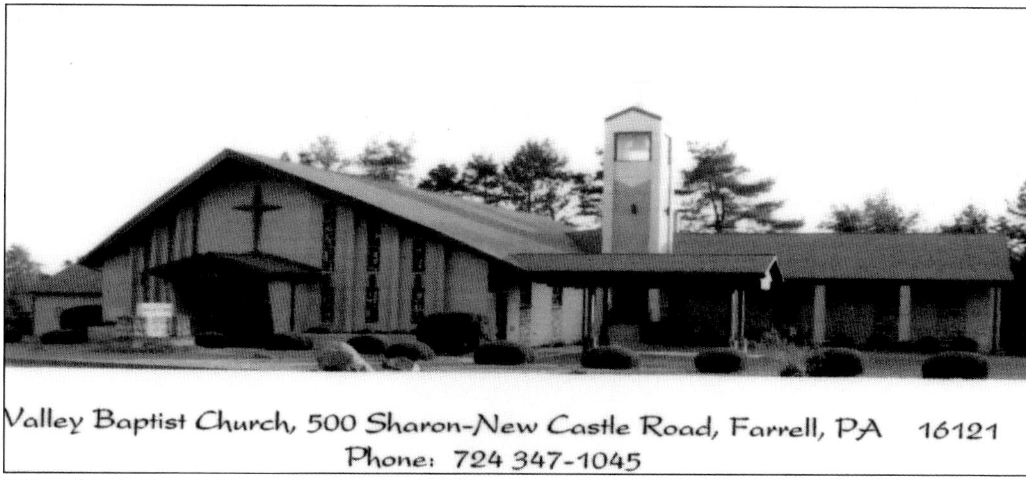

Wheatland councilman Charles S. Butler (1892–1990) operated Butler Riding Stables at 39 Morton Street near the tennis courts. In 1953, Valley Baptist Church began construction of a new building under Rev. S. J. Waller. In 1985, a tornado destroyed the church and neighboring vicinity. In 1986, under the leadership of Rev. Anderson T. Tatum, the longest-serving pastor, Valley Baptist Church rebuilt in Farrell.

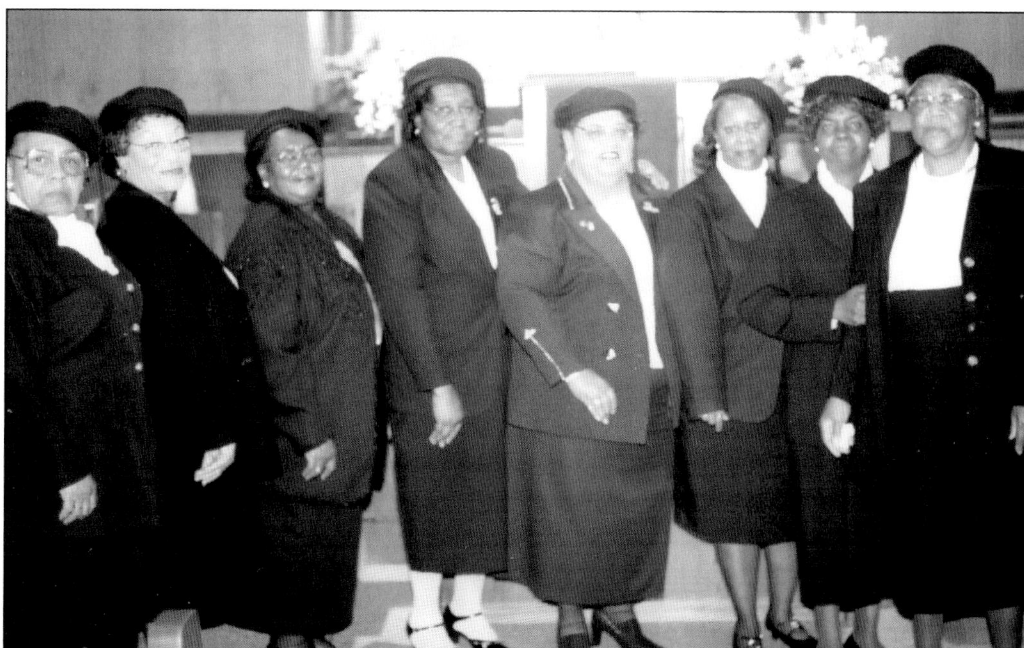

Shannon Funeral Home, operated by Wilbert L. Shannon Sr., the first African American chairman of the Pennsylvania State Board of Funeral Directors, and son his Wilbert L. Shannon Jr., continues as a landmark on the hill in Wheatland. From left to right, Valley Baptist Church deaconesses Ethel Johnson, Mary Ray, Martha Cromartie, Mardyn Coleman, Carolyn Roberts, Eileen Batchelor, Alma McCoy, and Aurelia Hosey are pictured at the mortgage burning in the 1990s. (Courtesy of Veral Adair.)

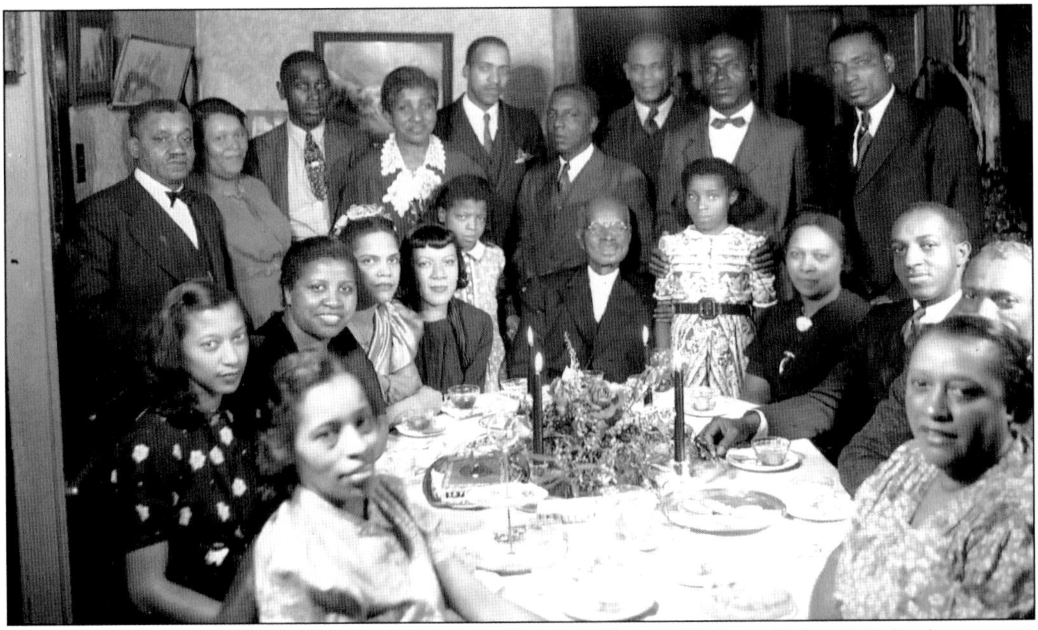

Before World War I, Rev. Elijah Flemon (seated at the head of the table), a Methodist circuit rider, traveled by horse and buggy from Brookfield, Ohio, across the rivers through Sharon, alternating routes going to churches in either Mercer or Greenville on Sunday. In African Methodist Episcopal Zion connection's sanctuaries, the community discussed vital issues of the day, engaged in intellectual pursuits, and developed leadership. Mercer had a Colored Literary Society. (Courtesy of Frances Flemon Ward.)

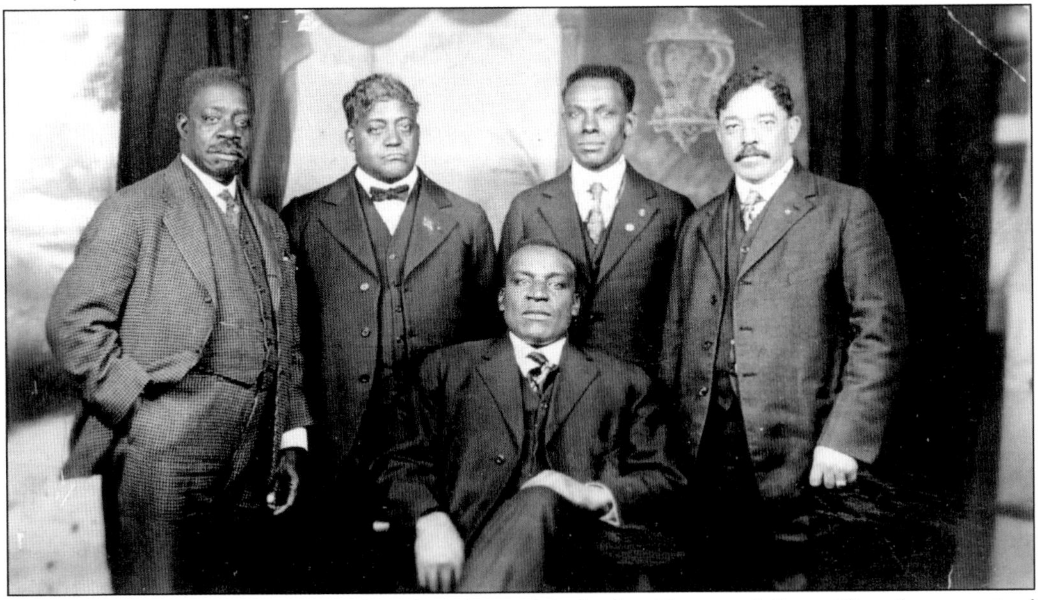

Rev. Janifer D. Meade, pastor of Ruth African Methodist Episcopal Zion Church, organized Calumet Lodge No. 25, Prince Hall Affiliation in 1917. A steward at National Malleable, Harry S. Molson (standing, second from left); an inspector at the Farrell nail plant, Thomas Dillard (standing, second from right); and a tinner, Edward B. Hodge (far right), were the first worshipful masters. The men are pictured at a Masonic event in Erie around 1922.

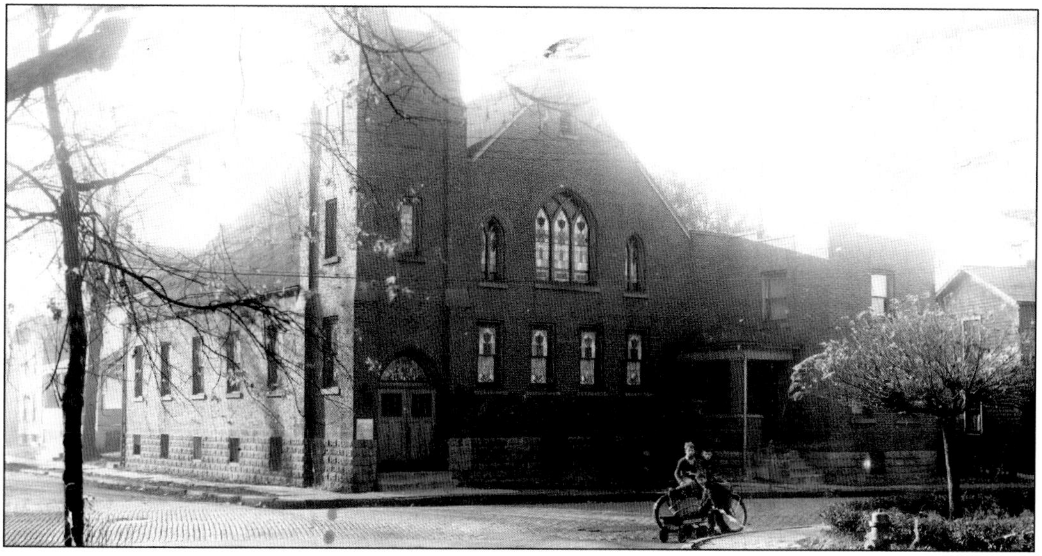

In 1888, Rev. P. R. Anderson became the first pastor of the Ruth African Methodist Episcopal Zion Church in Sharon. The Sharpsville, Greenville, and Mercer African Methodist Episcopal Zion Churches no longer existed. The African Methodist Episcopal Zion Church, hailed as the "Freedom Church," was formed by free persons of color and reached Mercer County in the 1870s. In 2009, the pastor of Ruth African Methodist Episcopal Zion Church is Rev. Geraldine Williams. (Courtesy of Ulysses Ward.)

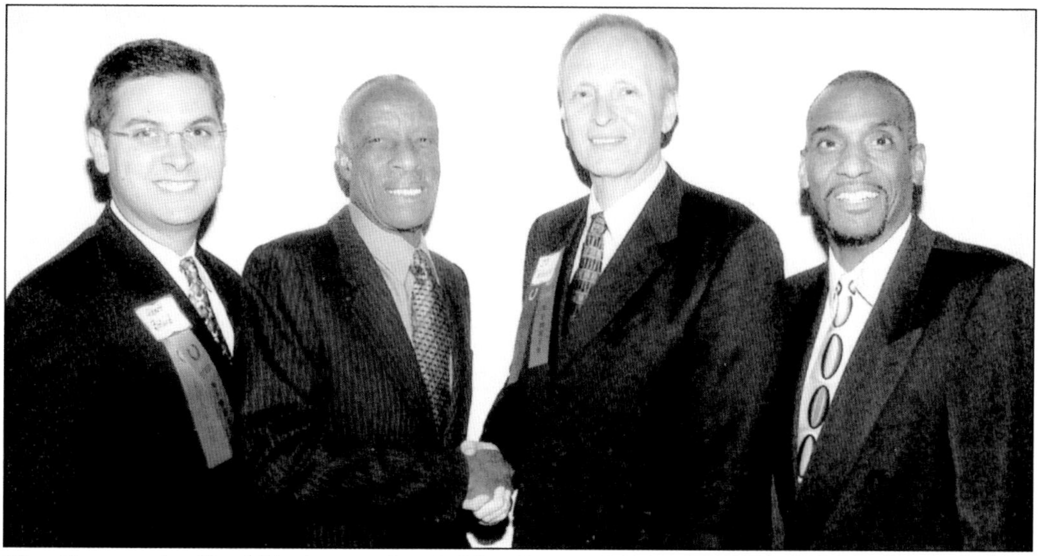

The Community Food Bank, spearheaded by Greater Mount Zion Church of God in Christ, operated out of Ruth African Methodist Episcopal Zion Church during the administration of Dr. Samuel Perry, who served as its president. The Community Food Bank, formed by a group of 14 black churches to assist those "being turned down by the Salvation Army," received financial support from African American churches and fraternal groups. Heavy traffic required a change of facilities after a year and a half, due to damage suffered from flooding in 1959. Pictured here, Michael Wright (far right) salutes Johnny B. McClean (second from left) for years of dedicated service to the Community Food Warehouse of Mercer County, a separate entity, in Farrell. (Courtesy of Michael Wright.)

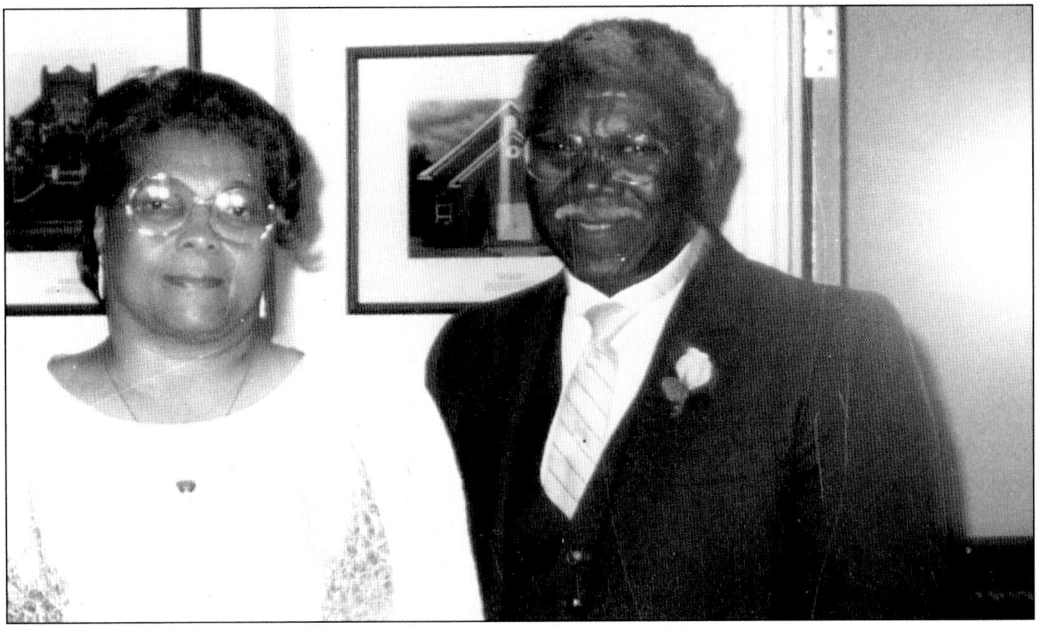

A cadre of community leaders, ranging from civic to fraternal leaders, arose from Ruth African Methodist Episcopal Zion Church. Dr. Theodore L. Yarboro, a Buhl Day honoree in 1999, and Deanna M. R. Yarboro, a Buhl Day honoree in 1997, are pictured at a wedding ceremony for their son. Local organizer Dr. Theodore L. Yarboro served on the board of directors of the National Urban League from 1973 to 1978. (Courtesy of Dr. Theodore L. Yarboro.)

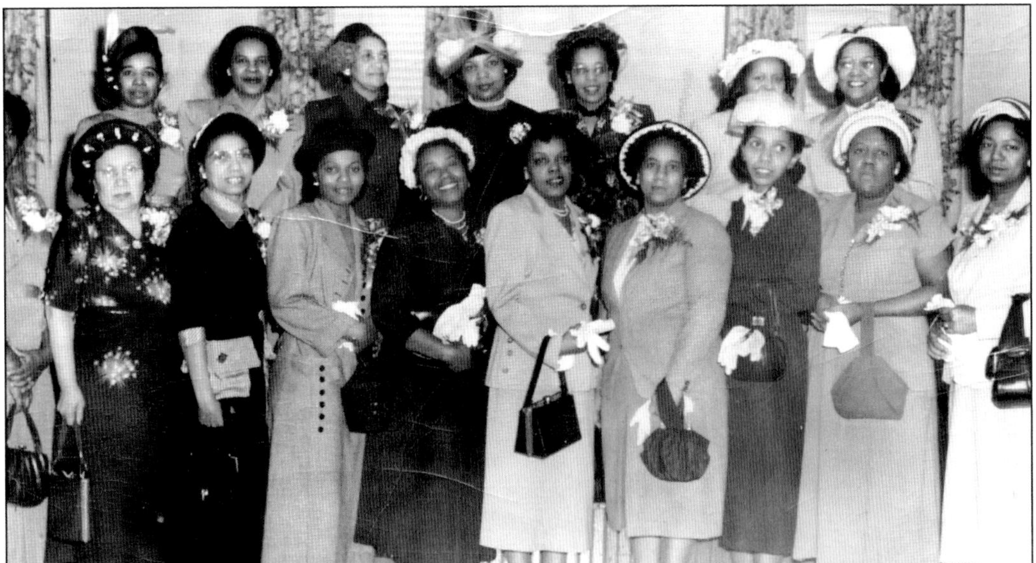

In the 1940s, Rev. Ira B. Lavigne organized the Willing Workers at Ruth African Methodist Episcopal Zion Church. Pictured in the 1950s at the Carver Community Center in Farrell are, from left to right, (first row) Agnes Matthews, Mary Johnson, Helen Green Wilson, Lottie Johnson Lampkins, Modestine Green, Catherine Matthews, Freda Palm, Elva Mae Truman Jones, Erma Grayson, and ? Bruce; (second row) Virginia Greene, Violet Flemon, Grace James, Wilma Mitchell, Catherine Flemon, Evelyn Johnson, and Jean Arkward. (Courtesy of Ulysses Ward.)

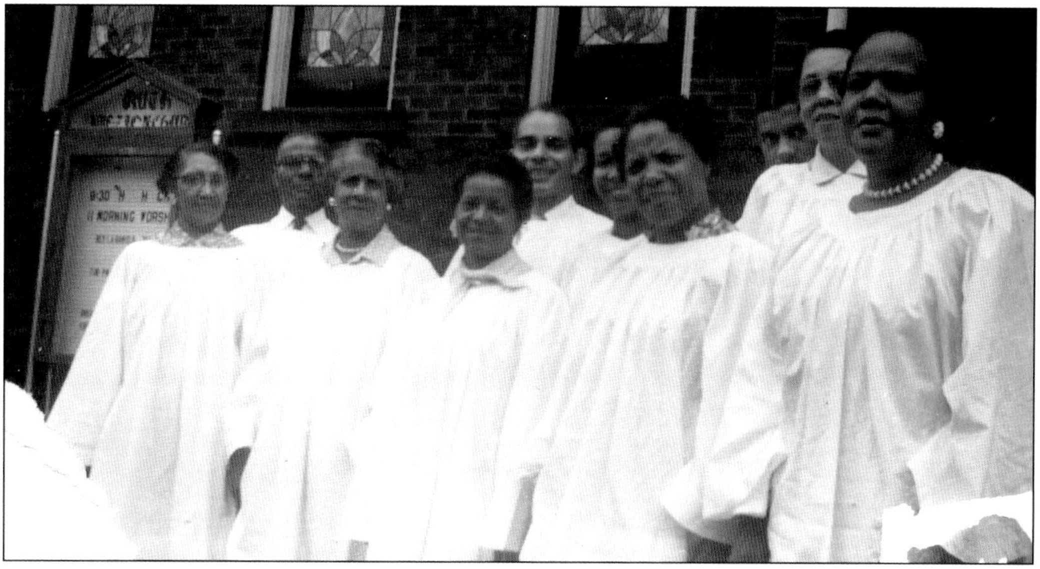

In 1977, the Mercer County Housing Authority's Ira B. Lavigne Manor, located at Dream Boulevard and Cathedral Drive in Farrell, was named in honor of Lavigne. During the civil rights era, Rev. K. Melvin Taylor was instrumental in enrolling the first African American student nurses at the Sharon General Hospital of Nursing, which was a milestone. Ruth African Methodist Episcopal Zion Church choir members pictured include Freda Palm, Evelyn Johnson, Wilma Mitchell, Ruth Haynes, Sylvester Ward, Edward Cooper, Cleo Overton, and Kenneth Matthews. (Courtesy of Frances Flemon Ward.)

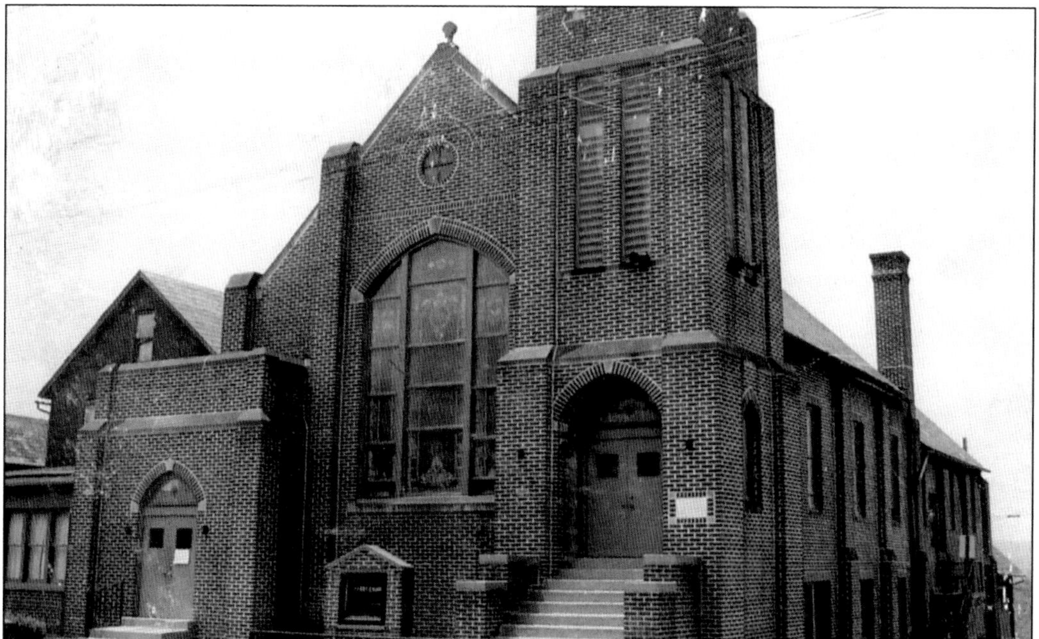

In 1901, the First Baptist Church was organized at the home of Chestina Jones when she resided at 1116 Hamilton Avenue in South Sharon. The church moved to a school on Idaho Street and then to a storefront on Greenfield Avenue, later known as Market Avenue, in Farrell. The present site is at the corner of Darr Avenue and French Street. (Courtesy of Joe C. Pulliam.)

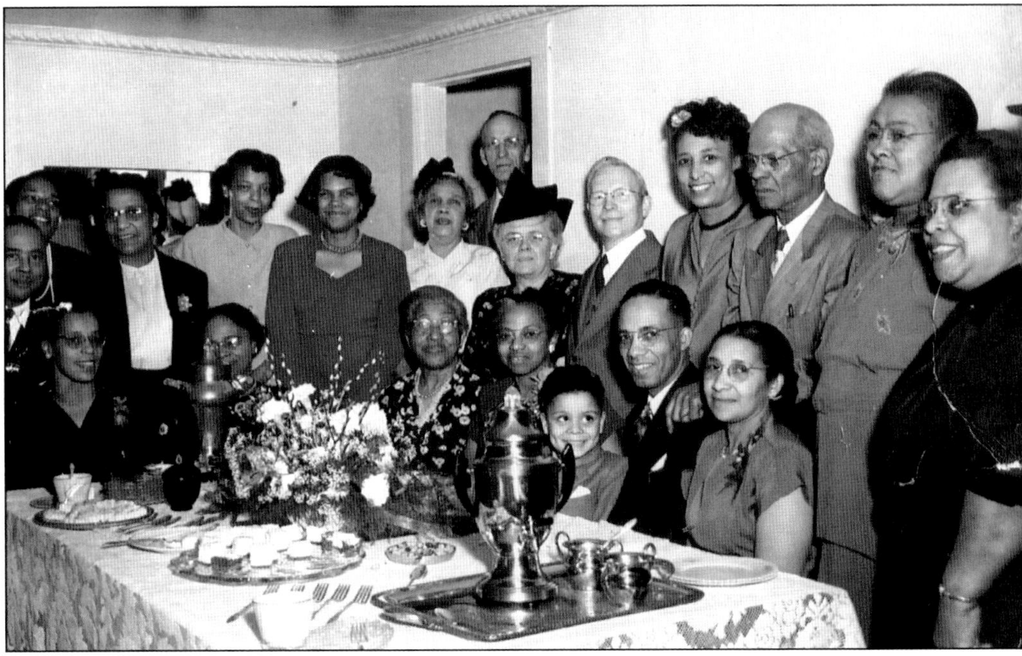

Rev. Ira B. Lavigne (seated), who was called in 1949, served 27 years, the longest-serving pastor at First Baptist Church in Farrell. In 1978, he was followed by Rev. D. Lee Owens, Rev. Lowell T. Williams, Rev. Phillip King, and Rev. Sidney B. Walker. (Courtesy of Ulysses and Frances Flemon Ward.)

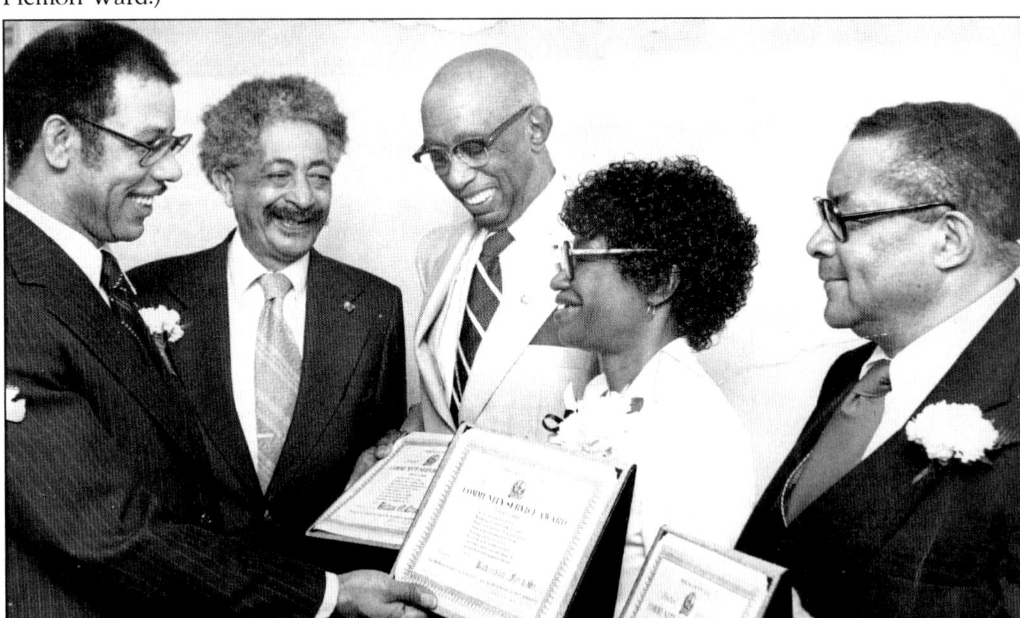

The Community Prayer Band, conceived by Robinson Ford Sr. along with members of First Baptist Church, was organized in 1953. Maurice Cary (far left), president of the Mercer County Frontiers Club, presents the 1981 community service awards to Ford; Artie Mae Russell Johnson, member of New Hope Baptist; and Belton Crim, member of Greater Morris Chapel African Methodist Episcopal Church. (Courtesy of Mercer County Frontiers Club.)

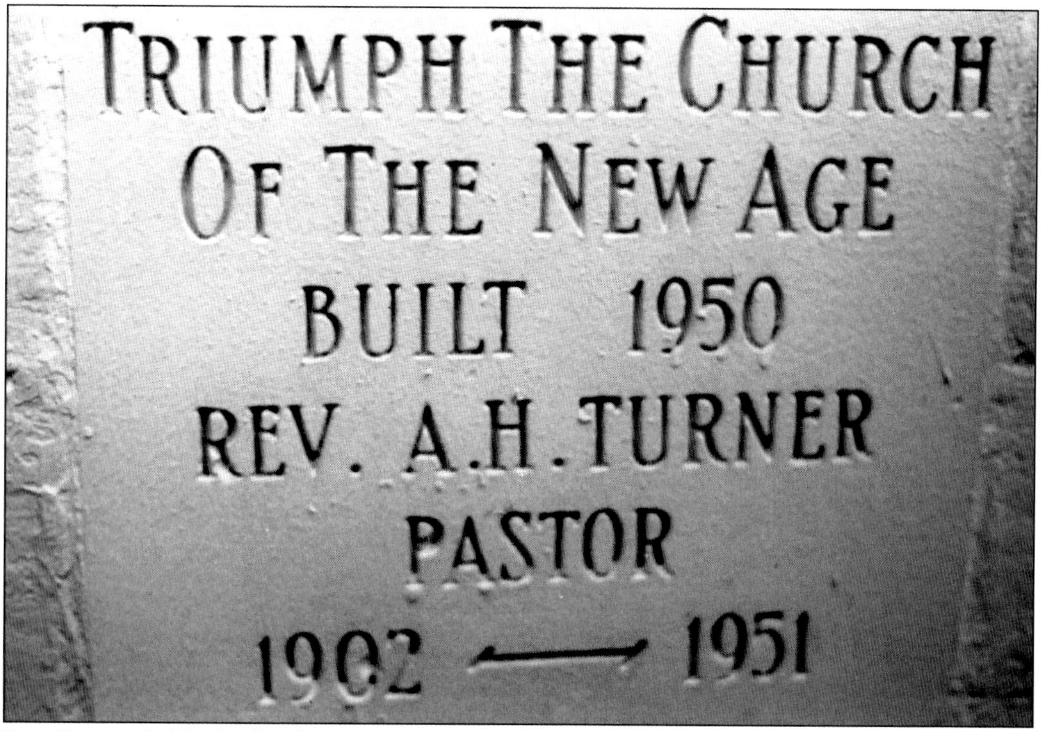

Rev. George Gibbs, Richard Campbell, Alphonso Ford, Henry Ford, Joseph Logan, Toby Morris, George Staley, and Melvin Wilson assisted in establishing the Community Prayer Band. Triumph the Church of the New Age was organized in 1902. The first pastor was Rev. E. D. Smith, and the church location was at 929 Lee Avenue in Farrell. The church is no longer in existence.

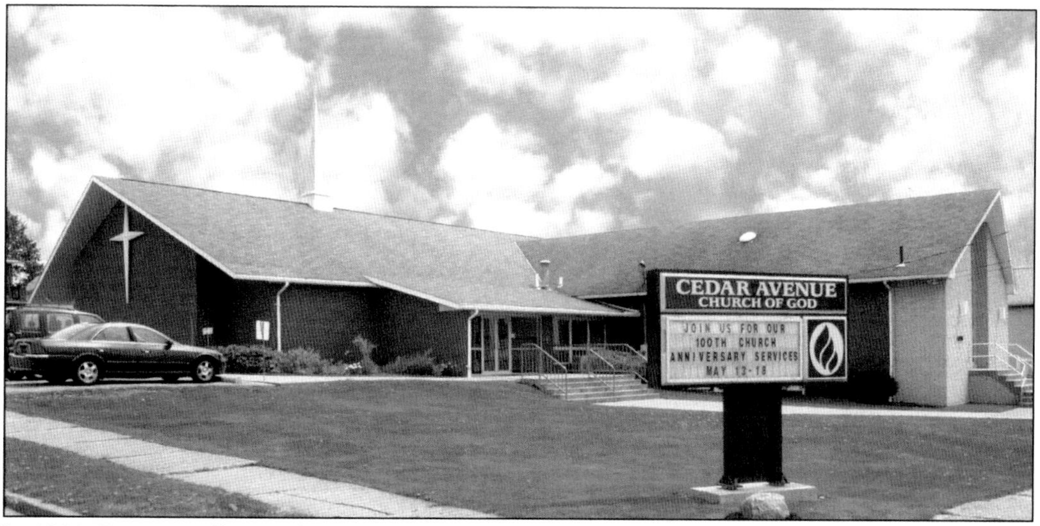

In 1908, Rev. Priscilla Wimbish and Rev. Ida English served as first pastors of the Cedar Avenue Church of God. In 2009, the pastor is Rev. Charles S. Johnson. Former pastors include Rev. William Blackburn, Rev. Purnell White, Rev. G. R. Dixon, Rev. J. L. Blake, Rev. J. Bonner, Rev. L. M. Turner, Rev. Hattie Smoot, Rev. J. W. Butler, Rev. I. W. Mitchell, Rev. T. J. Sawyer, Rev. Noah W. White Jr., Dr. Michael A. Smith, and Dr. Angel Dela Cruz. (Courtesy of Cedar Avenue Church of God.)

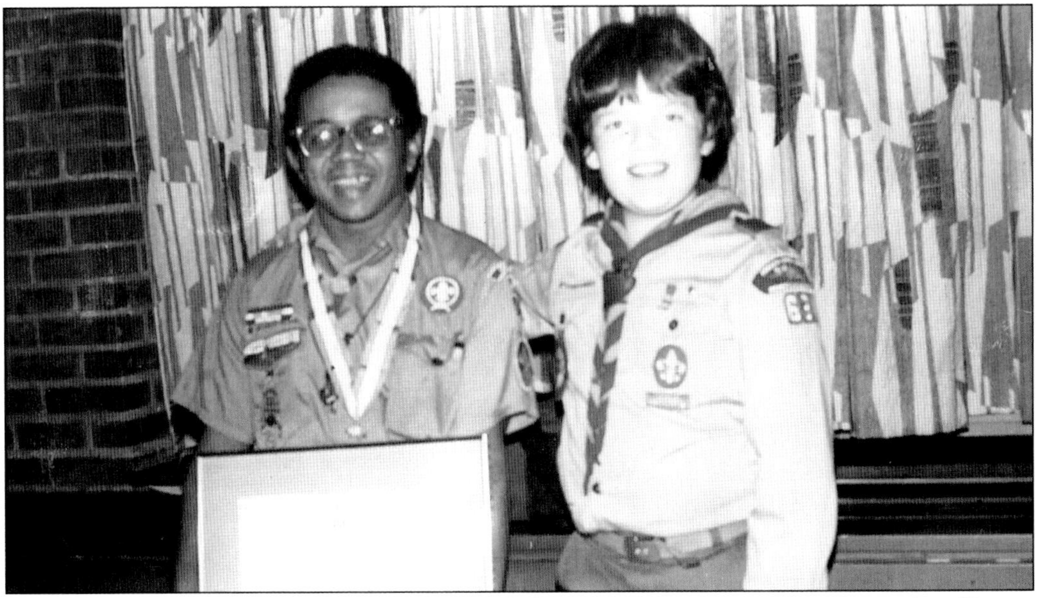

The Mercer County Frontiers Club presented the 1992 community service award to Dewey Lorance, a member of Cedar Avenue Church of God, for organizing Cub Scout pack No. 11 in Farrell. In 1980, David Torrence, scoutmaster for Boy Scout troop No. 72, which was sponsored by the Salvation Army in Greenville, received the Silver Beaver Award at Edinboro College. Torrence, of Greenville, served as a commissioned officer in the Salvation Army. (Courtesy of David Torrence.)

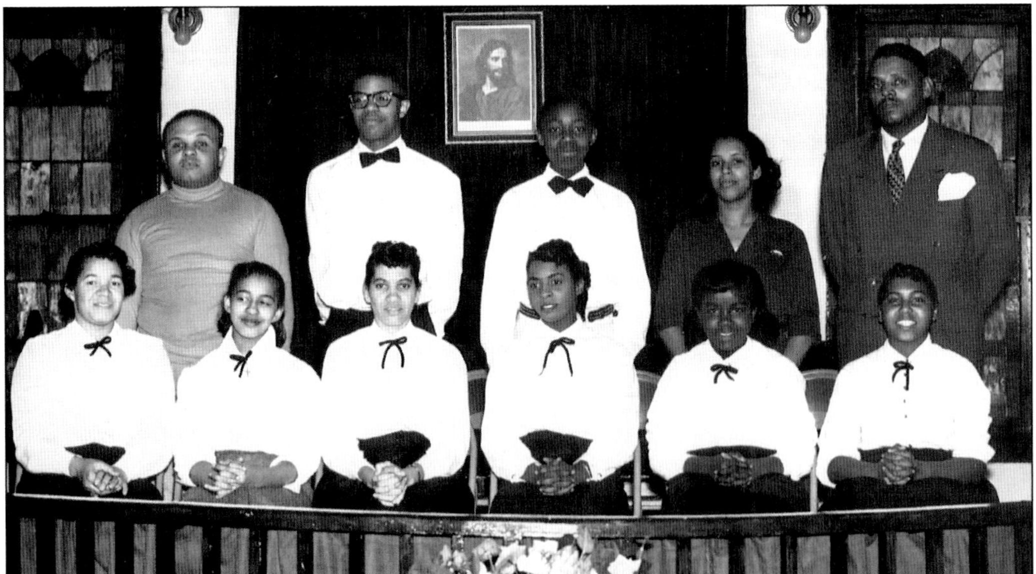

Pictured around 1950, the Cedar Avenue Church of God orchestra includes, from left to right, (first row) Grace Mitchell Pleasant, piano; Julia Steele, flute; Shirley Matthews Williams, piano, xylophone, and barbell; LaVerne Culp Porter, xylophone and piano; Wilda Amos, clarinet; and Bertha Jean Askerneese, clarinet; (second row) Albert Phillips, trombone; Fred Culp Jr., saxophone; Sterling Culp; Dorothy Polley Matthews, violin; and director William Alford. Not pictured is Charles Pleasant, bass violin. (Courtesy of Shirley Matthews Williams.)

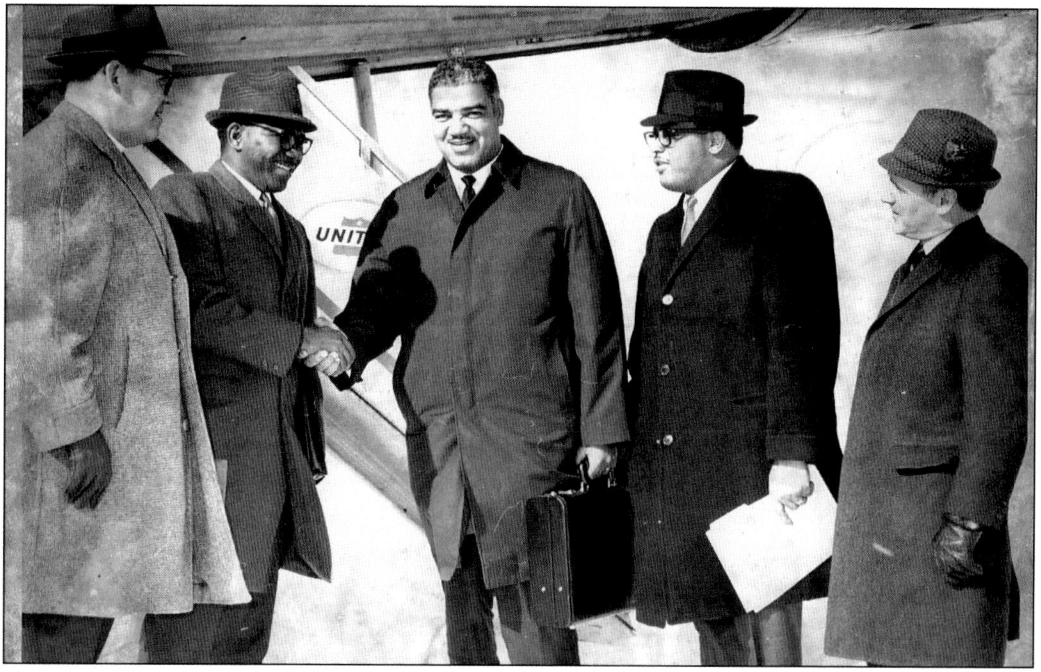

Pictured are, from left to right, Rev. Malcolm McMillan, Dr. Theodore L. Yarboro, Whitney Young Jr., executive director of the National Urban League, local affiliate executive director Ernest Prince, and Ernest Tobin at the Youngstown Airport. Young attended the Shenango Valley Urban League (SVUL) charter banquet presentation at St. Michael's Center, Hermitage, in 1969. (Courtesy of Dr. Theodore L. Yarboro.)

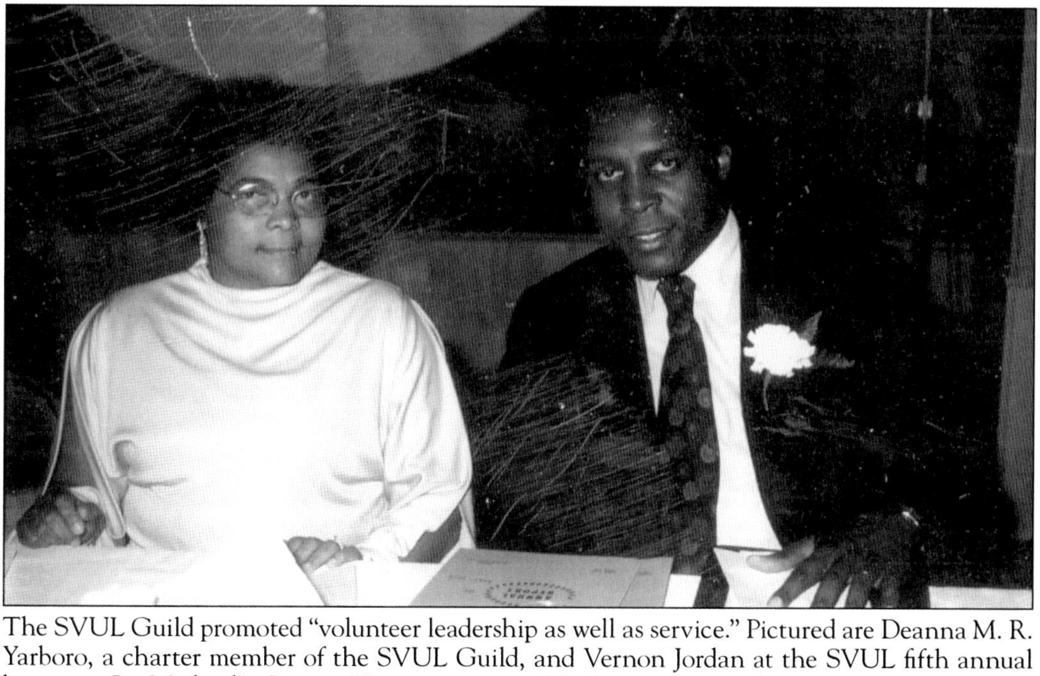

The SVUL Guild promoted "volunteer leadership as well as service." Pictured are Deanna M. R. Yarboro, a charter member of the SVUL Guild, and Vernon Jordan at the SVUL fifth annual banquet, St. Michael's Center, Hermitage, in 1973. Over 700 people attended. (Courtesy of Dr. Theodore L. Yarboro.)

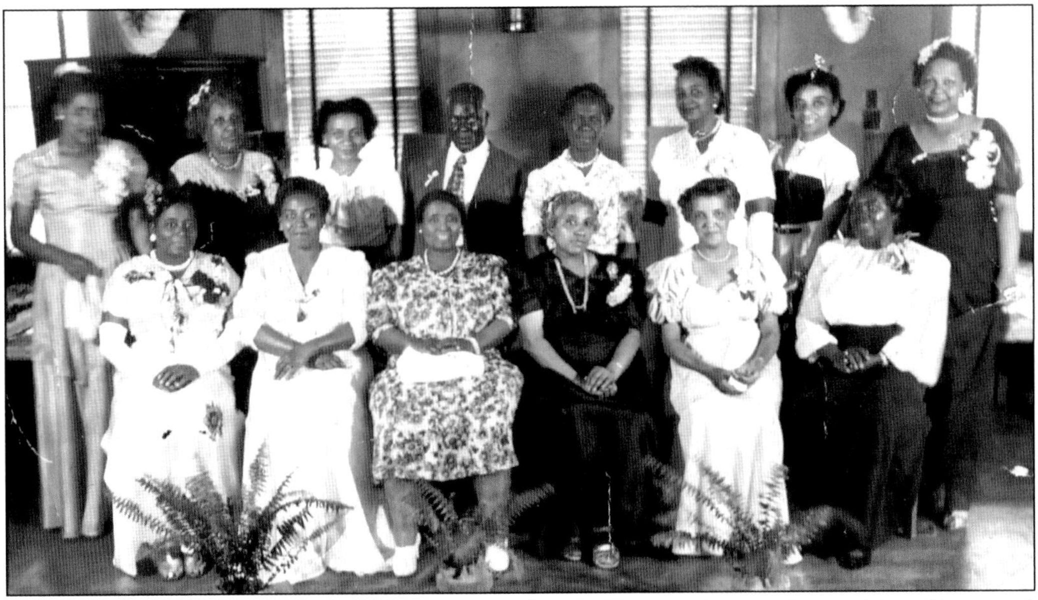

Gathered for an unidentified celebration in the 1940s are, from left to right, (first row) unidentified, Anita Fitzpatrick, Harriet B. Wright (wife of the Greater Morris Chapel African Methodist Episcopal Church's pastor), unidentified, ? Cherow, and unidentified; (second row) Margaret Robinson, ? Gaddy, Merrel Phillips Robinson, Adam Jenkins (class leader), ? Lancaster, Arlillian Jeter, Mabel Phillips, and unidentified. (Courtesy of Greater Morris Chapel African Methodist Episcopal Church.)

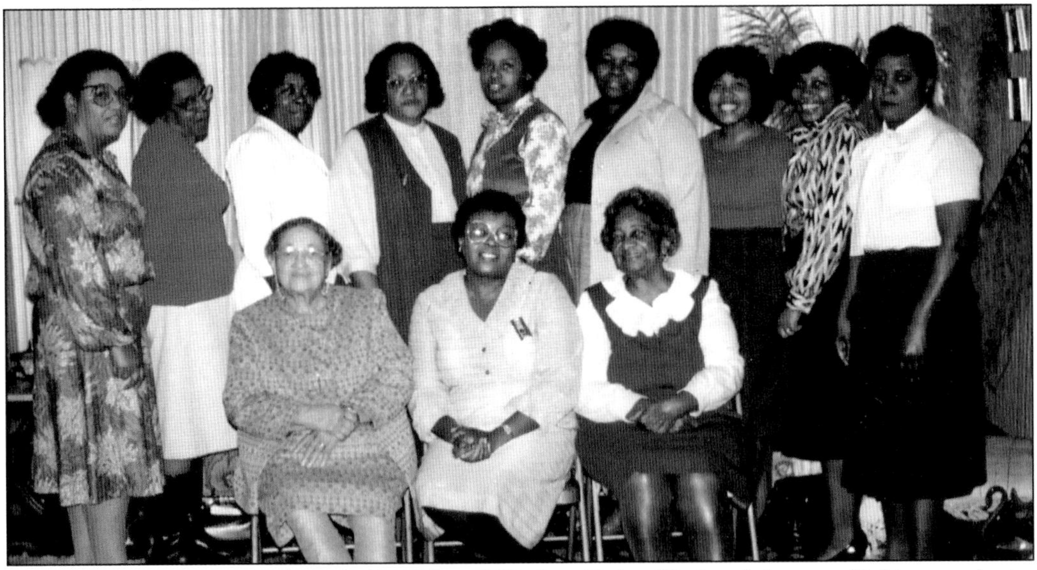

The Gospel Echoes, which included Edward Hodge, Helen Hodge, Margaret Robinson, Anita Nixon Daniel Fitzpatrick, Carl Stewart, Mildred Perry Stewart, and Merrel Phillips Robinson, sang on radio station WPIC. Pictured in the 1970s, Harriet B. Wright Missionary Society members are, from left to right, (first row) Mamie Miller, Frances Jackson, and Arlillian Jeter; (second row) Carolyn Miller Roberts, Alfreda Crim, unidentified, Rev. Virginia Wiley, Reverend Taylor, unidentified, Rev. Jeanette Hooks Hubbard, Gloria Wright, and unidentified. (Courtesy of Greater Morris Chapel African Methodist Episcopal Church.)

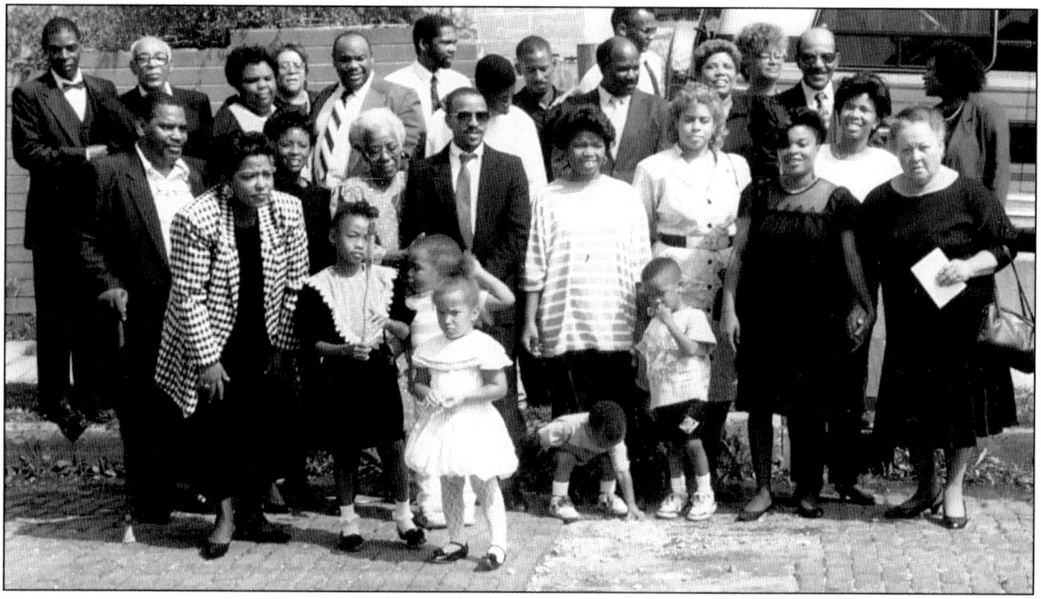

Merrel Phillips Robinson raised 11 children by herself and brought them all from out in the country to Greater Morris Chapel African Methodist Episcopal Church in town. Sunday school superintendent Mildred Cannon, recognized as valedictorian of her West Middlesex High School class, had the Cannon Room named in her honor. Following the service, the Cannon family gathers outside Greater Morris Chapel African Methodist Episcopal Church in Farrell around 1989. (Courtesy of Toby and Dorothy Jackson.)

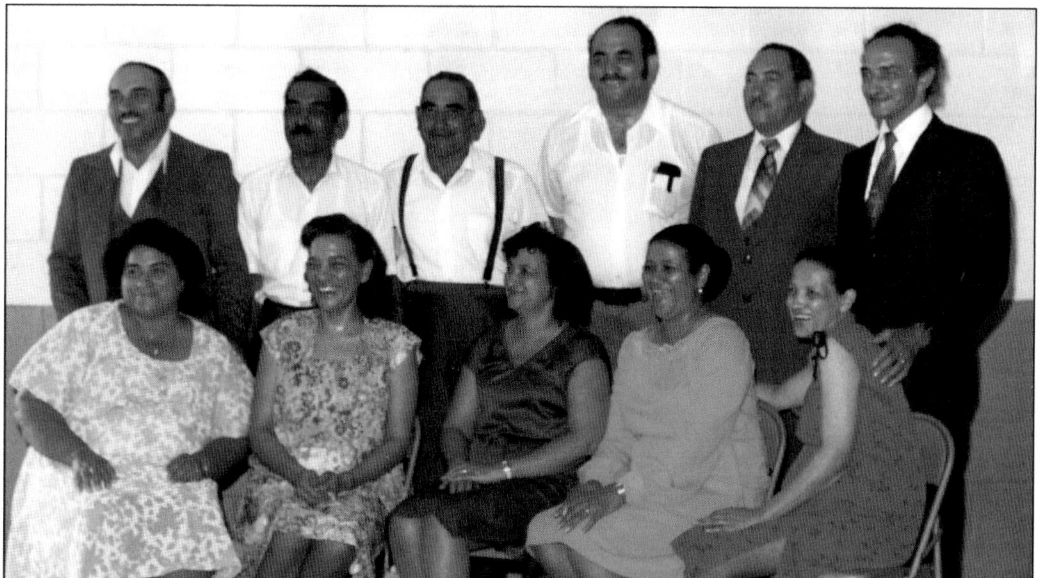

Expecting her 11th child when her husband passed, Robinson raised the family alone. Adult children of Robinson include, from left to right, (first row) Gloria Elaine Boatwright, Sarah (Sally) Pinson, Marie Mathews, Margaret Walker, and Marian Bush; (second row) Cornelius Emery Robinson, Gordon Thomas Robinson, Jeremiah Samuel Robinson, James Ambrose Robinson, Harry Alexander Robinson, and Charles Albert Robinson. They are pictured at the Wheatland American Legion in 1977. (Courtesy of Sarah Pinson.)

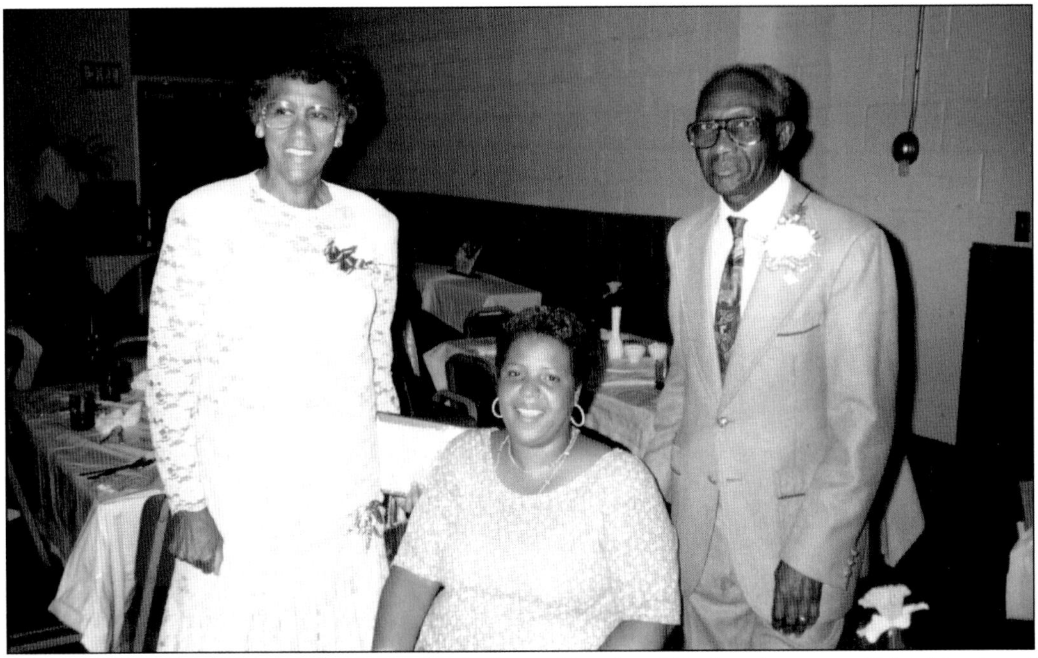

Pictured are, from left to right, Dorothy Jackson; Rosalyn Wright, director of Neighborhood Based Family Intervention Center; and Toby Jackson at the first officers banquet of Greater Morris Chapel African Methodist Episcopal Church, held at the Keystone Blind Association in Sharon about 1995. (Courtesy of Toby and Dorothy Jackson.)

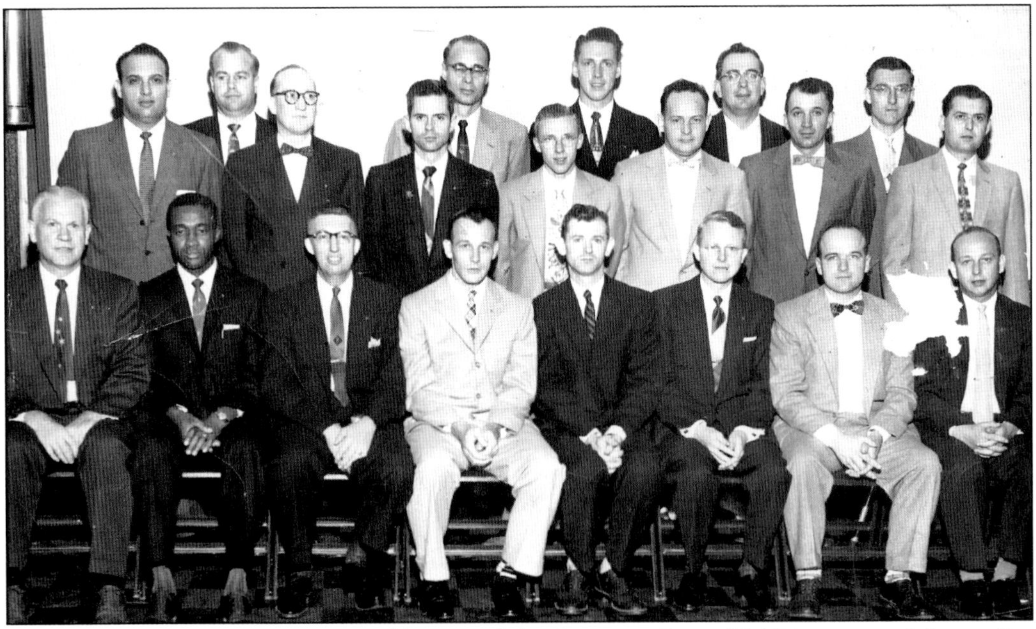

On August 27, 1917, the *Sharon Herald* reported the Carnegie Camp YMCA improved the quality of life for southern migrants. In 1917, M. S. Lennon, a Shaw University graduate, ran a YMCA for 45 African American men at the Carnegie Camp in Farrell. Toby Jackson (front row, second from left) serves as part of the Wiseman, an organization that founded YMCA in Hermitage. (Courtesy of Toby and Dorothy Jackson.)

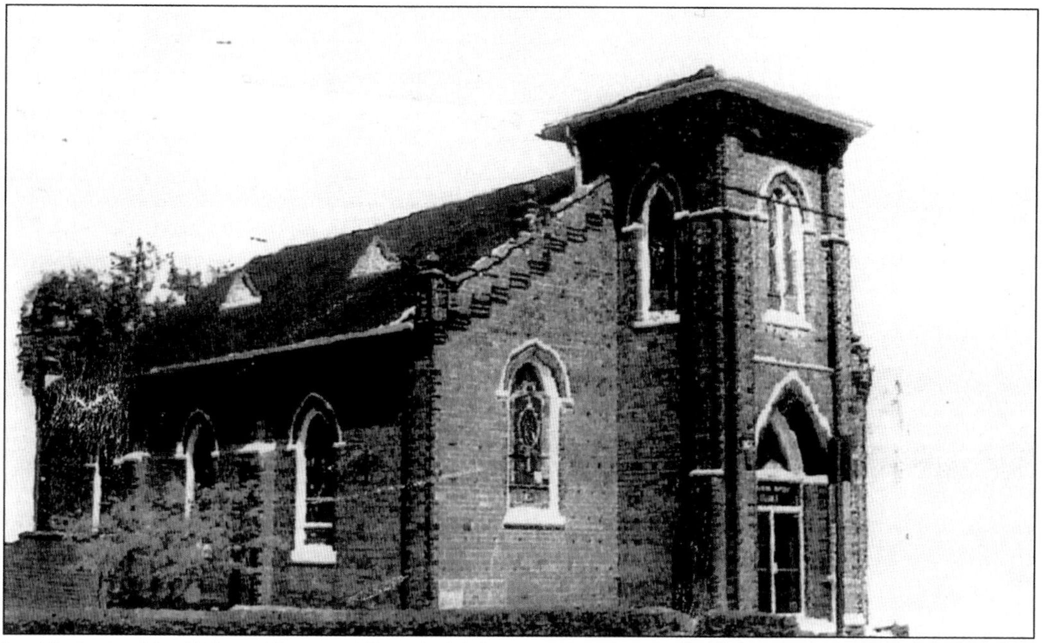

In 2007, the Bethlehem Baptist Church 86th anniversary souvenir book included the image of the present building at 858 Wallis Avenue in Sharon. The pastor is Rev. Leon Avery. (Courtesy of Bethlehem Baptist Church.)

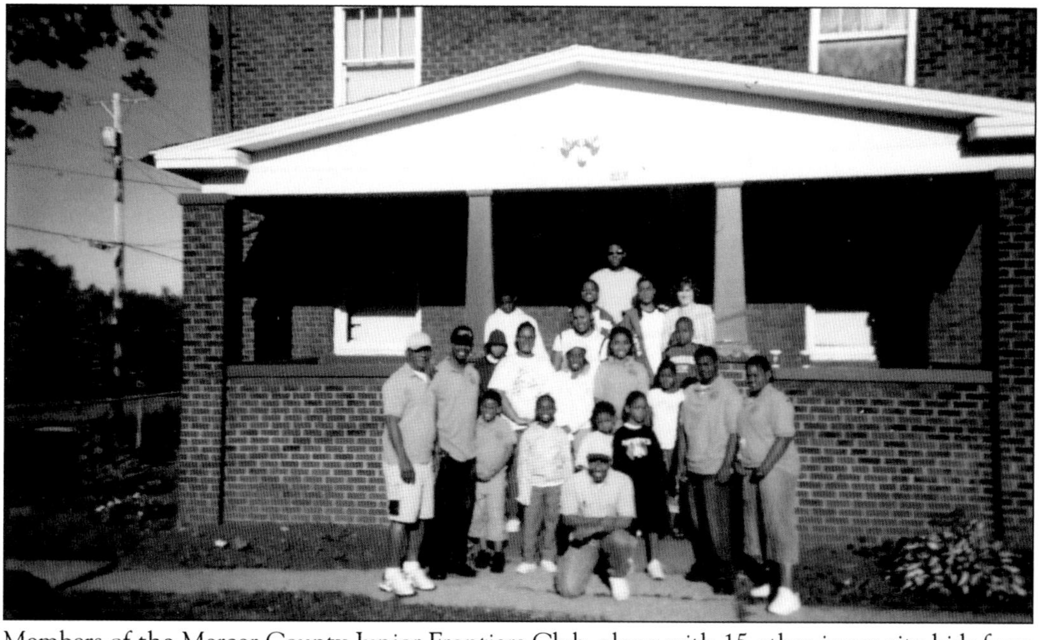

Members of the Mercer County Junior Frontiers Club, along with 15 other inner-city kids from the Bethlehem Baptist Church, gather in front of Noah's Ark Educational Center to attend Youth Field Day, where they learned how to canoe and fish. Dea. Milton Wilson (kneeling) provided experience for youth to enhance their quality of life and help them to grow socially and economically.

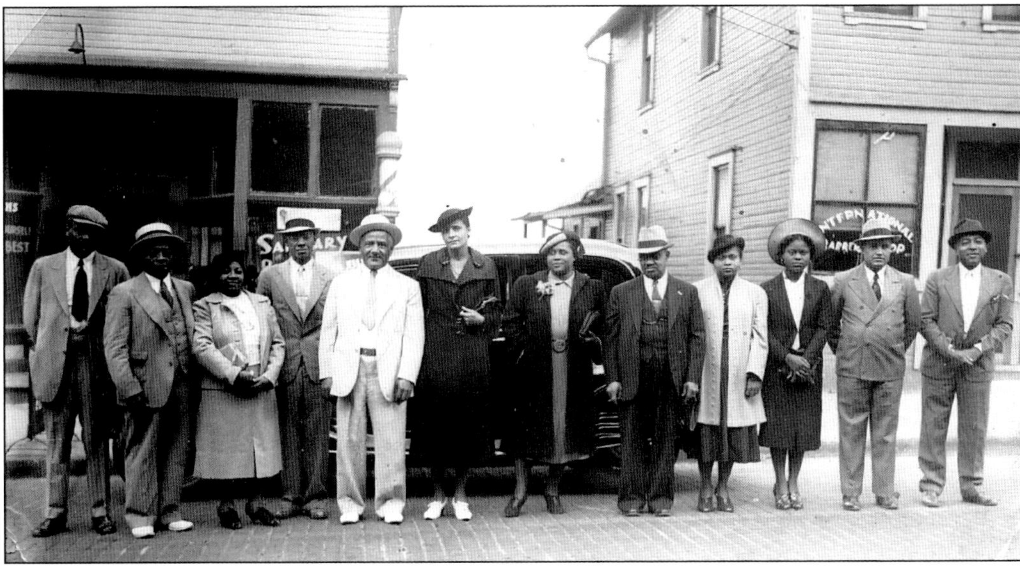

Prior to 1919, the association's executive secretary commended the Mercer County branch of the NAACP branch for its firm stand against racial prejudice. Branch members are, from left to right, Robert Bruce, Rev. Oscar Singletary of Friendship Baptist Church, unidentified, James Elmer Matthews, unidentified, unidentified, Mabel Bruce, Lincoln Watson, Violet Bruce Crowder, Margaret Bruce Campbell, Thomas Dillard, and ? Counts on the Market Avenue African American business corridor in the 1940s. In 1926, Rev. Oscar Singletary (1891–1974) served as the branch president. (Courtesy of Ethel McClain.)

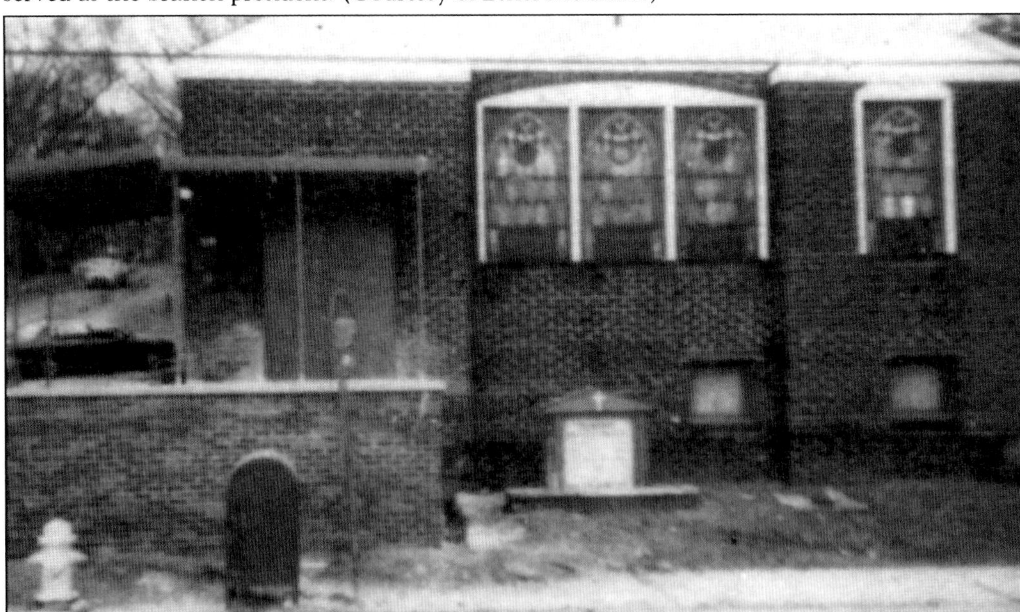

The Friendship Baptist Church 75th anniversary souvenir book included the image of the church building located at the corner of Spearman Avenue and Stevenson Street in Farrell in 1994. In 1919, five men from First Baptist Church of Farrell organized the Sixth Mount Zion Baptist Church in Sharon, the predecessor of Friendship Baptist Church in Farrell. The first pastor was Rev. P. C. Bailey. (Courtesy of Friendship Baptist Church.)

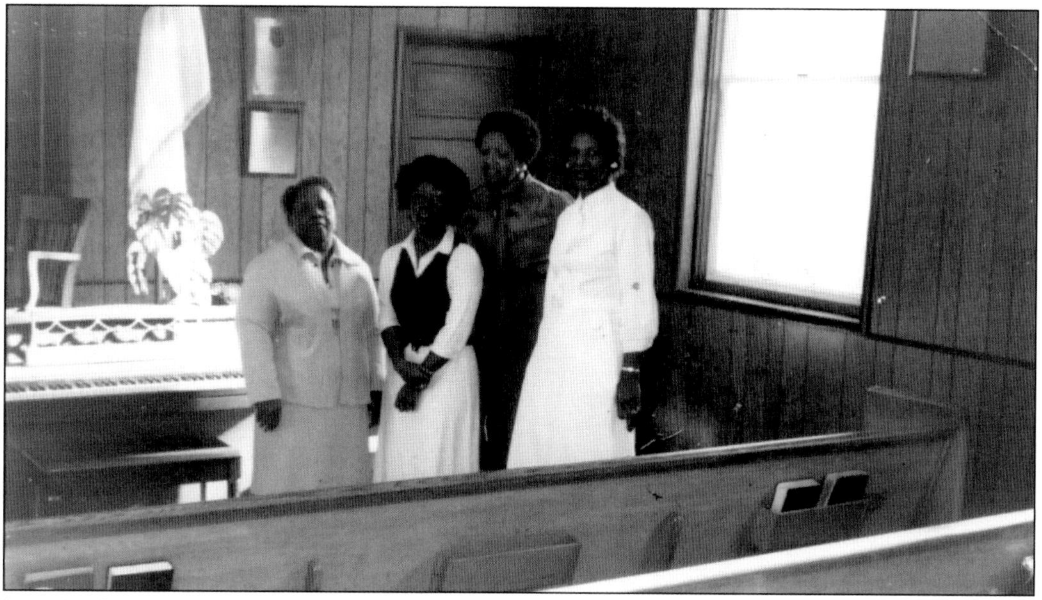

In 1929, Dea. James Renshaw, cofounder of the Sixth Mount Zion Baptist Church, became the first African American city councilman in Farrell's history. Cofounders included R. S. Breedlove, J. R. Johnson, Dea. Fate Rome, and Dea. T. J. Fernside. In 1930, the merger of the Sixth Mount Zion Baptist Church and Union Baptist Church produced Friendship Baptist Church in Farrell. Pictured from left to right, Friendship Baptist Church's ushers are Elizabeth Wright, unidentified, Martha Richards, and Charlotte Pegues. (Courtesy of Martha Richards.)

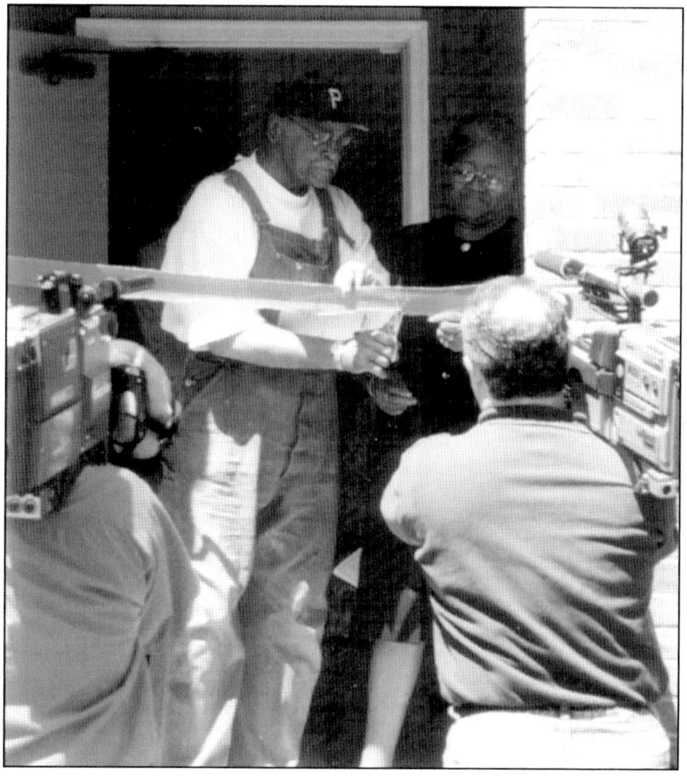

The former home of Rev. Oscar Singletary serves as the Ark House, a transitional home for women. During World War I, the development of the Baptist Church spread to Sharpsville. Pictured are trustee Marion N. Lampkins Sr. (1932–1999) of the Second Baptist Church in Sharpsville and Martha Richards at the ribbon cutting for the Ark House in Farrell. In 2009, the pastor of the Second Baptist Church in Sharpsville is Rev. James McKeithan. (Courtesy of Martha Richards.)

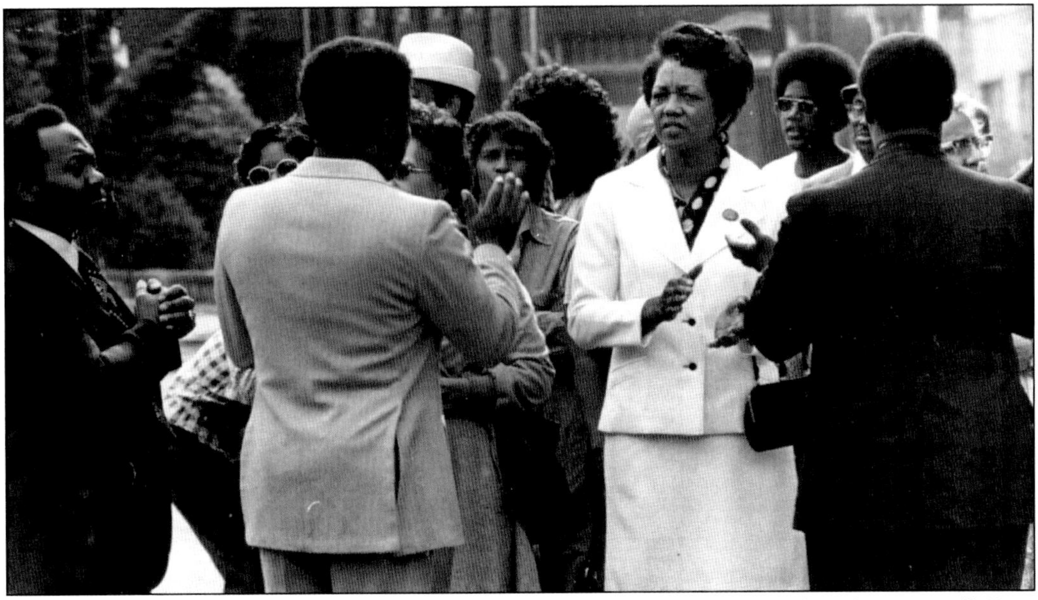

Rev. W. M. Wingfield Jr. (far left), pastor of Second Baptist Missionary Church in Farrell; Rev. Walter Gillespie, pastor of Second Baptist Church in Sharpsville; and Rev. Clyde Crooks, pastor of Triumph Church of God in Christ in Farrell, lead the Mercer County branch of the NAACP rally in support of the Boston branch of the NAACP's struggle for equal education. The 1954 United States Supreme Court decision *Brown v. Board of Education of Topeka*, which officially ended segregated public education is commemorated. (Courtesy of Martha Richards.)

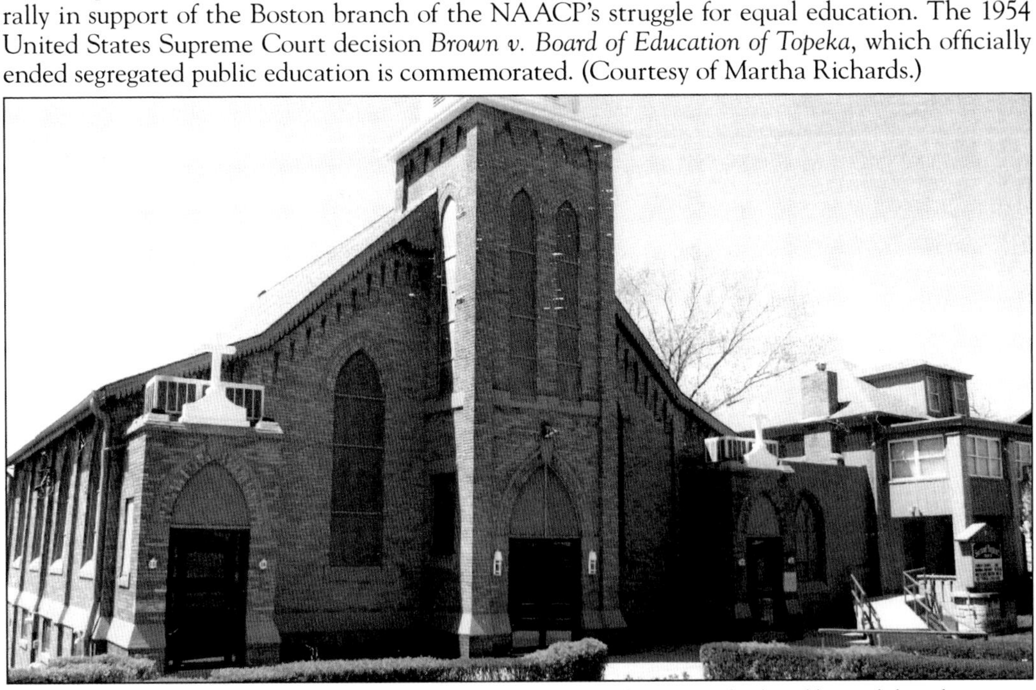

The Mercer County branch of the NAACP education rally began at the local branch headquarters on the corner of Spearman Avenue and Union Street and concluded at the historic Second Baptist Missionary Church, where Dr. C. H. Butler, the Pennsylvania NAACP president, spoke. In 1956, a tornado damaged the former church building at 1116 Market Avenue. In 1971, the church moved. Shown is the current site of Second Baptist Missionary Church at 1140 Spearman Avenue in Farrell. (Courtesy of Second Baptist Missionary Church.)

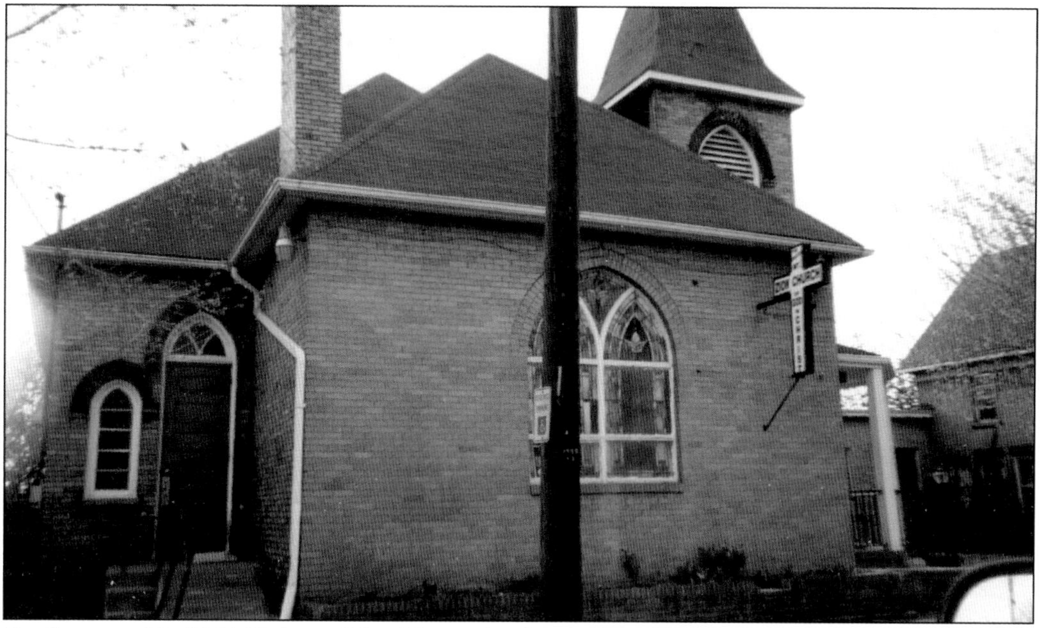

On January 18, 1947, Bishop Odis Alexander, his wife, mother Virginia Alexander, and five others came to Farrell. Services were held at the home of mother Louise Blackwell and mother Shepherd in Sharon. Bishop Charles Segers served as assistant to the pastor. Pictured is Greater Mount Zion Church of God in Christ at 414 Fruit Avenue in Farrell in the 1980s. (Courtesy of Greater Mount Zion Church of God in Christ.)

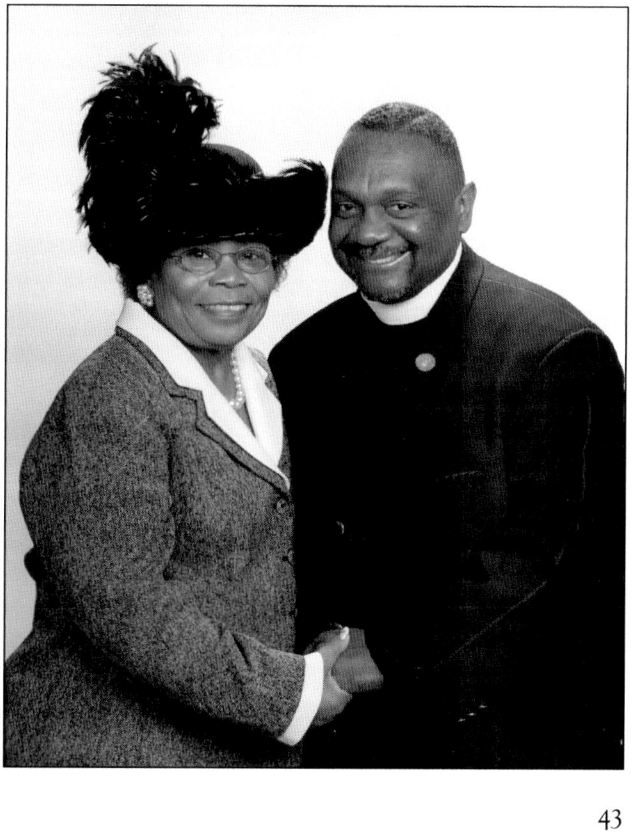

According to the Greater Mount Zion Church of God in Christ 50th anniversary booklet, "Superintendent Wilbert G. Hadden became the pastor of Greater Mount Zion Church of God in Christ upon the death of Alexander in 1985." Eight years later, under the leadership of Hadden, a new church and housing for senior members were purchased. Pictured are Wilbert G. Hadden, pastor, and Hazel M. Hadden, copastor. (Courtesy of Greater Mount Zion Church of God in Christ)

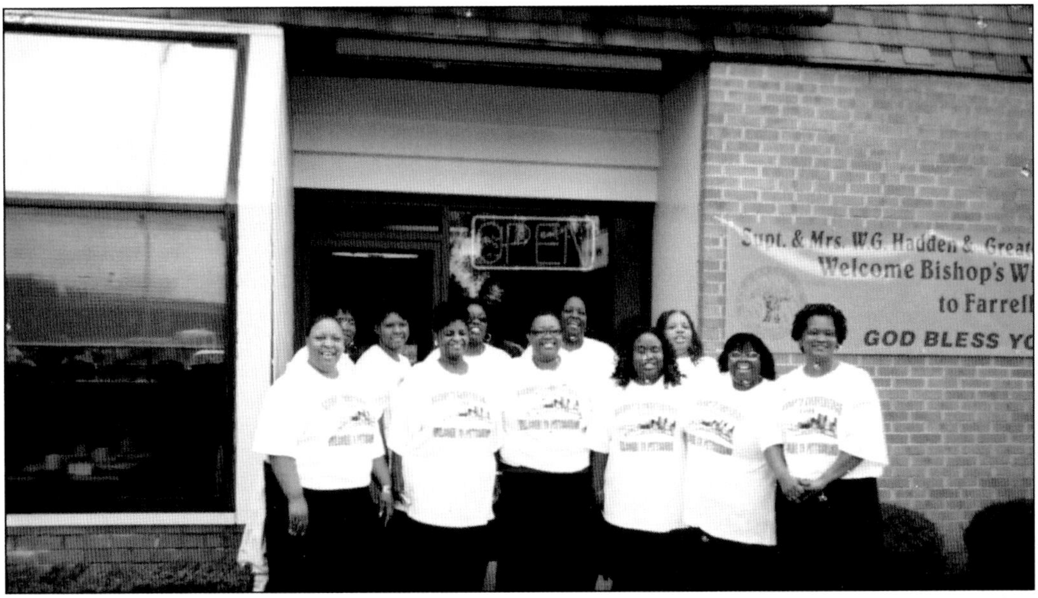

In 1988, the death of Olive Brown-McKeithan's son Todd was defining moment. Following her own group support, she provided bereavement services to others for three years. She harnessed the dormant power of churchwomen to form the Minority Health Advocacy Committee, which was birthed out of her personal struggle. The Pennsylvania regional Target Area Local Leader (TALL) team graduation for Aliquippa, Erie, and Farrell was held at Zion's Daily Bread, a family restaurant in Farrell. (Courtesy of Greater Mount Zion Church of God in Christ.)

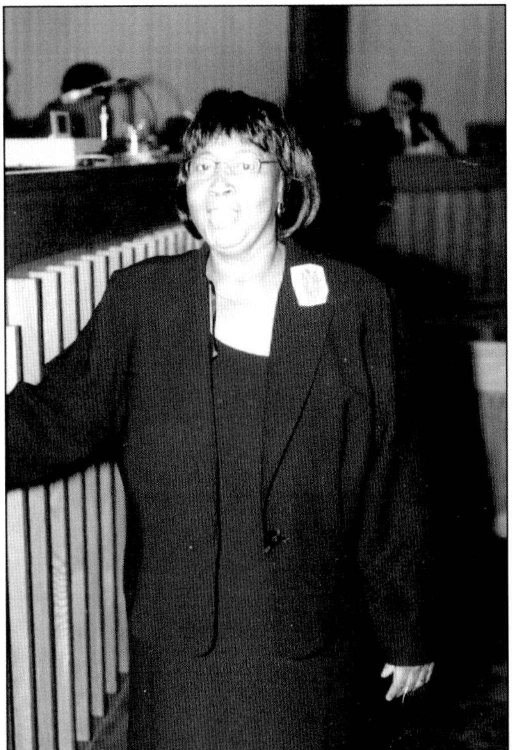

Brown-McKeithan is recognized as a tireless community organizer and missionary at Greater Mount Zion Church of God in Christ. For 13 years, she served as executive director of the Minority Health Center and Endorse Resistance of All Substance Abuse Everywhere (ERASE) Anti-Drug Coalition, whose programming included Art and Soul and Phenomenal Woman, before being elected the first African American and first female mayor in Farrell. She is pictured here in January 2008, presiding from the city chamber. (Courtesy of Veral Adair.)

Three

Greenville, Mercer, and Sharon
The Intelligentsia

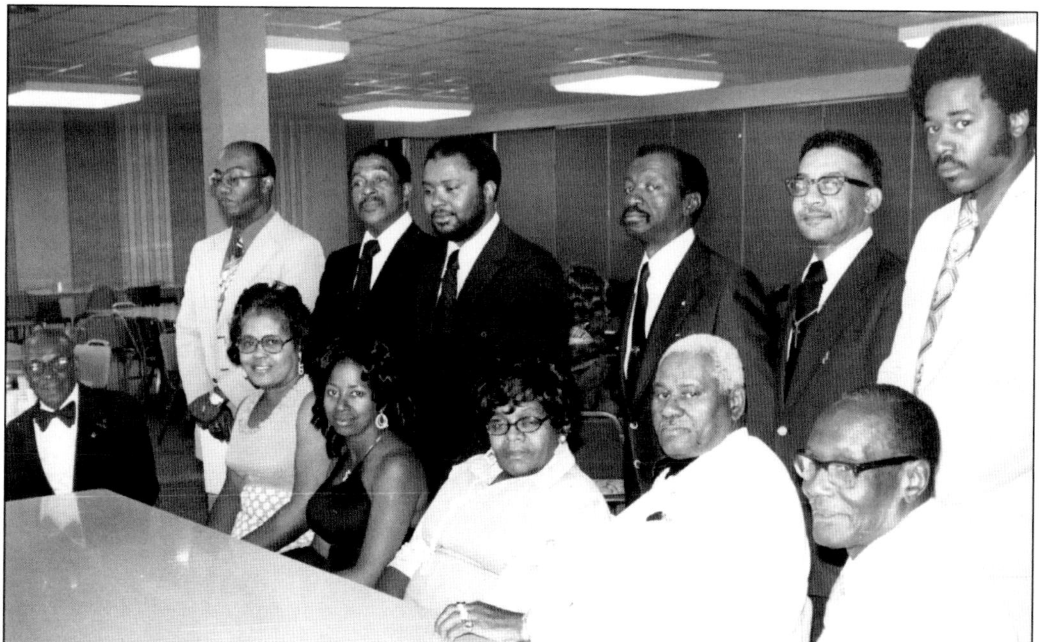

The Masonic board of regents for Knights of Pythagoras Odell B. Matthews Sr. No. 11 planned fund-raisers, and in conjunction with the advisors of the Felicitares, the female youth auxiliary, it held an annual cotillion. Board members include William Hobbs, David Myers, Issac Clarke, Odell B. "June" Matthews Jr., and Jesse Dobie at the third annual youth benefit banquet dance held at the Oak Tree Country Club in West Middlesex on September 17, 1977.

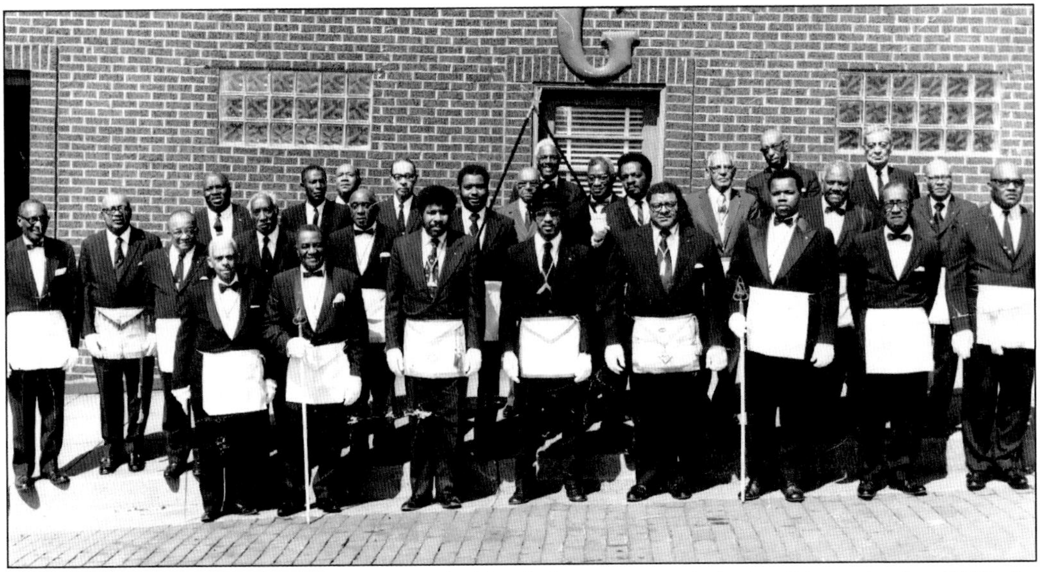

Prince Hall Masonry became a stronghold of the community's intelligentsia. In 1920, its 41 members reflected the middle class. Its ranks included four chefs, three clergymen, two barbers, two proprietors, two chauffeurs, two teamsters, a postal employee, a policeman, a mechanic, and a messenger. Calumet Lodge No. 25, organized by Rev. Janifer D. Meade, pastor of Ruth African Methodist Episcopal Zion Church, gathered in front of the lodge hall at 106 Idaho Street in the 1970s. Among those pictured are Henry Wells, Nelson Miller, John Singleton, Maurice Cary, Henry K. Sanders, George B. Thomas, Shade Speight, Edward Dunlap, John Hatwood, Samuel Ford, Henry Johnson, David Myers, John Reed, Charles S. Butler, William D. Mason, William Jones, Jesse Dobie, Bennie Ousley, Franklin Wilson, Julius Heath, Ralph Jefferson, John Overton, Alphonso Ford, Robinson Ford, and Roy Thomas. (Courtesy of David Myers.)

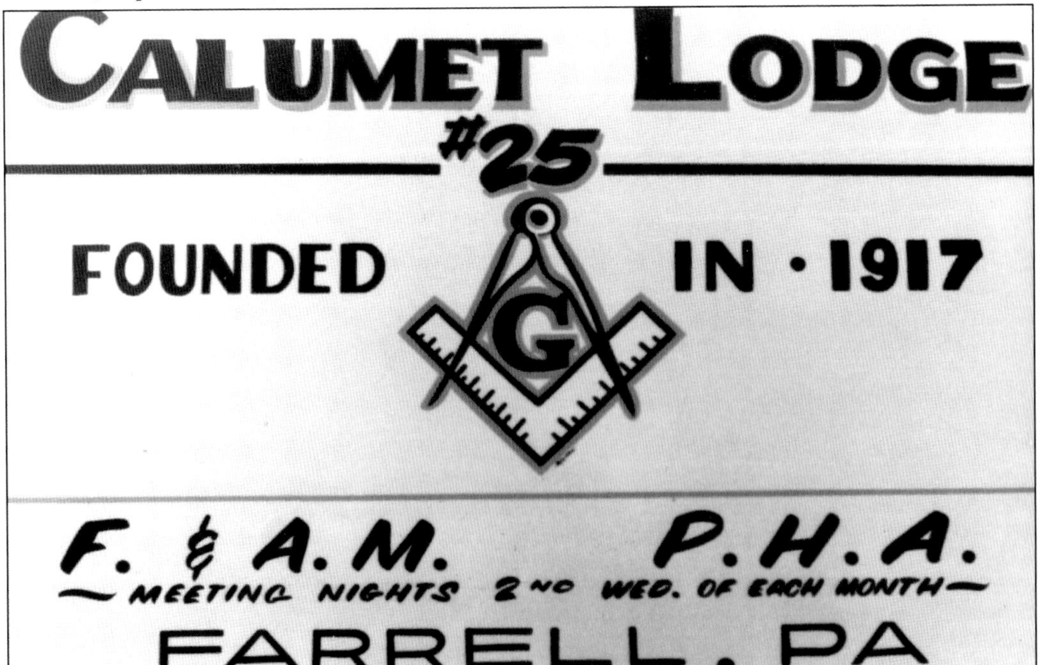

During the 1930s, Sara Dillard Austin (1916–2003) wrote that Abraham Lincoln did not free the slaves at Sharon High School. Mother Elizabeth Stoney Dillard, descendant of Pandenarium, shared how the collective efforts of the people contributed to their own freedom. Jeffrey Cromartie pins flowers on his cousin Martha Cromartie, a Sharon teacher, for a Knights of Pythagoras program at the Community Baptist Church in Farrell in 1977. Sharon educators included Guy Chavers, Cheryl Gibbs, Rachine Mazyck, and Marshall Norman. In 1969, Kathleen "Kitty" Culp (1920–1970) was the first African American schoolteacher in the Sharon School District.

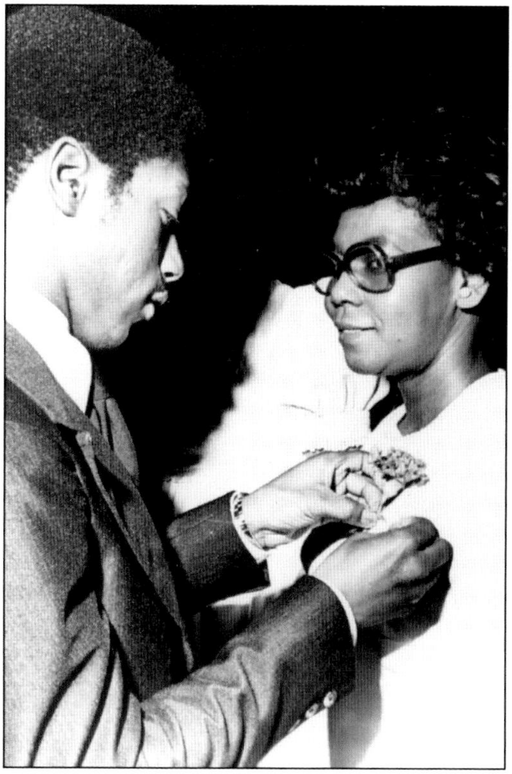

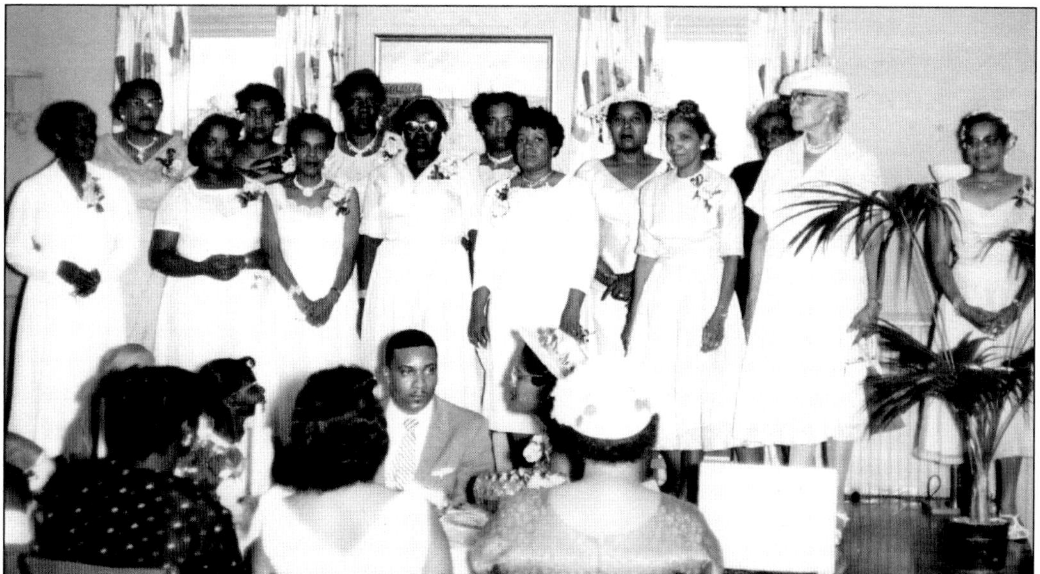

Sara Dillard Austin, a 1989 Buhl Day honoree, served as statewide grand worthy matron, Order of the Eastern Star, from 1973 to 1975. At the annual calendar tea around 1950, members of the Miriam Chapter include (first row) Belle Wright, Chrystina James, Sara Dillard Austin, Elizabeth Jackson, Rosetta Satterwhite Ragster, Helen Wilson, Elizabeth Thomas, and Catherine Flemon; (second row) Ollie Belle James, unidentified, Mary Prince, Nancy Alston, Josephine Arkward, and Florence Stitt.

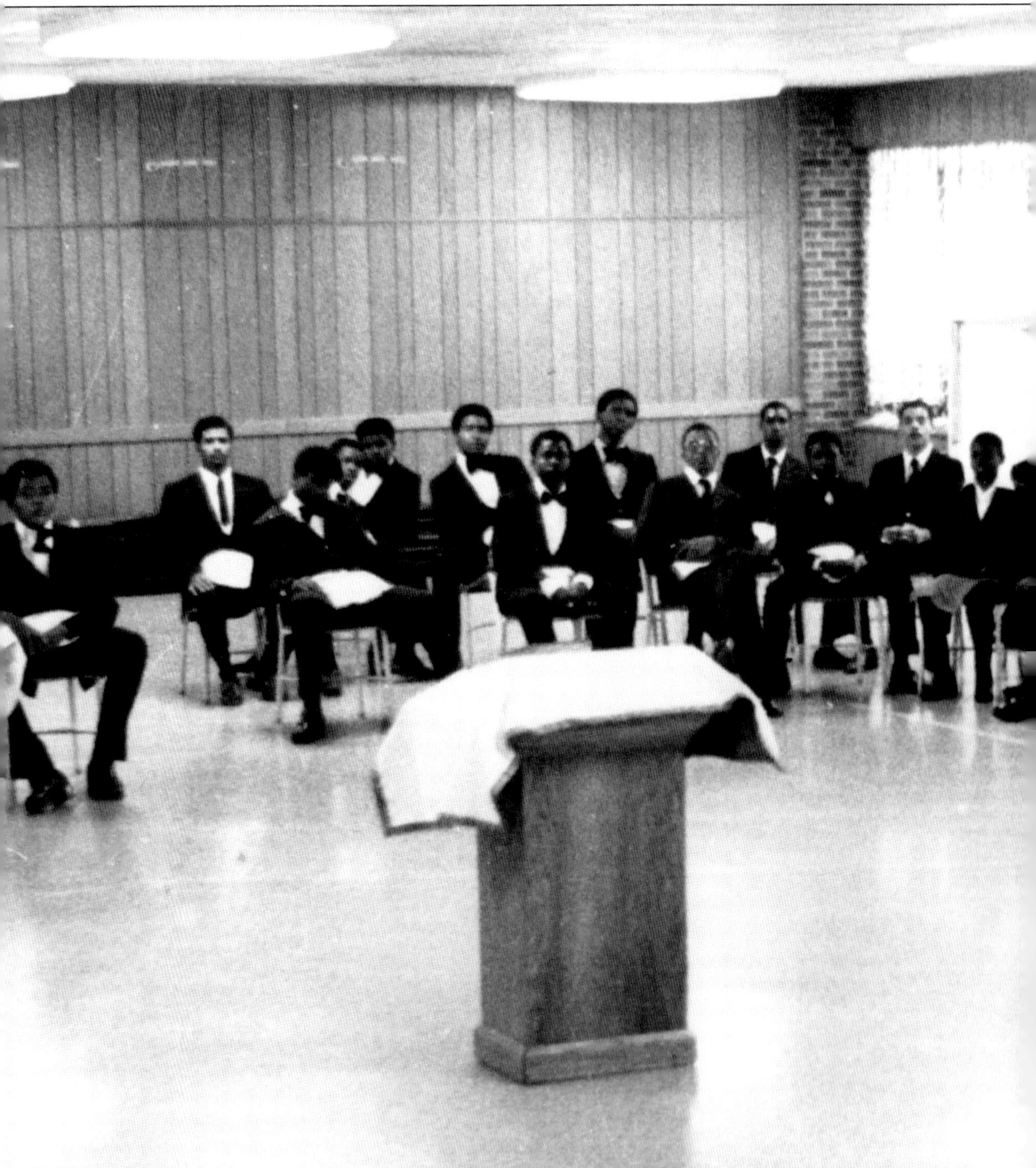

The Masonic youth group of Knights of Pythagoras Odell B. Matthews Sr. Council No. 11, Prince Hall Affiliation, hosted the statewide convention at Thiel College in Greenville on June 18–20, 1976, which attracted hundreds of youth. The local youth group, organized in 1975, included Rev. Rayford Harris, Gregory Claiborne, James C. Dixon Jr., Mark Hailey, Roland Barksdale-Hall, Vincent Barber, Charles Smith, Odell B. Matthews III, Mark Dungee, David Dungee, Anthony Seltzer, Cornelius Holmes, Dana Smith, Eugene Matthews, Jeffrey Cromartie,

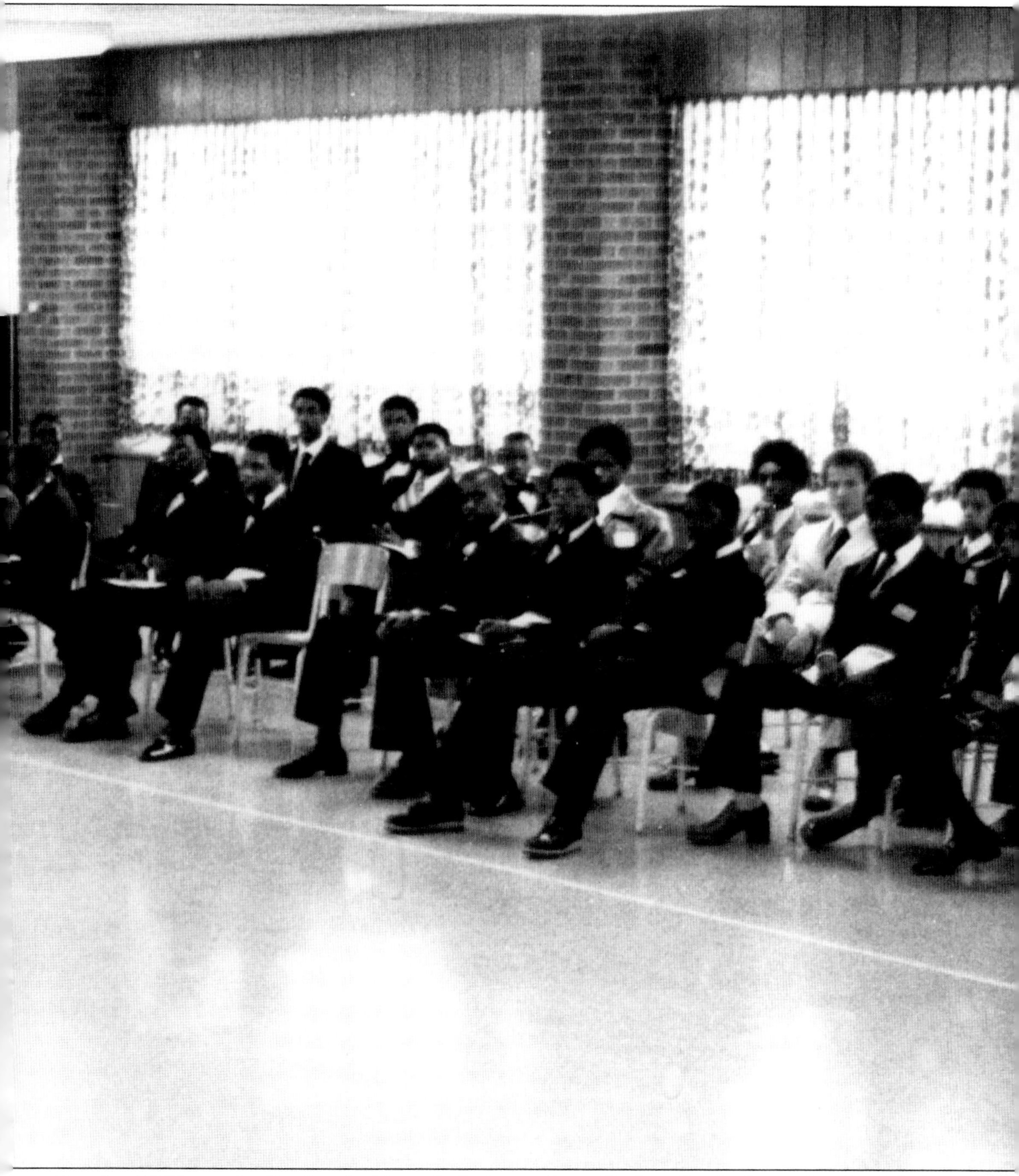

Douglas Williams, Leslie Smith, Derrick Pickens, Gary Hailey, Frank Lewis Brodie, Mark Lindsey Robinson, Michael Brodie, Sheldon Allen Matthews, Jesse Edison Graham Jr., John Dunlap, Larry Dunlap, Lawrence Edward Miller, Roderick Willard Miller, Morgan Shannon, Wilbert Shannon, Lawrence Huntley, James Snow, Jeffrey Bolling, James Dixon Jr., Kevin Harris, Cornelius Holmes, and Jeffrey Singleton. The first master knight was Rev. Rayford Harris.

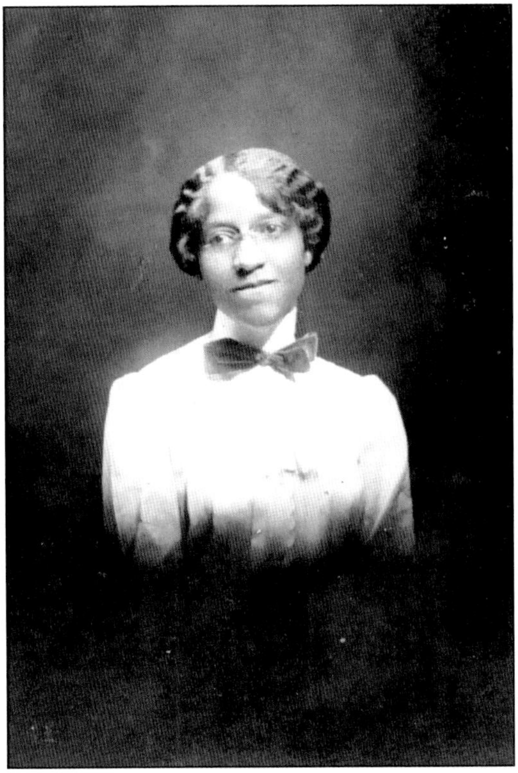

A native of Coraopolis, Ethel Brown Lewis studied cosmetology before moving to Sharon around 1915, where she opened a beauty parlor with an exclusive white clientele. She was a member of the female auxiliary of Masons, and self-employment placed her among the rank of the elite in the community. Calumet Lodge, organized in 1917, became a stronghold of Farrell's black intelligentsia. However, it was no less susceptible to factional strife than other African American organizations.

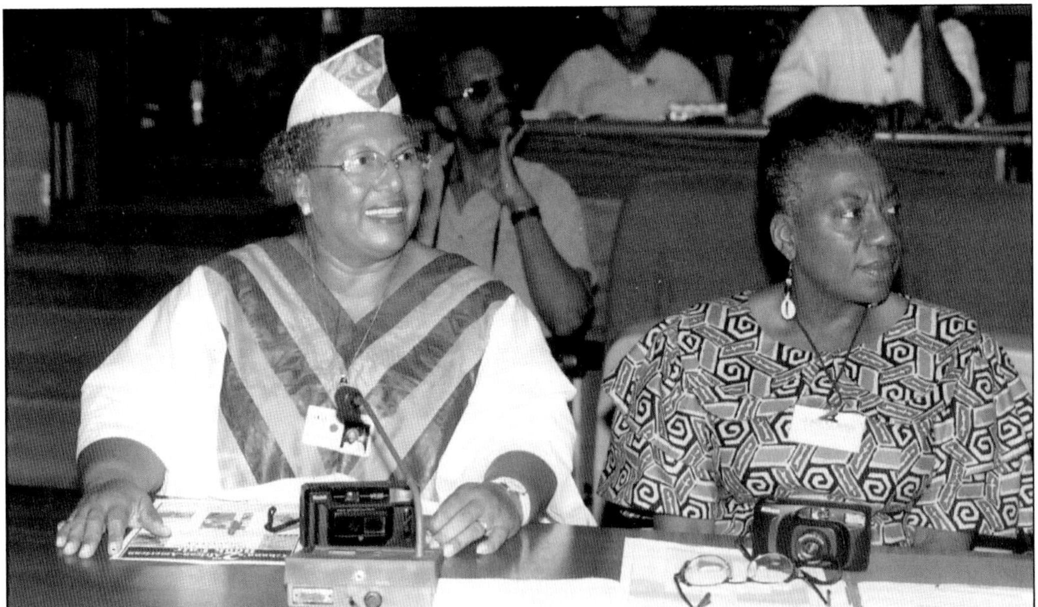

In 1920, there was a challenge to the status quo when a group of African American men moved to establish another Masonic lodge in Farrell. Appeals for unity thwarted this drive, yet a rift among the wives of those involved meant that two female auxiliaries operated until 1929, when attrition forced a merger. Shown is Dr. Travis Mattox (left), a descendant of Ethel Brown Lewis, on a research trip in Ghana, West Africa. (Courtesy of Dr. Travis Mattox.)

With more money and property than any of its competitors, the African American Knights of Pythias lodge was not only the richest fraternal group, it was also recognized as one of the best organizations in the nation. Shown with his immediate family around 1920, Odell B. Matthews Sr. (1879–1971) held a prominent position in the Knights of Pythias. He is the brother of James Elmer Matthews, the first elected NAACP branch president.

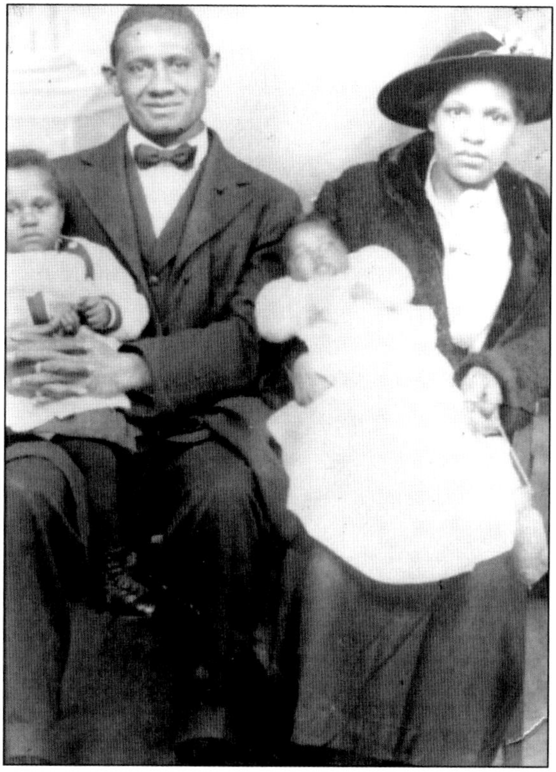

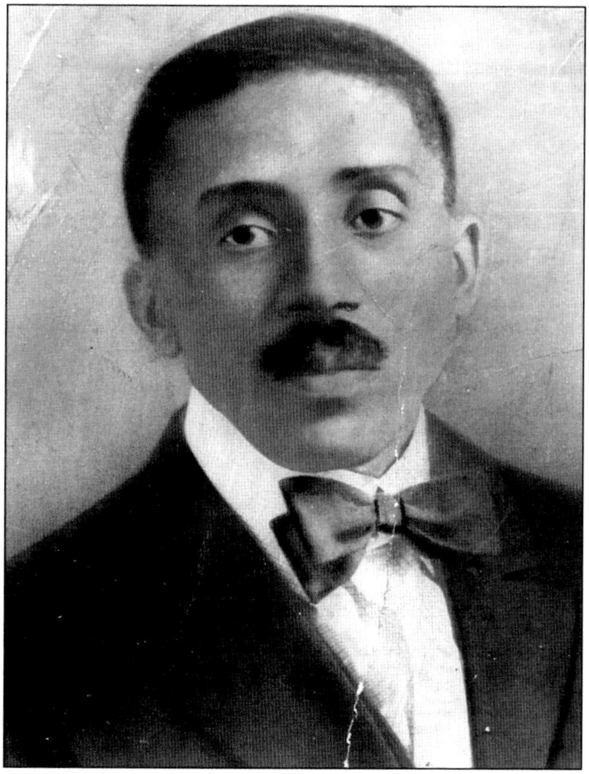

Robert Torrence, an African American barber, recalled meeting "Dad" Johnson, an African American barber, upon arrival in Greenville from North Carolina. Henry R. Sovell, another African American barber, had a barbershop in the National Hotel in Greenville. Torrence replied to an advertisement for a barber servicing an all-white clientele in Greenville around 1917. (Courtesy of Ken and Marlene Torrence.)

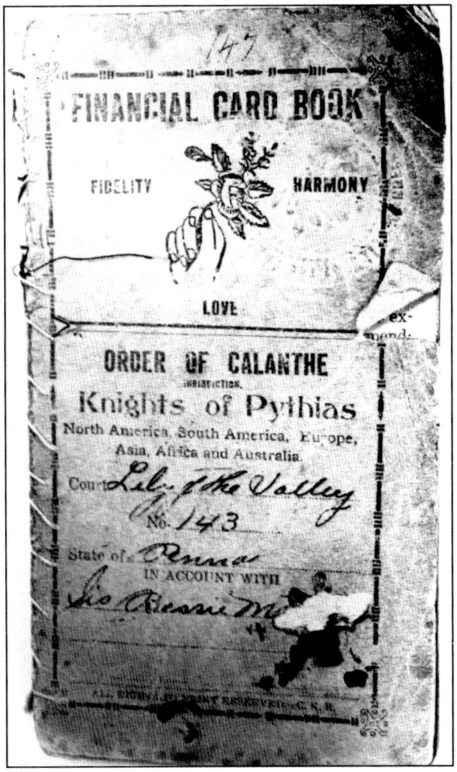

In Farrell, the Knights of Pythias Golden Rule Lodge and its female auxiliary, the Court of Calanthe, lacked mass appeal; membership in the latter never exceeded 40. Its rich endowment did attract semiskilled African American workers, but exorbitant fees and exclusionary practices worked against it. Bessie Matthews's financial card book of the Lily of the Valley No. 143, Order of Calanthe, from 1927 to 1929, shows a record of dues, taxes, and endowment payments made.

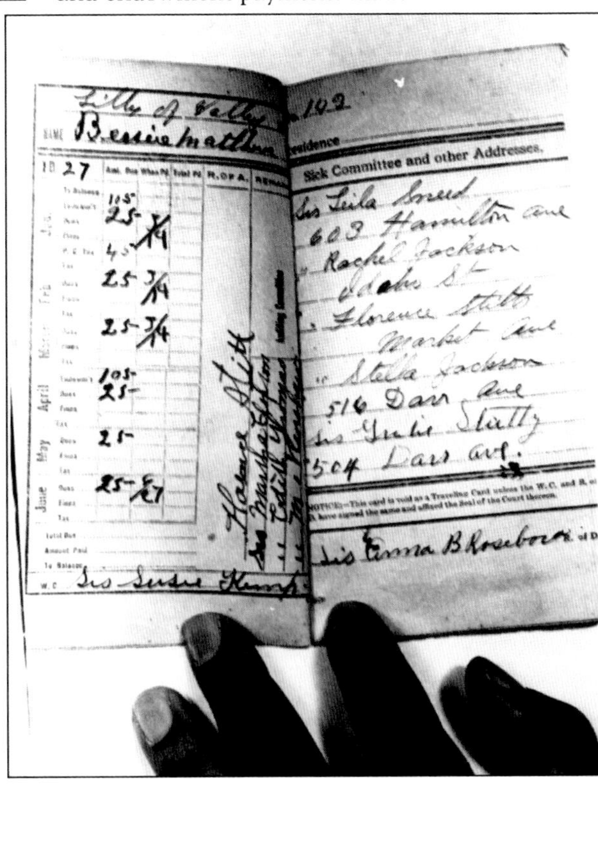

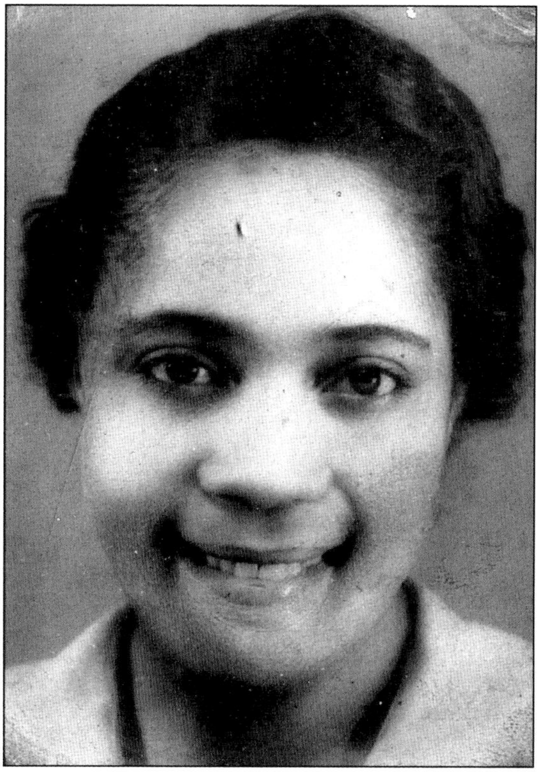

J. Fountain Reed (born in 1806), a barber, moved from Carlisle to Mercer and married Cynthia Adams in the 1830s. Seen below, John Fountain Reed (died in 1941), a chef, gave daughter G. Isabel Reed Moore (1917–1987), at right, her wings to soar as a graduation gift in 1936. Cosmetic surgery corrected scarring that stopped her from singing. Moore, recipient of the Marion Anderson Negro Opera Award, attended Julliard School of Music and toured the country as a concert soloist. (Courtesy of Samuel Moore.)

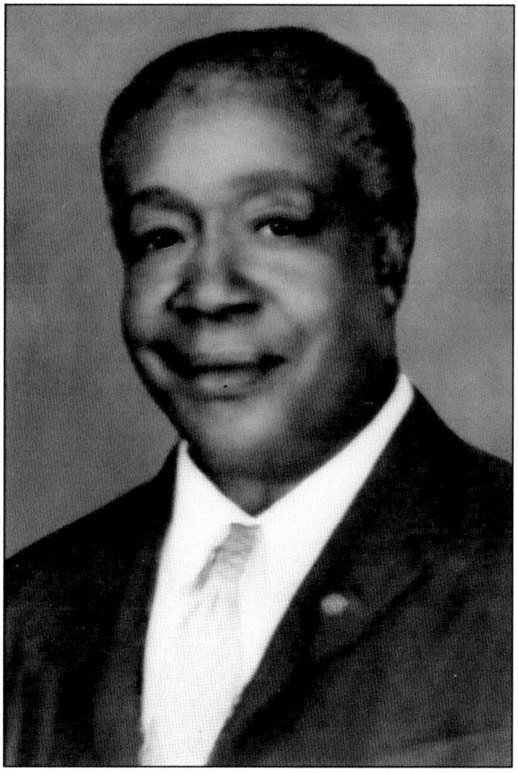

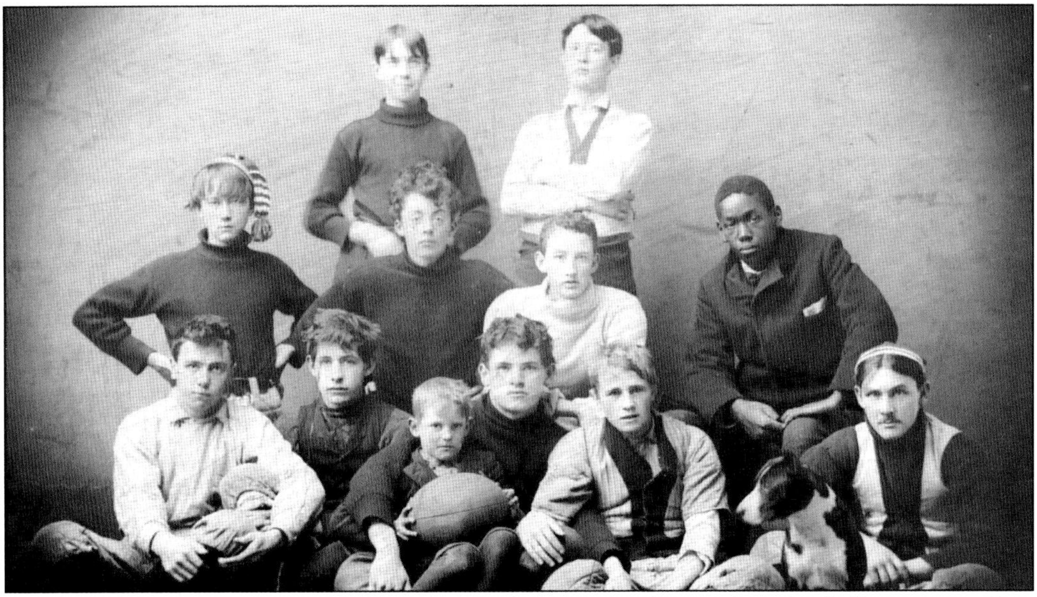

Pictured from left to right around 1897, members of the first Mercer football team are (first row) ? Thompson, George Proctor, team mascot Jimmy Gibson, ? Hope, Jim Byers, and Stewart McKean; (second row) Walter Truehard, Will Montgomery, Art ?, and Les Ford; (third row) Ross Calvin and Frank Elliott. Les Ford likely was a descendant of William Ford (*c.* 1846–1924) of the United States Colored Troops, who came to Mercer from Toronto, Ontario, Canada. (Courtesy of Mercer County Historical Society.)

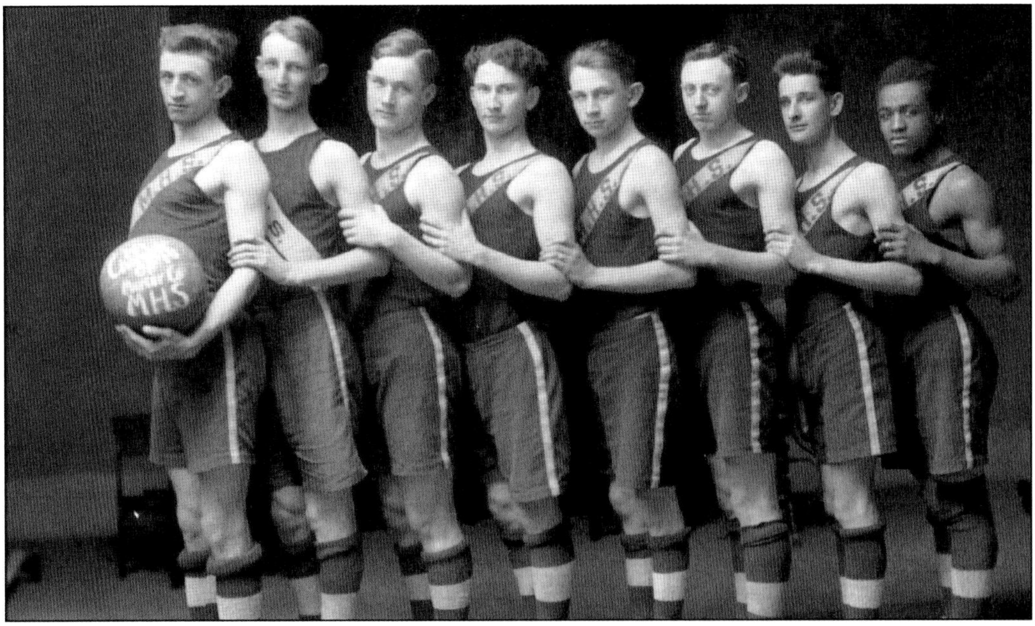

Arthur Leroy Richards, a descendant of Pandenarium, played football and was on the 1915 Mercer championship basketball team. He was the grandson of Crosby Richards and Milly Bell, a citizen of Pandenarium. During World War I in 1917, he enlisted and served as a bugler in Company C, 506th Engineers. Upon discharge in 1919 from Camp Dix, New Jersey, he resided in Mercer. (Courtesy of Mercer County Historical Society.)

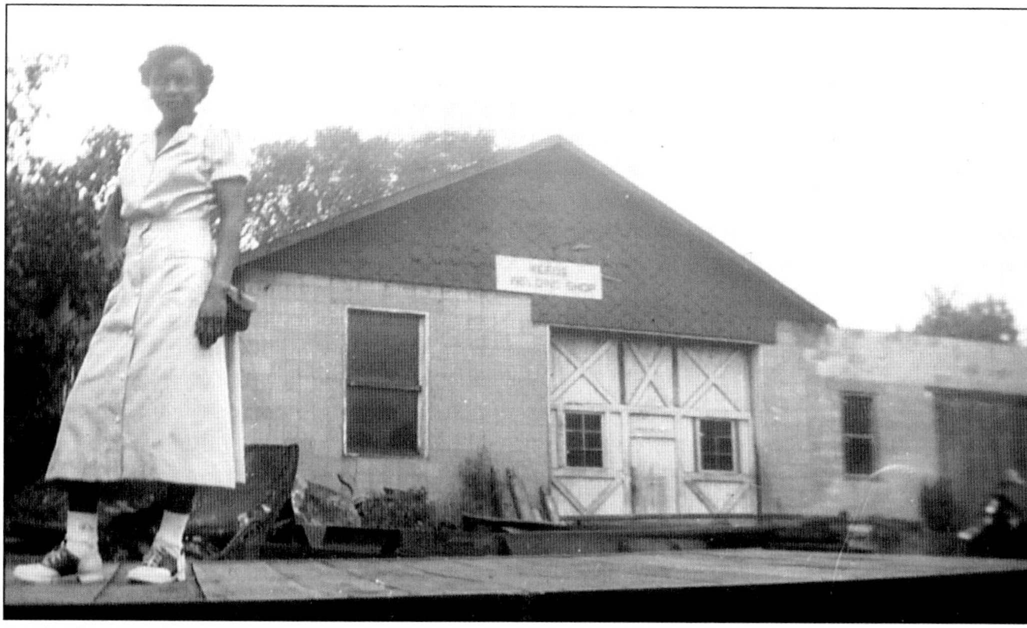

In the last graduating class from old Mercer School in 1952, Clara Mae Rucker (later McMillan) received a $50 savings bond and blue Samsonite luggage for her essay "I Am a Negro" at an assembly. Graduates received a brick from the building. She stands in her Isaly's uniform on a stage built by James F. Reed in front of Reed's Welding Shop on Butler Street around 1950. (Courtesy of Clara Mae Rucker McMillan.)

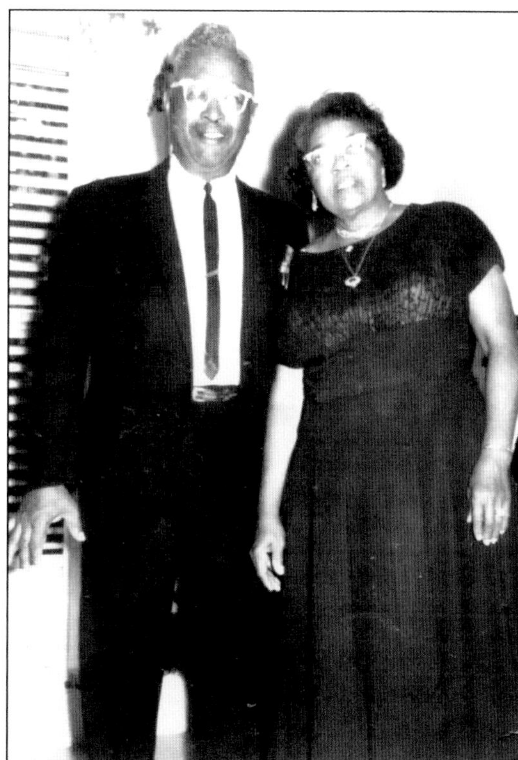

In West Greenville, African American roots in service industries date back as far as 1850 when Bazeal Stewart, a barber, and Peter J. Williams, a carpenter, worked in town. Ollie Whiteside, an African American plasterer, moved from Tennessee to Greenville. Shown on their 50th wedding anniversary are Ollie and Geneva Tolliver Whiteside in their living room on Straub Avenue in Greenville in 1966. The Whiteside-Tolliver extended family continues to reside in Greenville. (Photograph by Lininger Photo, courtesy of John Whiteside,)

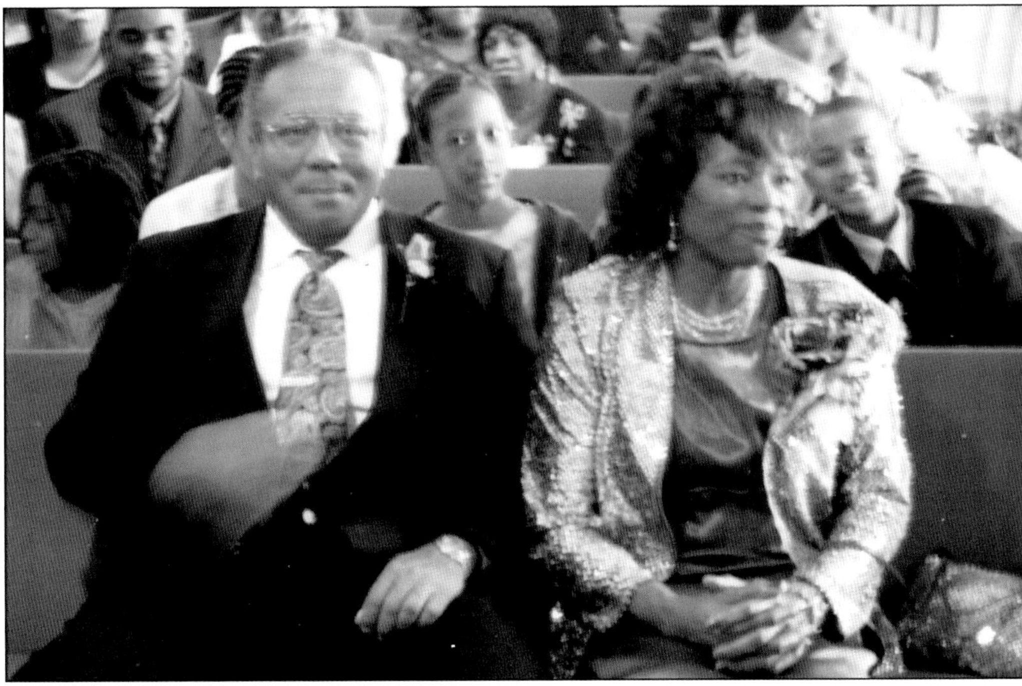

Robert "Ken" Torrence, descendant of Robert Torrence, served as a Sharon policeman from 1973 to 2000. Ken Torrence made an unsuccessful bid for coroner in 1995. His son Daryl Torrence was appointed the first African American firefighter in Sharon by Mayor Robert Price in 2002. Ken and Marlene Torrence attend the wedding ceremony of their son Calvin Torrence and April Avery held at Greater Mount Zion Church of God in Christ in Farrell in 2004. (Courtesy of Ken and Marlene Torrence.)

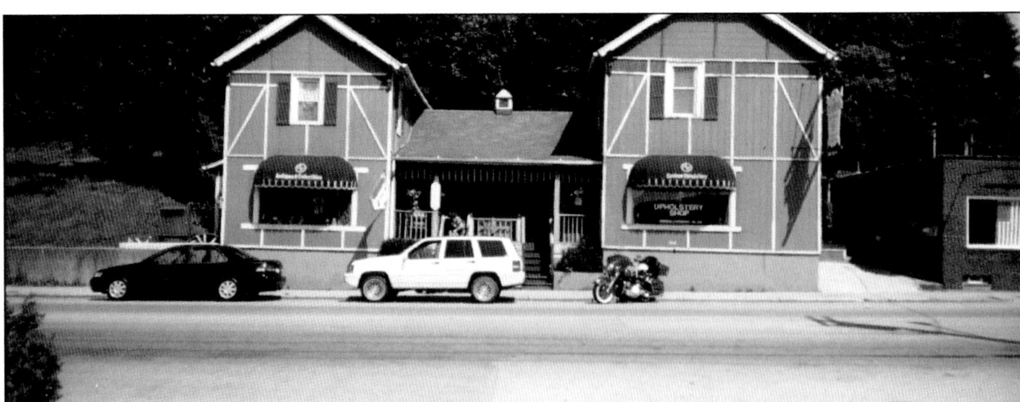

Doyle Tutt was the first African American policeman in Sharon, yet Ken Torrence has the longest record of service. Marlene Torrence, an African American entrepreneur, began an upholstery and antique business in 1989. Three years later, she bought two separate buildings, undertook an extensive renovation project, combined the buildings, and opened an expanded shop. Shown is Treasure Chest at 110 North Sharpsville Avenue in Sharon. (Courtesy of Ken and Marlene Torrence.)

Four

STEEL HERITAGE

AMERICAN MADE

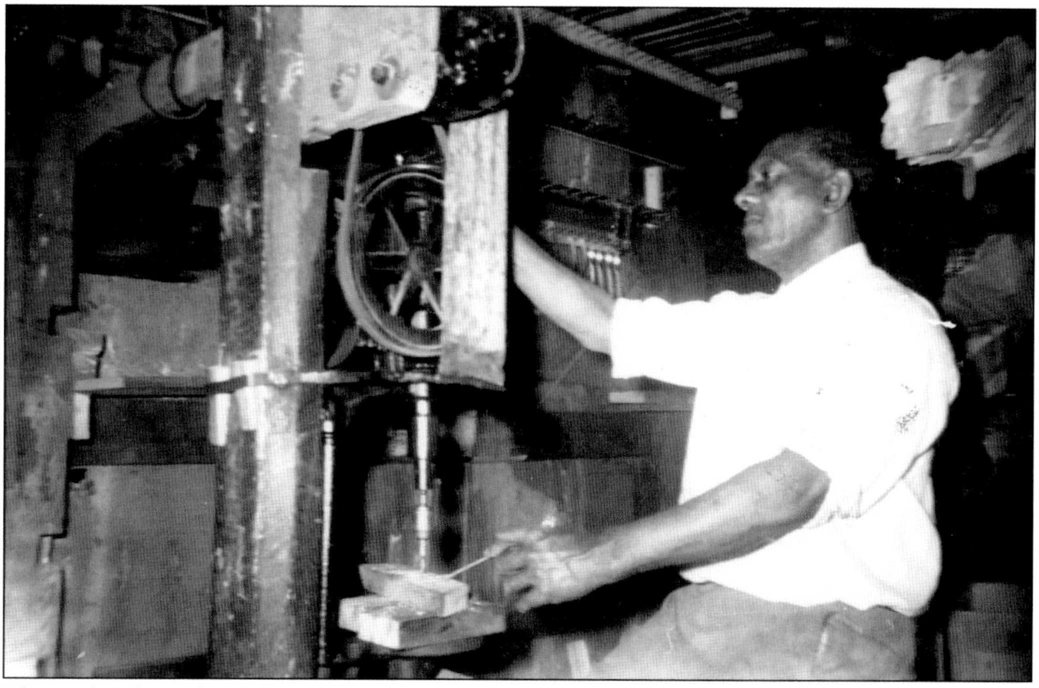

The technological revolution of the 19th century initiated an era in which all people could not only realize the benefits of advancement but also make meaningful contributions. Mill worker James Elmer Matthews (1886–1976) moved from Homestead to South Sharon and found employment at the South Sharon Works of the American Sheet and Tin Plate Company (which became the U.S. Steel Corporation), where in 1916, he invented a shear guide that was used for snipping tin evenly and safely.

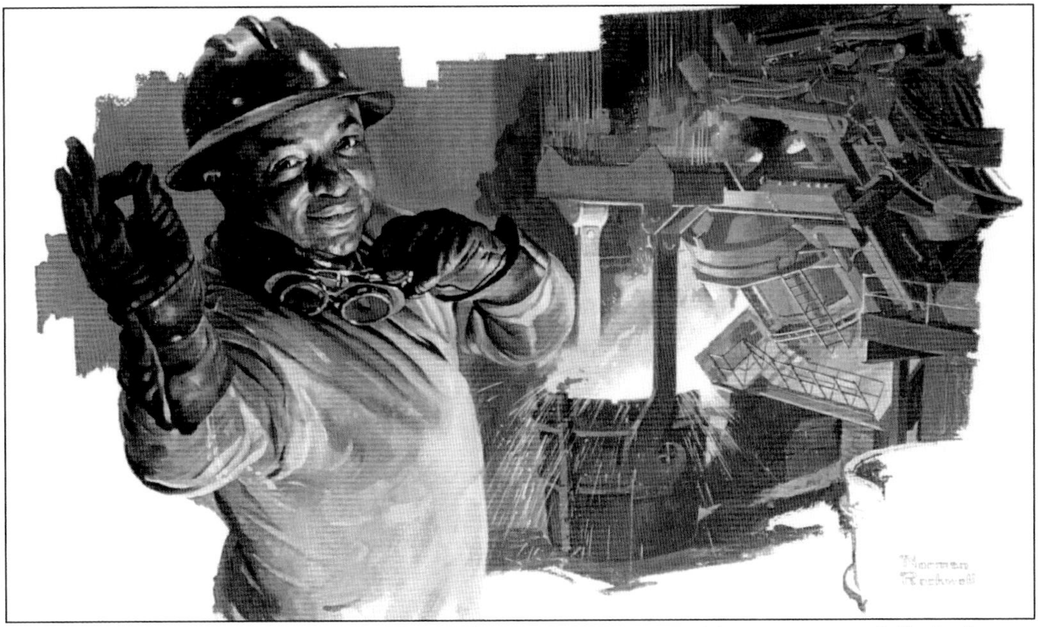

Due solely to race, there was a time when African Americans could not get an unskilled job even working on a labor gang in the steel mills in western Pennsylvania and eastern Ohio. Between 1909 and 1923, there were two waves of African American migrations to Farrell. Shown is Johnson Ragster, an African American steelworker who appeared in a series of paintings about Sharon Steel by artist Norman Rockwell around 1968.

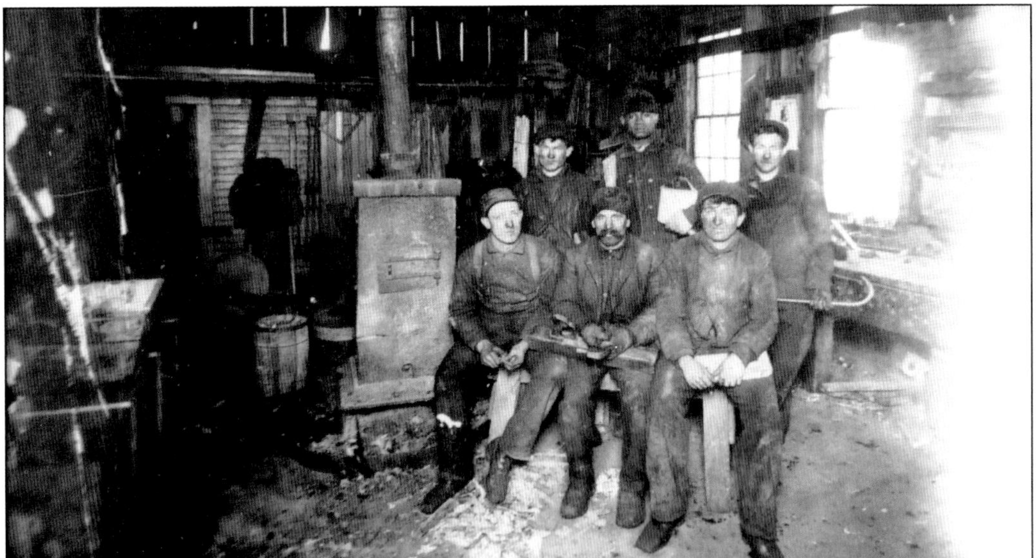

During the first wave of migrations, the American Sheet and Tin Plate Company exploited racial antipathies in an attempt to break the union. When the Amalgamated Association of Iron and Steelworkers called a 1909 strike, local company officials employed African Americans as skilled, nonunion workers. H. Russell Wayne (1888–1982) and Marshall Wayne (1881–1925) came here as tin men. Behind the scenes maneuvering was going on for the highest-skilled rolling position.

Pittsburgh native William Hunter Dammond (1873–1956) was recognized as a mathematical genius and the first African American graduate of the Western University of Pennsylvania, today known as the University of Pittsburgh. His patents included a signaling system (1903) and safety system for operating railroads (1906). In 1916, Dammond moved to Farrell and located employment as a draftsman at the Farrell Works of the Carnegie-Illinois Steel Corporation (U.S. Steel Corporation).

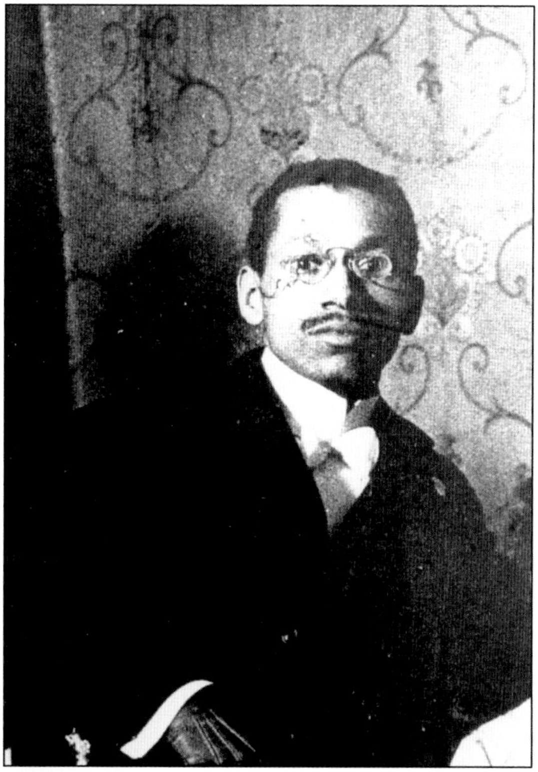

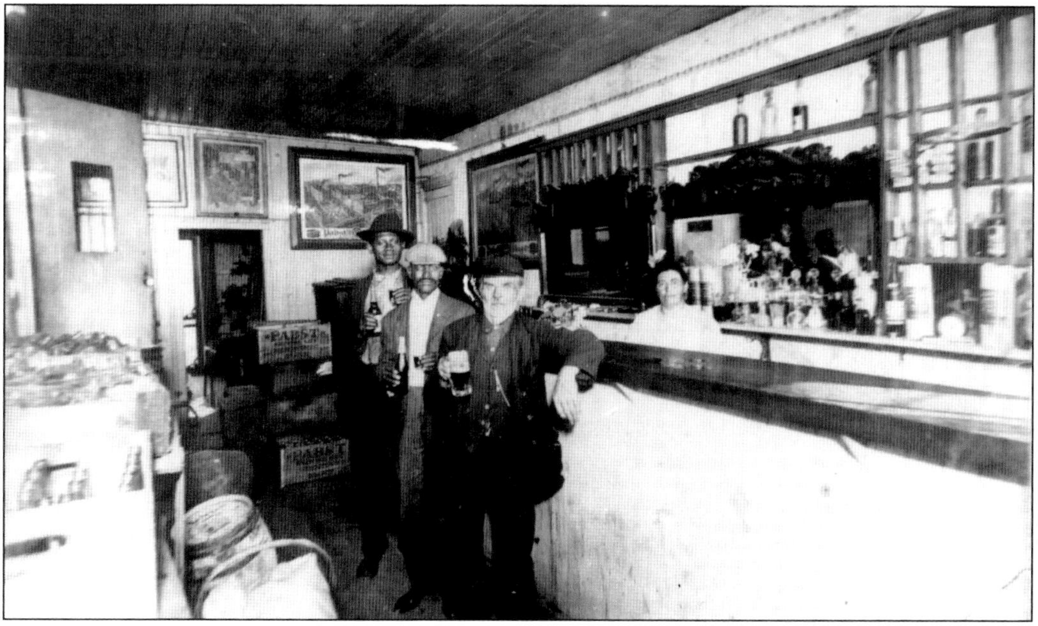

Before World War II, families in Farrell lived in mixed neighborhoods where neither they nor any of the borough's numerous white ethnic populations were able to maintain a majority. In 1921, James Elmer Matthews was elected first president of the Citizens of the Neck Club when the majority of residents were of eastern European descent. Under these circumstances, a degree of social mixing occurred.

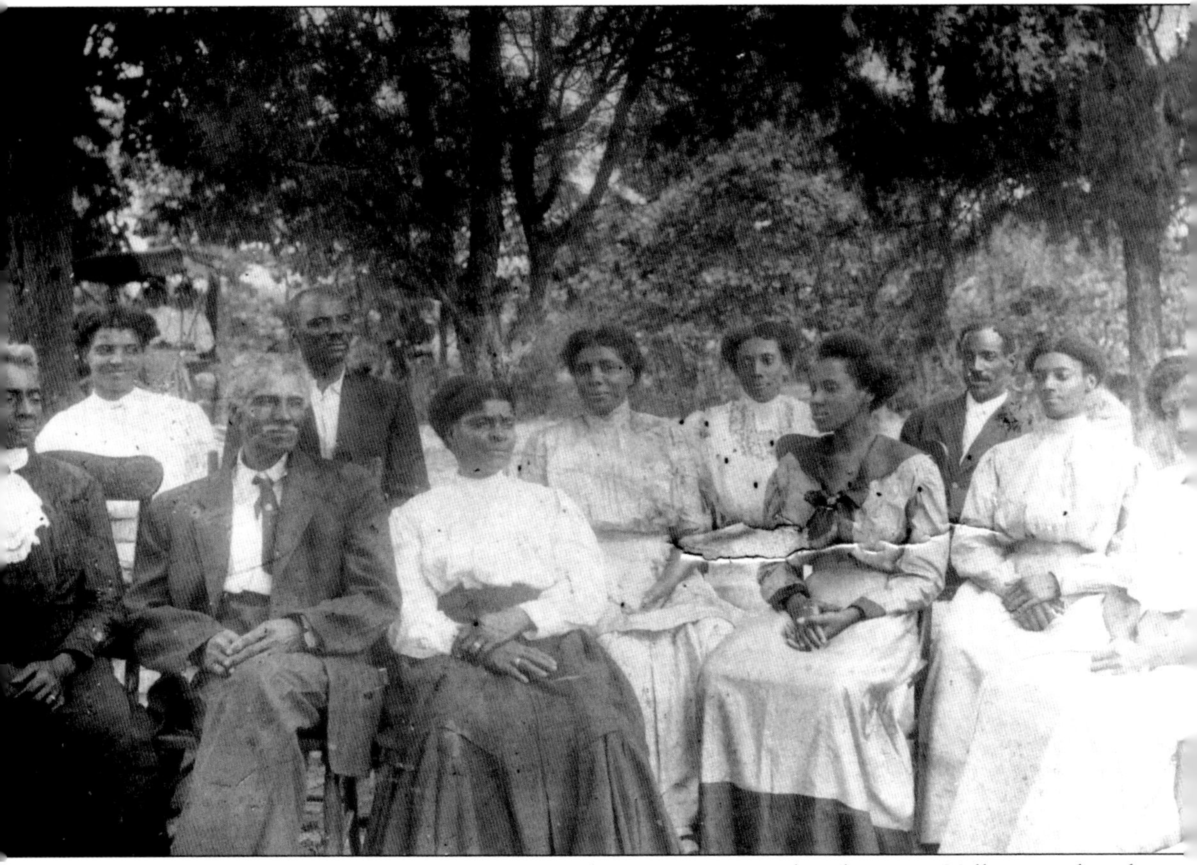

Between 1916 and 1930, the majority of southern migrants to the Shenango Valley were hired as unskilled workers. During the great migration, former slave Wilson Steverson (1838–1948) (second from left, front), Mary Steverson McClendon (second from right), and Etania Steverson (third from right) left the South and moved to Farrell. Etania Steverson found employment as an unskilled worker in the American Sheet and Tin Plate Company mill. (Photograph by Thomas E. Askew.)

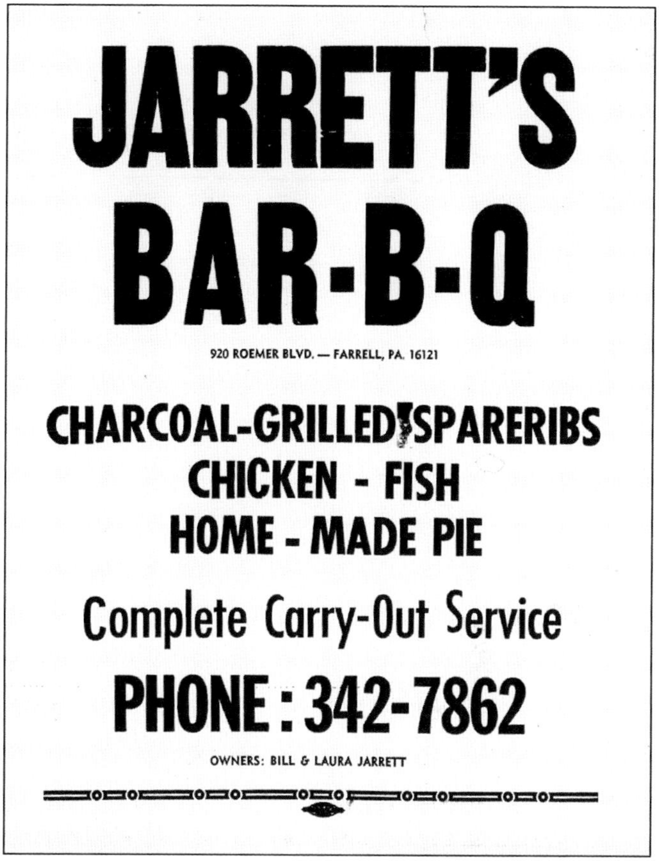

During a 1919 strike, southern migrants were heavily recruited. Most came from the Carolinas, Georgia, and Alabama, with others migrating from Florida, Mississippi, Tennessee, and Kentucky. Coal miner Joseph S. McClendon (1884–1963) was employed by the Tennessee Coal and Iron Company in Ensley, Alabama, before immigrating to Pennsylvania after World War I, where he worked as a burner's helper in the Farrell mill of the Carnegie-Illinois Steel Corporation. William Jarrett, a descendant of the large enterprising Adair-James-Jarrett family, owned Jarrett's Bar-B-Q on Roemer Boulevard in Farrell around 1970. He later reopened the barbecue on Victor Posner Boulevard, Wheatland, around 1980. (Courtesy of William Jarrett.)

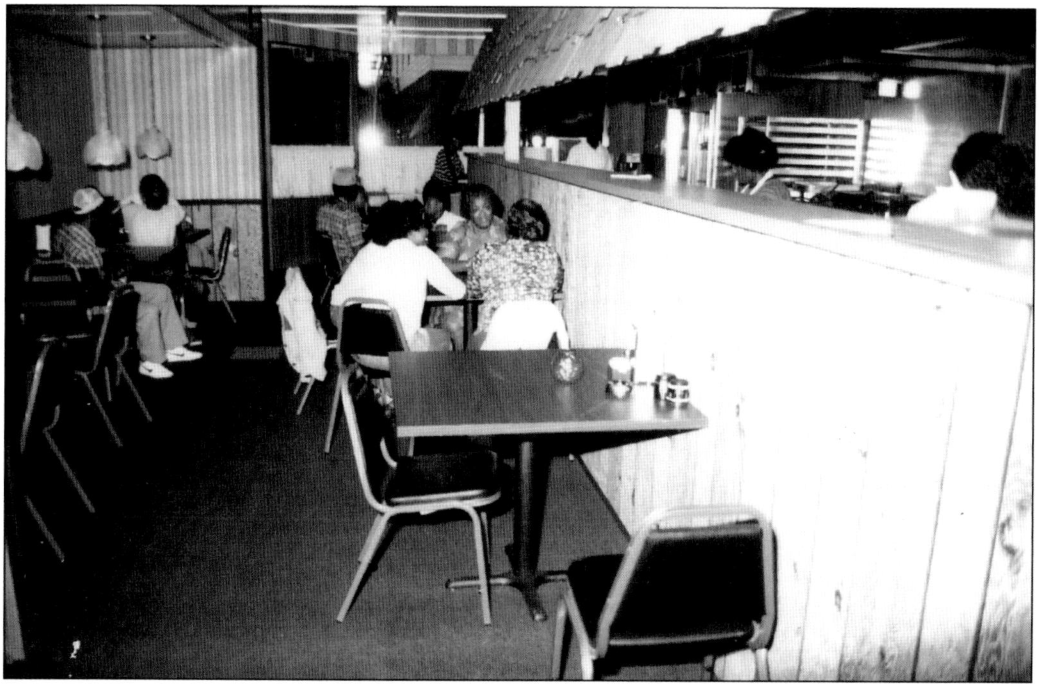

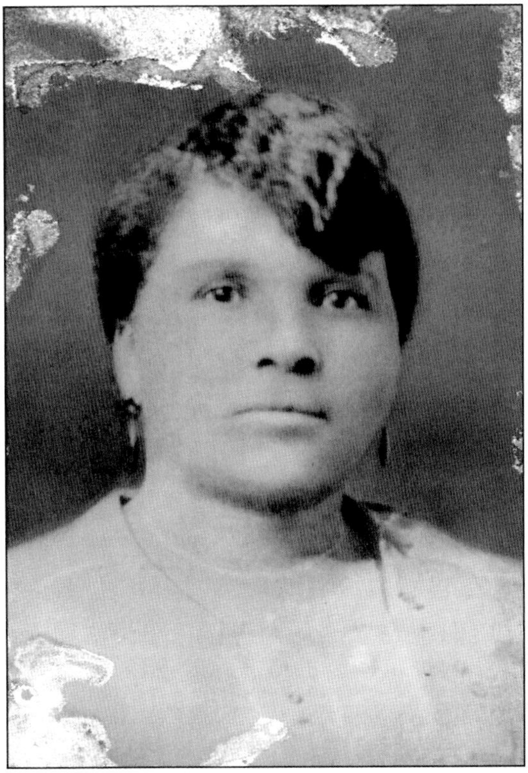

In 1916, Frank Wilson Sr. (1889–1972) moved from Cheraw, South Carolina, to Farrell and located employment at Sharon Steel. A year later, Daisy Hammond moved from Cheraw, South Carolina, and opened a snack shop on Broadway. Hammond, Samuel Stitt, and Harvey Satterwhite formed the leadership of the Afro-American Progressive League. Sharon Steel recruited heavily from Cheraw, South Carolina, because of residents' work ethic. (Courtesy of Rudolph Hammond.)

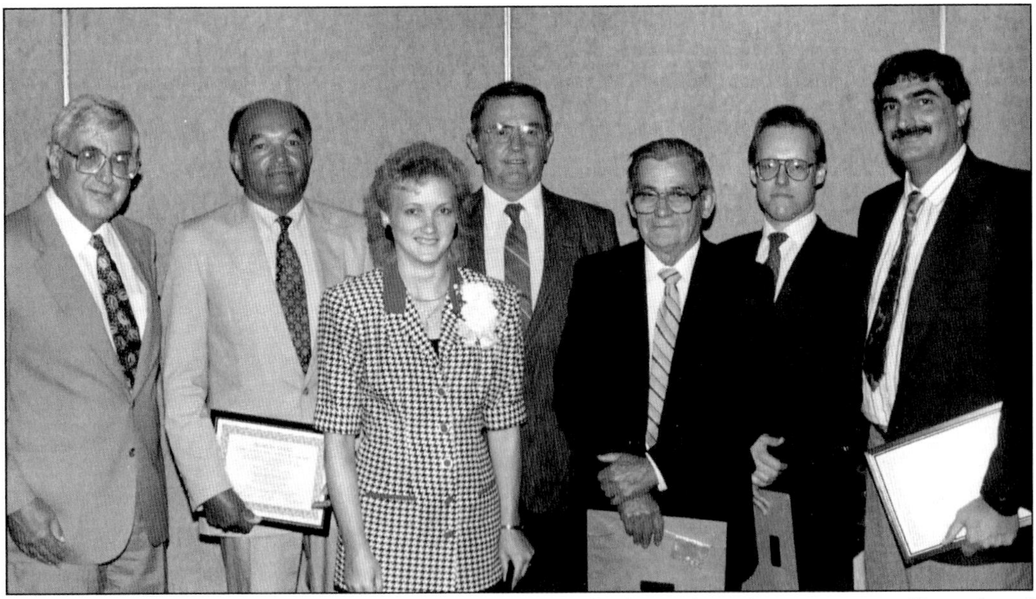

Rudolph Hammond, descendant of Daisy Hammond, devised a plan to move idle railroad cars from the stockyard at a cost savings of $200,000 per month. He was the recipient of the Mercer County branch of the NAACP's James Mendez Matthews Community Service Award for his longtime service as a Farrell city councilman in 2008. Here he receives the Sharon Steel Chief Executive Officer's Award from the chief executive officer in 1991. (Courtesy of Rudolph Hammond.)

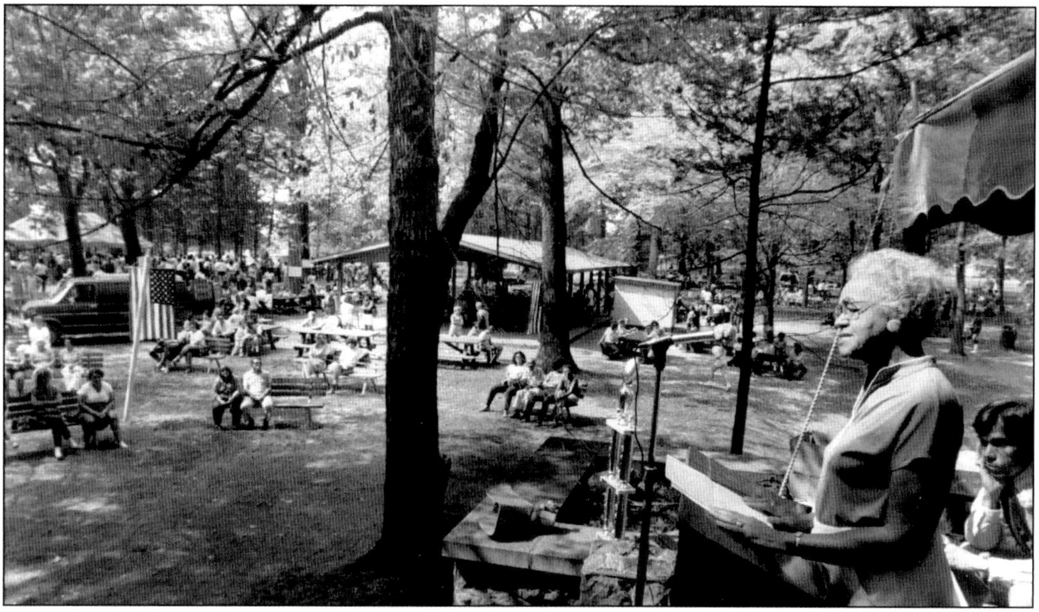

Pictured is Louise Ponder (1908–2000), Buhl Day honoree, reading an original poem, "Tribute to Farrell City Park," at the annual homecoming celebration on September 22, 1985. Due to the closing of Sharon Steel and economic woes, Farrell City Park no longer exists. Ponder, author of a book of poetry called *The Preacher*, was a founder of the Farrell Area School District Parent-Teacher Association. In 2009, Ponder descendant Vernon Scott is a teacher in the Farrell Area School District. (Courtesy of Martha Richards.)

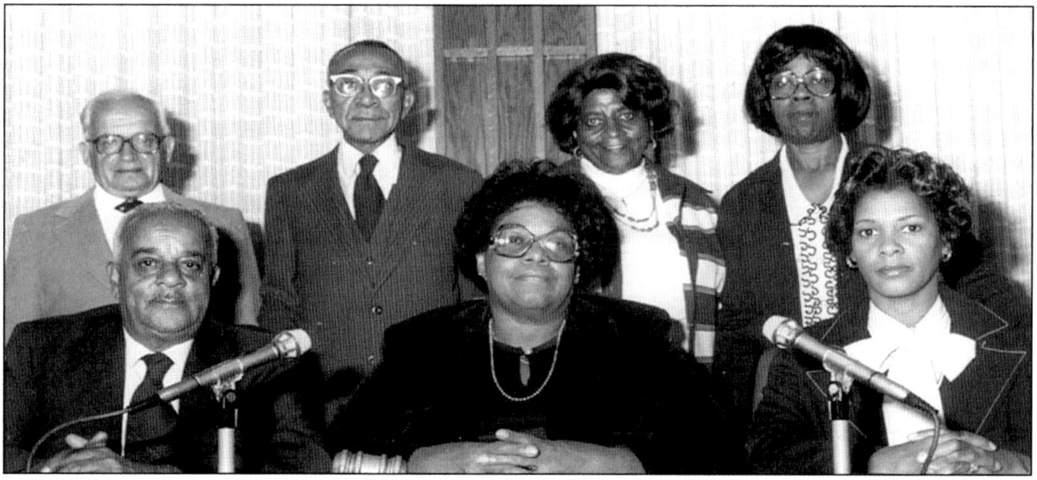

During the 1930s, Henry G. Walker had a fish market at 206 Idaho Street in Farrell. Nellion Ponder, a nephew, made the deliveries. Shown around 1981 at a press conference held by Southwest Gardens Economic Development Corporation are, from left to right, (first row) Aaron Smith, first vice president; Mary Harvey (1920–1987), president of the board of directors; and Shirley McLean, secretary; (second row) Steve Holler, second vice president; Nellion Ponder; Maxine Pulliam; and Ann Scarbarough.

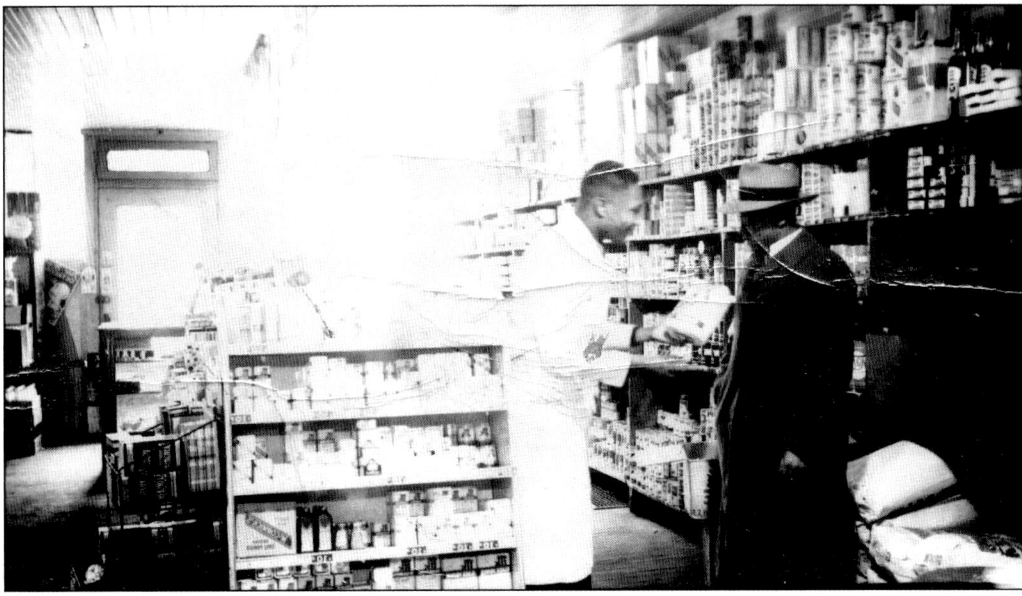

In 1929, Rev. Samuel Delane Jr., a native of South Carolina, established Delane Food Market, a grocery store, in the 900 block of Greenfield Avenue, later known as Market Avenue, where a thriving African American business district emerged. Across the street, Hailstock's Bakery distributed its sweet potato and cream pies to grocery stores. Dan the Barber, a barbershop, and Edmunds Hotel were located in the same block. A Mr. Green is pictured on the left in Delane's grocery store. (Courtesy of Althea Jennings.)

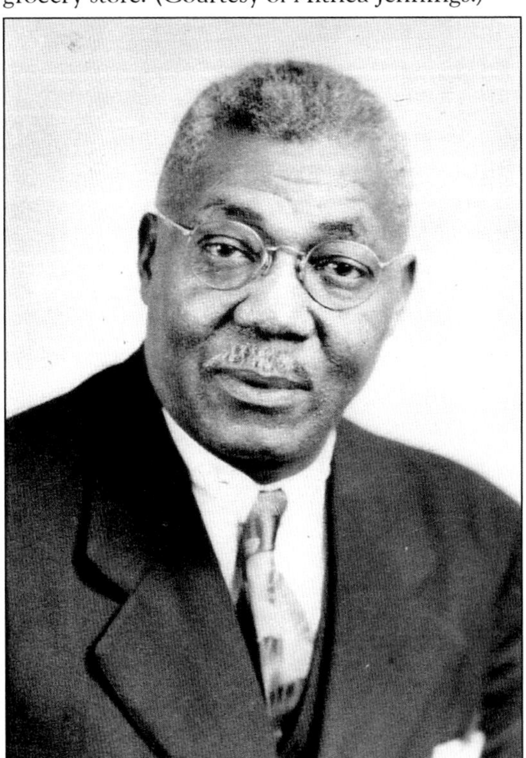

In 1914, James Abraham Christman Sr. (1879–1966), left, established the Christman Transfer Company located in the 900 block of Darr Avenue in Farrell. He owned and operated the major business concern for 33 years yet served as a member of the board of directors of the Interstate Commerce Commission. He had three trucks and three employees per truck. "Mr. Farrell" was painted on the side of the largest truck. (Courtesy of Darlynna Thompson.)

The Christman family was multifaceted. Brothers Harry Benjamin Christman (1922–1972) and James Abraham Christman Jr. (1908–1984) owned and operated Christman's Garage at 928 Market Avenue in Farrell in the African American business corridor in the 1940s. Pictured is James Abraham Christman Jr., who received a patent for a brake safety device in 1958. He developed a cold welding process for cracked engines, which attracted considerable interest by major car manufacturers. During the 1920s, Michael S. Askerneese (1890–1975), a southern migrant, served as president of the Farrell Division Universal Negro Improvement Association. He independently owned and operated Liberty Canning at 306 Spearman Avenue in Farrell. He developed a process for canning collards, which attracted considerable interest, as the process was not common knowledge. In 1923, Marcus Garvey gave an address in Farrell. (Right, courtesy of Darlynna Thompson.)

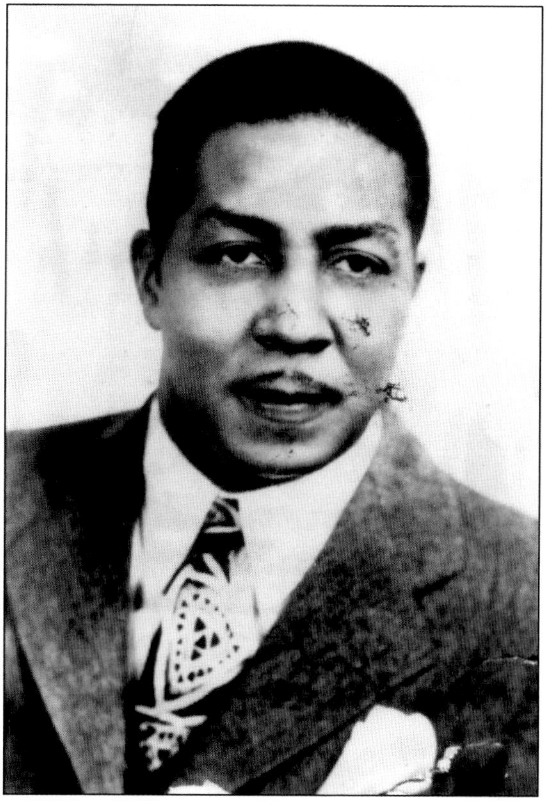

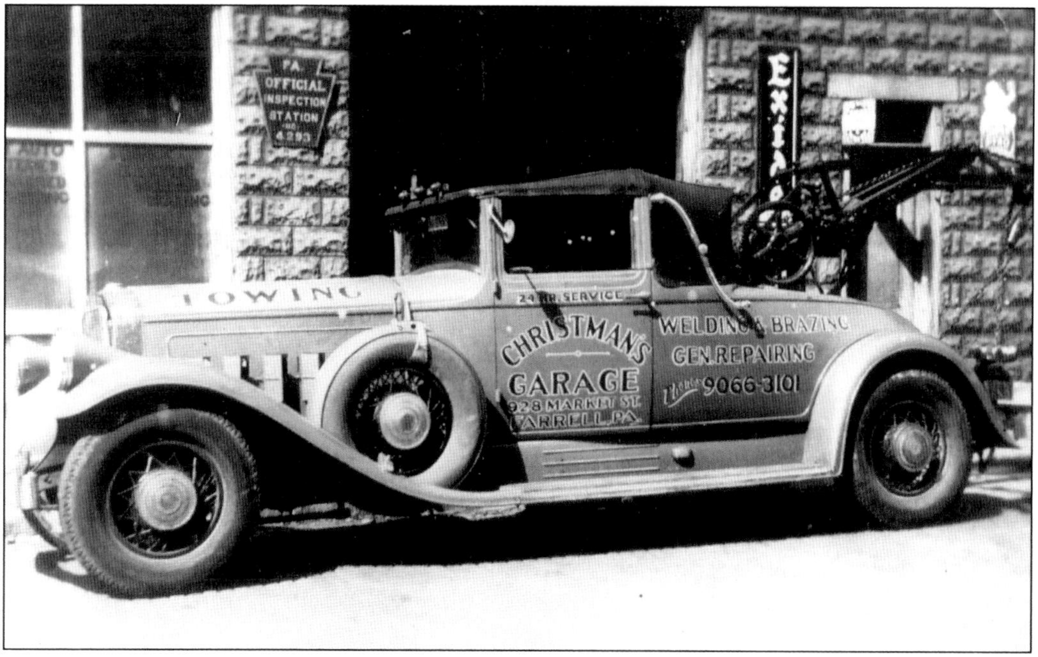

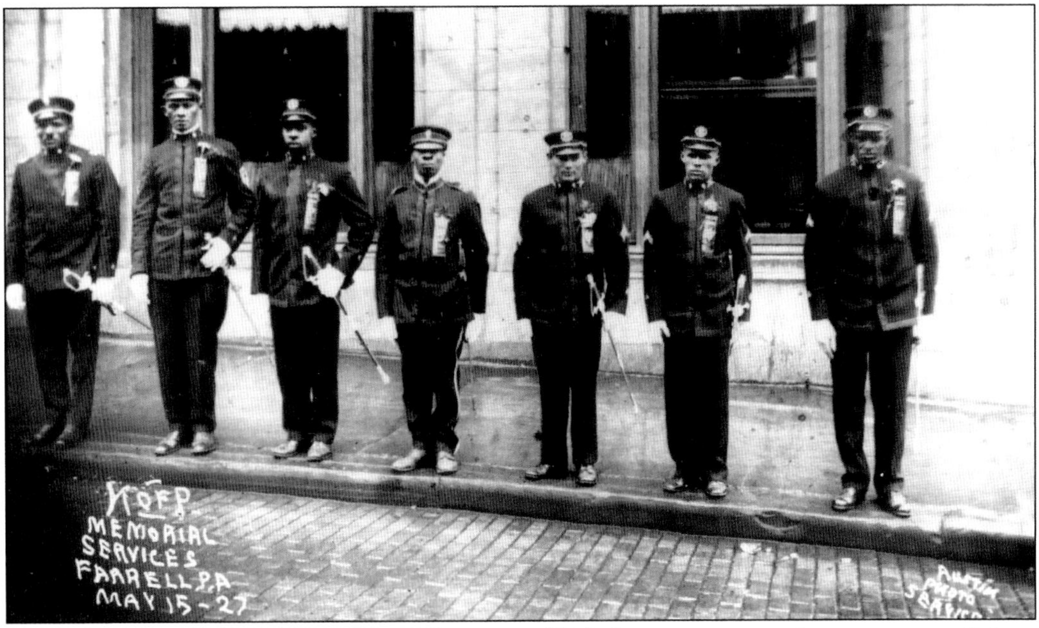

With prosperity came a rise in fraternal activity. With "more money and more property" than any of its competitors, the African American Knights of Pythias lodge not only was the richest fraternal group, but it also was recognized as one of the best organizations in the nation. Members of the Golden Valley Lodge No. 89 of the Knights of Pythias are at their memorial service in 1927.

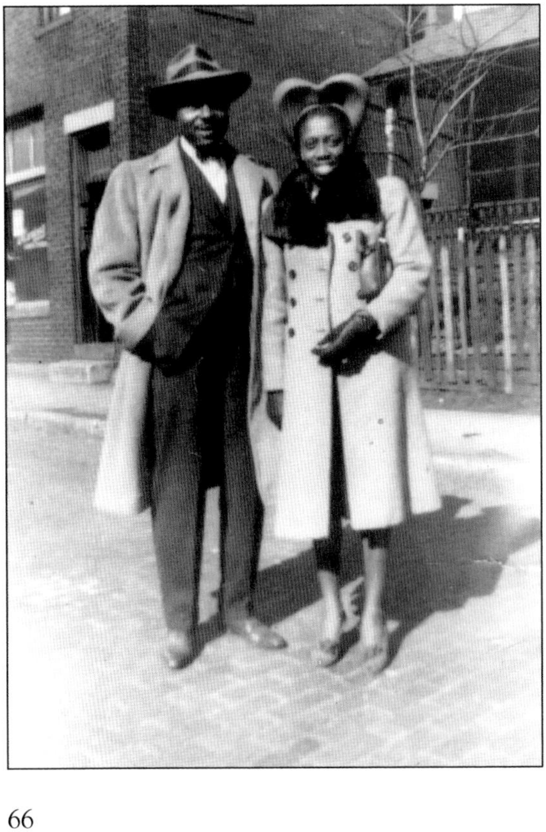

Shown are Samuel and Dorothy Steverson Malloy, out on the town on Market Avenue in the African American business corridor. He was worshipful master of Calumet Lodge No. 25, Free and Accepted Masons, Prince Hall Affiliation, and a member of the Knights of Pythias and Elks during the 1940s. Dorothy Steverson Malloy belonged to the female auxiliaries. During the 1919 mill strike, Samuel's grandfather Gus McDowell was pinned down by sniper fire and swam across the Shenango River.

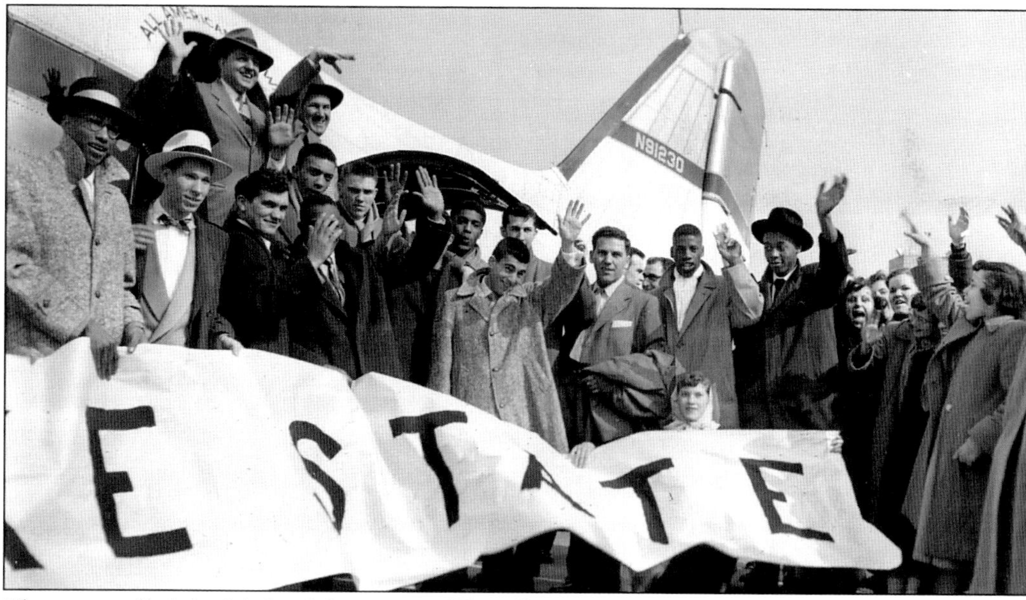

The team called the Mighty Mites secured Farrell's reputation as the city of champions. From left to right, the 1952 Pennsylvania Interscholastic Athletic Association (PIAA) state champions are (first row) Julius McCoy, Russell DeCarmen, assistant coach Bob Trambacco, Paul Flint, Tony Decello, assistant coach Felix Bonadio, Ronald Crosby, and Wilbert Shannon; (second row) Sy Alli, Bob Hoffman, Bates Johnson, and assistant coach Bill Canterna; (third row) athletic director Ralph Dresch and head coach Edward McCluskey. (Courtesy of William Jarrett.)

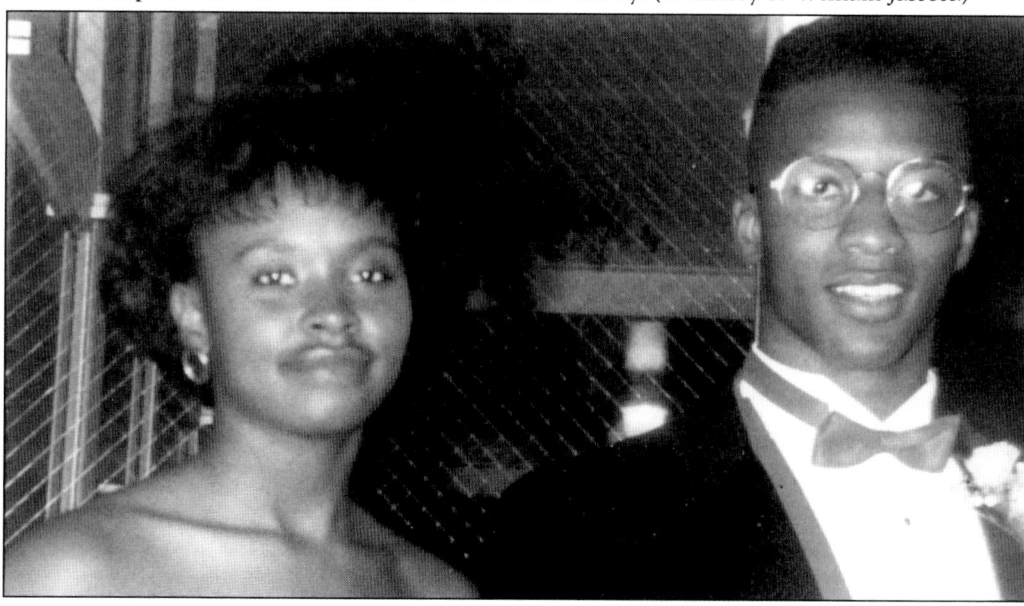

In 1989, coach Guy Gibbs and all-state running back Andre Coleman led the Hickory High School Hornets to the PIAA state championship. Coleman played with the Pittsburgh Steelers, Seattle Seahawks, and San Diego Chargers, where he made a record-breaking kickoff return in Super Bowl XXIX. He played five seasons and returned back home for football camps. Here Coleman attends a Hickory High School dance in Hermitage around 1989. (Courtesy of Martha Richards.)

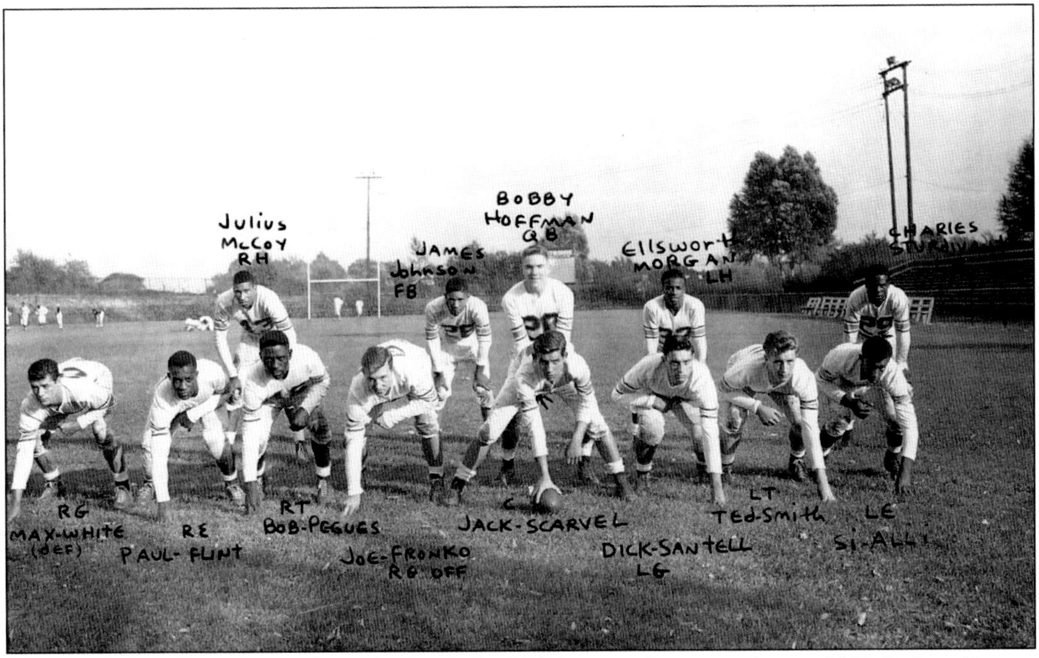

The Farrell High School Night Riders won the PIAA state championship in 1951. Robert Pegues was named honorary captain. Seniors on the football team included Sy Alli, Joseph Fronko, Robert Hoffman, James Johnson, Julius "Hooks" McCoy, Ellsworth Morgan, Robert Pegues, Alexander Pustinger, Richard Santell, and Maximo White.

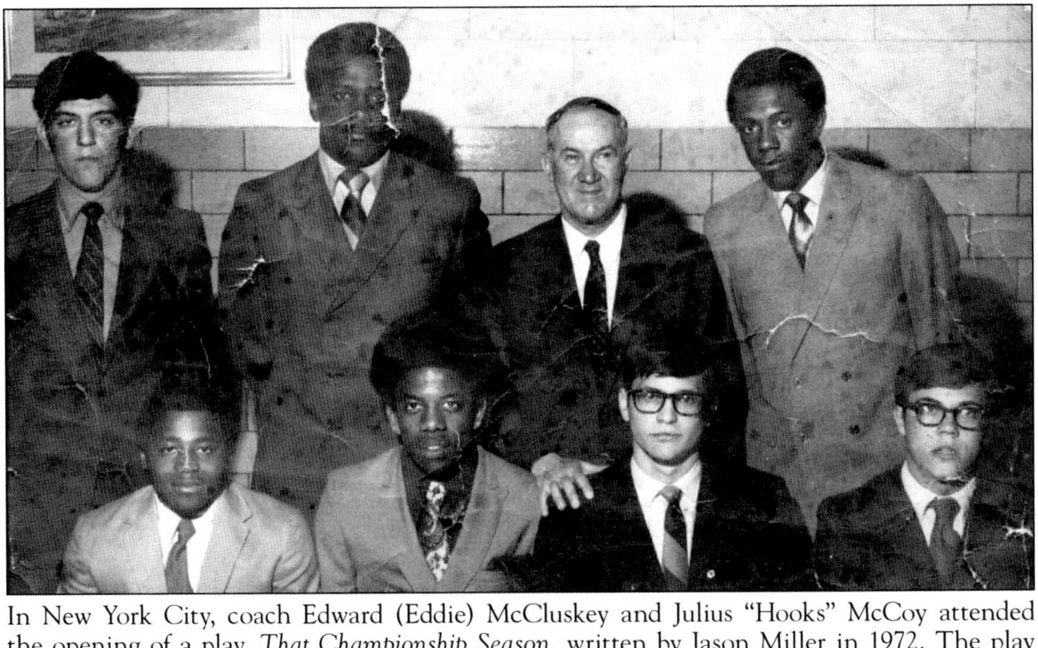

In New York City, coach Edward (Eddie) McCluskey and Julius "Hooks" McCoy attended the opening of a play, *That Championship Season*, written by Jason Miller in 1972. The play was based on Farrell's 1952 championship and what transpired over the next two decades, concluding with the 1972 PIAA state championship. Shown are All-America tackle Randy Crowder (second row, second from left), who went on to play for the Miami Dolphins, and McCluskey (second row, second from right) at Farrell High School.

Julius "Hooks" McCoy (1932–2008) of the 1952 PIAA championship team led the Farrell Steelers to the first of coach McCluskey's seven championships. McCoy played professionally with the Eastern Basketball Professional League and toured with the Harlem Globetrotters. His name was added to the Continental Basketball Association all-time team in 1996. McCoy appears in a Farrell High School Steelers uniform in the school auditorium around 1951.

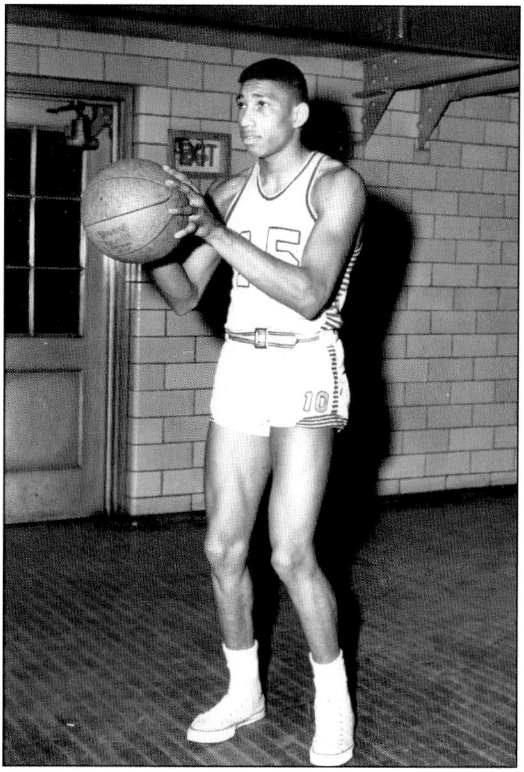

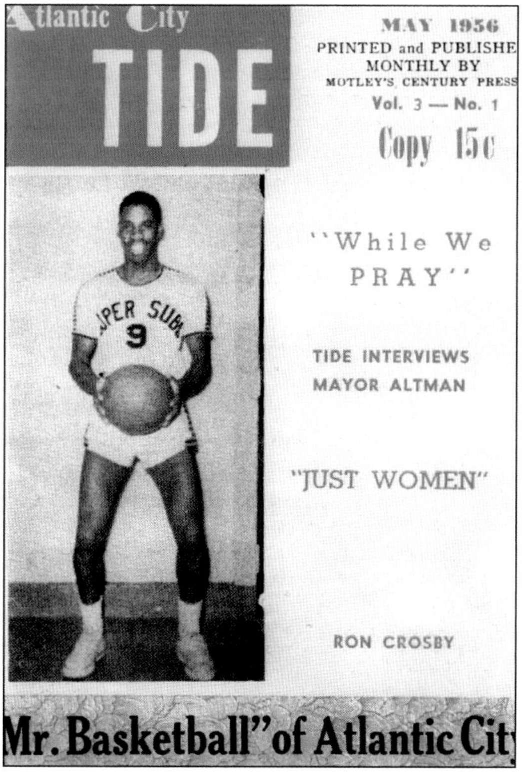

Ronald Crosby (1933–1994) of the 1952 championship team played for the Virginia State University Trojans and the Ettrick Lakers, an independent team that won the Virginia All-State Tournament championship, where he received most valuable player. In 1956, he played ball for South Jersey's Super Subs, where recognition as an all-around player on both defense and offense lead to being featured on the cover of the May 1956 *Atlantic City Tide* as "'Mr. Basketball' of Atlantic City."

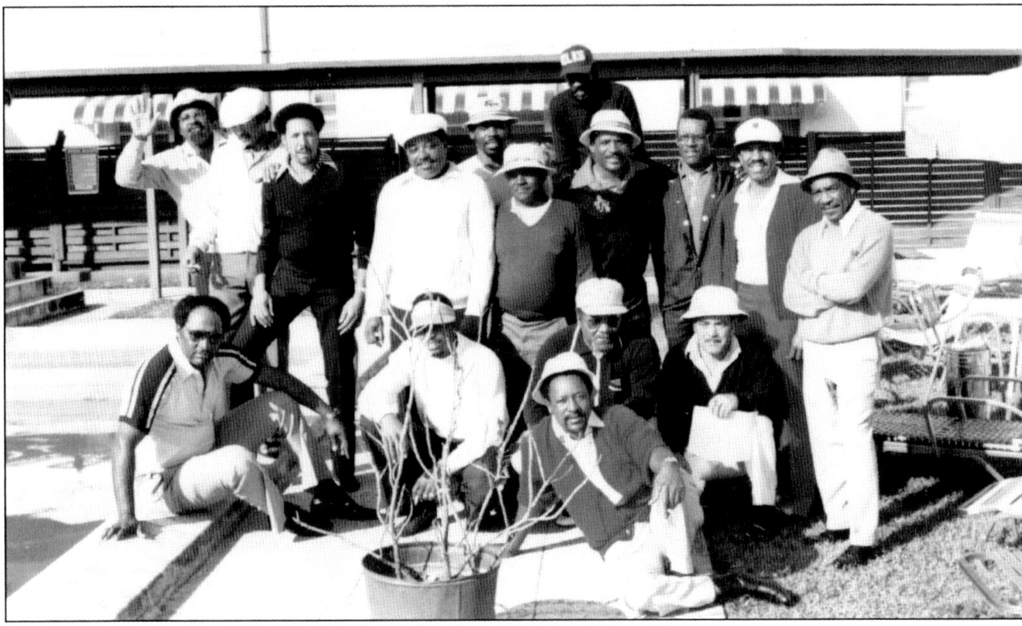

Leon Ponder, Ricky Gordon, James Mitchell, Charles Mitchell, Robert Flint, and some men from neighboring Warren and Youngstown, Ohio, are in the Caribbean for a winter golf outing. At its peak in 1980, 75 men participated in the bowling season at Sunset Lanes, which ran Saturday evening over 32 weeks from September into April. The roll-off concluded the season and awarding of team and individual prizes. Pictured at Sunset Lanes in Farrell are (first row) Ernie Saunders, Bob Smith, Jim Tatum, Walter Wright, Bill Capitol, Bob Johnson, ? Cain, Prentice Adams, Henry Richards, ? Robinson, Lawrence Richardson, David Richards, Tommie Daniels, and Gerald Mitchell; (second row) Hasco Darden, Harry Sam Boatner, Harvey Lights, Anderson Hilton, Cornelius Richardson, Marion Lampkins, Will Graham, Sam Malloy, Alphonso Allen, ? Dinkins, Al Juricks, Boshie Wells, Dave Truman, Tim Chapman, and Glenn Walker. (Courtesy of Helen Mitchell and Martha Richards.)

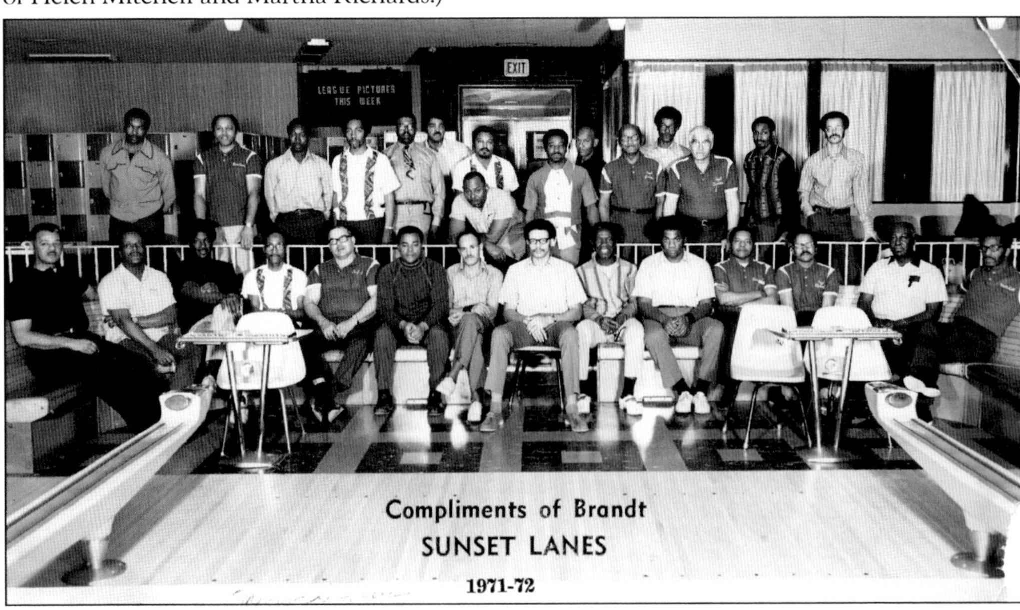

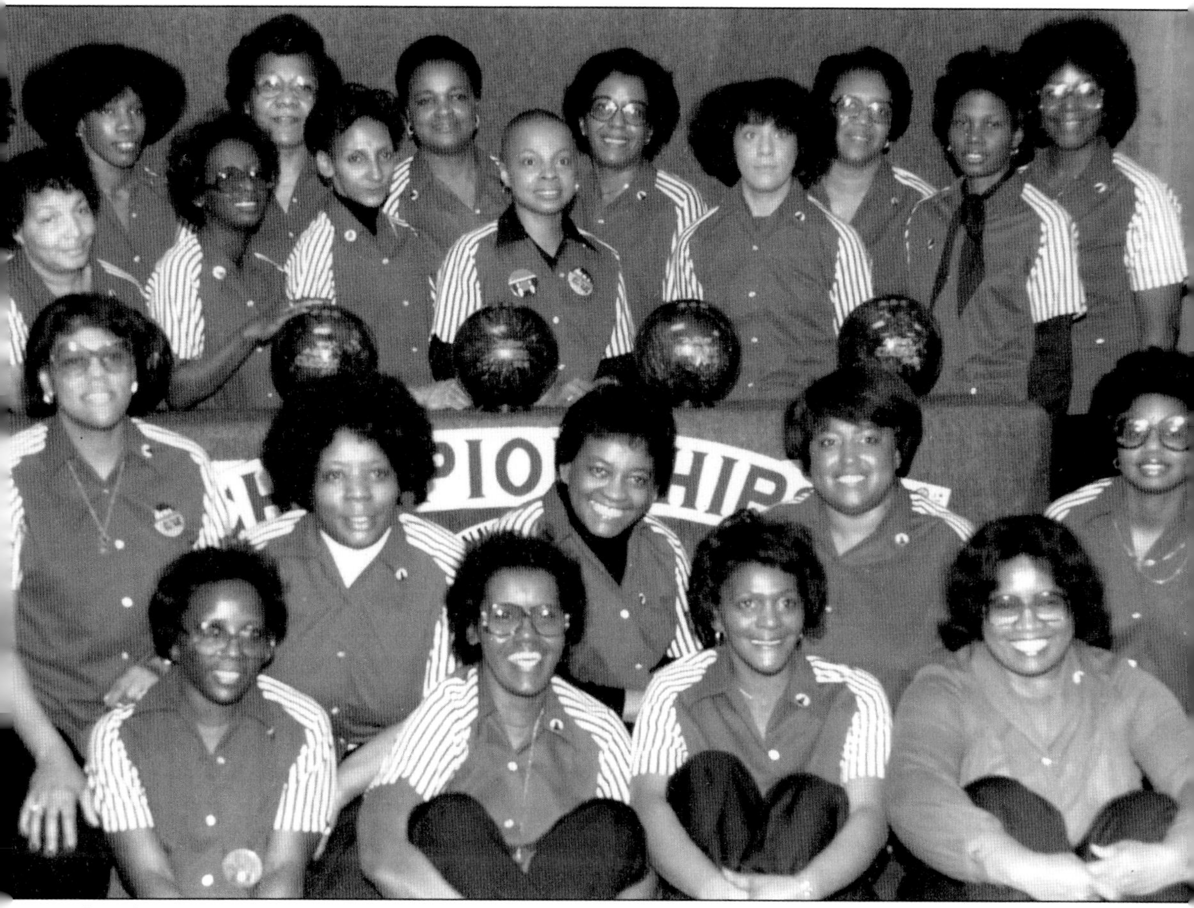

Almeda James, an avid bowler, member of the Ebonites, and charter member of the Keystone Mixed League, the oldest African American mixed league in Mercer County, operated through the support of the National Bowling Association with the help of Betty Marshall and Laura Harden a thriving youth bowling league for ages 6 to 18 in the 1970s and 1980s. The youth, known as bantams, bowled in the state tournament. In 1980, James, who had her undivided attention on bowling every Tuesday and Thursday evening, received a Mercer County Frontiers Club Community Service Award for the youth program. The Ebonites, an all-women league, have regularly attended annual National Bowling Association events across the country. Members of the Ebonites are, from left to right, (first row) Otie Cain, Alda Smith, Norman Tatum, and Sylvia Hunt Goodrich; (second row) Jasmine Ford, Becky Gordon, Betty Marshall, Phyllis Townsend, and Eleanor Quarles Houston; (third row) Almeda James, Gwynn Baker, two unidentified women, Wanda ?, and Roslyn Short; (fourth row) Peggy McDonald, unidentified, Valva Truman, Lois Moyer, Betty Lou Alston, Martha Richards, and Ernestine Campbell. (Courtesy Almeda James.)

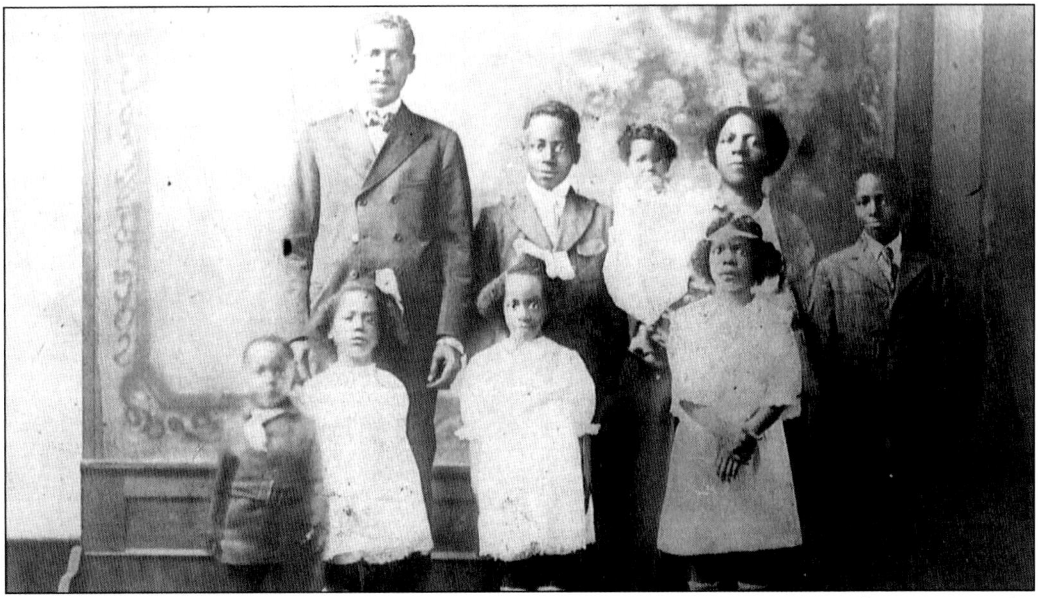

In 1912, Edward Robinson (1873–1979) moved to Farrell and located employment at the Carnegie-Illinois Steel Corporation, where he worked until 1937. His immediate family, pictured from left to right around 1920, includes (first row) Clarence W. "Buster" Robinson (1918–1988), Novella Ellen Robinson, Ruth Ethel Robinson, and Monzela Robinson; (second row) Edward Robinson, Charles "Sonny" Robinson, Sarah B. Inge Robinson, Ernest D. Robinson (in his mother's arms), and Joseph S. Smith. (Courtesy of Iris Robinson.)

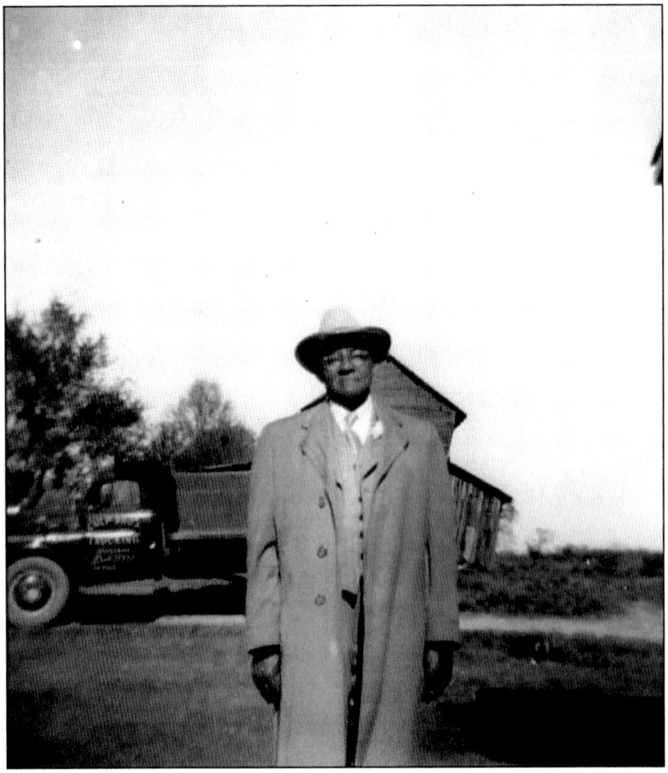

With expendable cash, some southern migrants considered long-term investments for the future. In 1929, Joseph and Mary Steverson McClendon purchased a 17-acre farm off Satterfield Road in Hickory Township near the Tam O'Shanter Golf Course. The family had a pig farm with orchards whose produce was donated to the campground in West Middlesex. Shown is Joseph S. McClendon on the farm. In the background is a truck owned by Culp Brothers Trucking of Sharon.

Five

Farrell's Twin City Elks Lodge
A Unifying Force

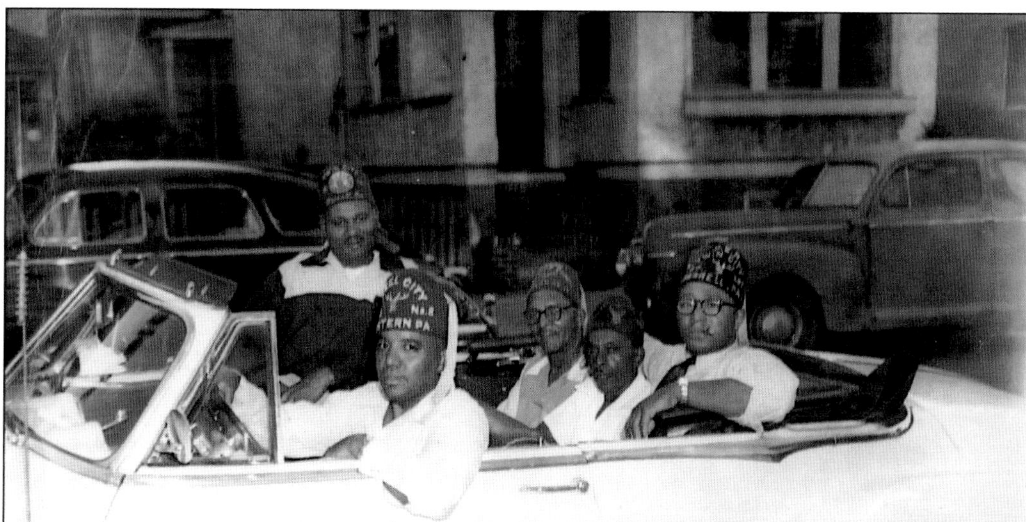

A national lodge dignitary, the dynamic J. Finley Wilson traveled across the country, telling people, "If you want to see somebody with money, go to Farrell, Pennsylvania." Shown are Twin City Elks officers Lewis Greene (1907–1990), driving; Odell B. "June" Matthews Jr. (born in 1914), sitting in the passenger's seat; and Charles Vactor Sr. (sitting in the middle of the backseat) in the late 1940s. Between 1938 and 1951, Vactor was the spokesman for Farrell's largest community-based African American organization.

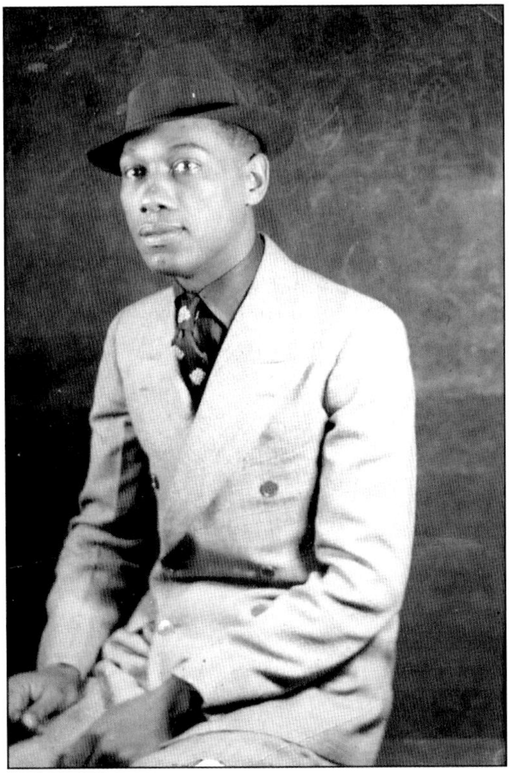

From the mid-1930s through the early 1960s, the Twin City Elks Lodge was "going to town." In the late 1930s, Elks members Charles Vactor Sr. and Dewey Brooks (1900–1999), at left, operator of Brooks' Shoeshine Parlor, bought James "Cootie" Callahan Jr. (1927–2004) a red wagon for the delivery of food, clothing, and coal from Murphy's Coal Company on Broadway to financially strapped people's homes. Charity was a cornerstone of the Elks' creed.

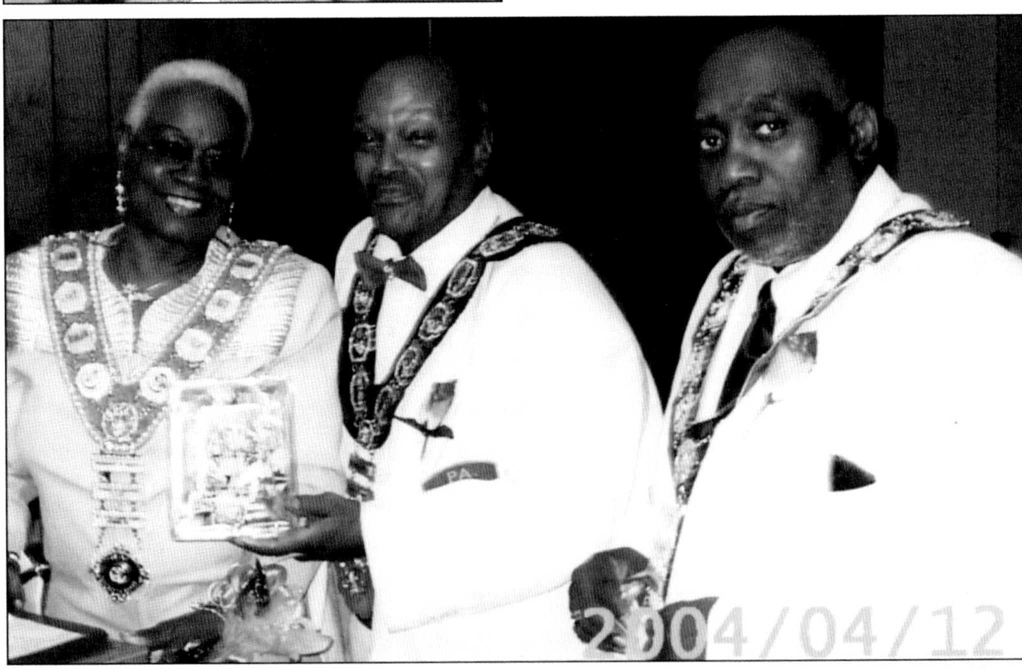

Callahan recalled the heyday of the Twin City Elks. During the 1930s, a strong softball and basketball league emerged from the Elks' ranks. Twin City Elks sports programming provided a constructive outlet to relieve pent-up frustrations. Due to segregation, African Americans built their own institution and established viable services and programming in the North.

In 1926, Lewis Henry "Duke" Greene Sr. (1907–1990), Farrell High School's former standout who lettered in basketball and football for three years, organized the Twin City Elks basketball team. Greene later coached the team for a year and served as exalted ruler. He played basketball until 1942, mentored Bobby Rapper, Ike Mitchell, Harry Boatner, Johnny Hammond, and James Callahan Jr., and had an influence upon the development of the basketball program.

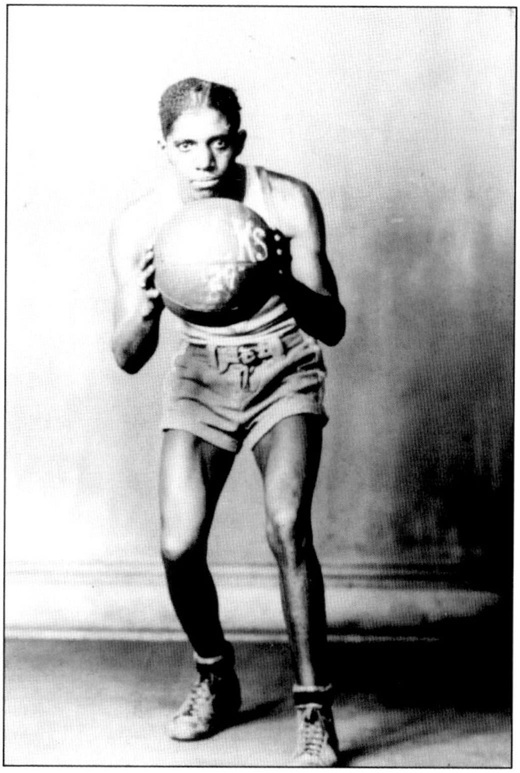

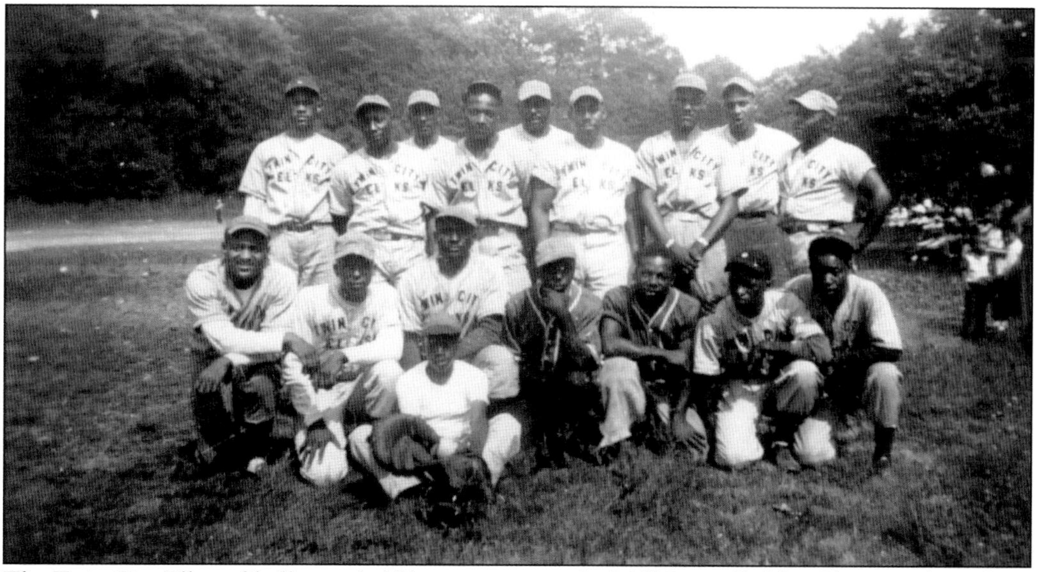

The Twin City Elks softball team held home games at the Mill Street Field in Sharon's Flats where 1,000 people attended. One team member recruited and offered a good job by Westinghouse to play for its independent team was Samuel Malloy (pictured back, center). Other team members pictured at the Pine Hollow Field in Sharon around 1955 are Clindo Truesdale, T. Johnson, ? Kellum, ? Henderson, and William "Kitty" Hyatt (rear, far right). Hyatt was a 1993 Buhl Day honoree.

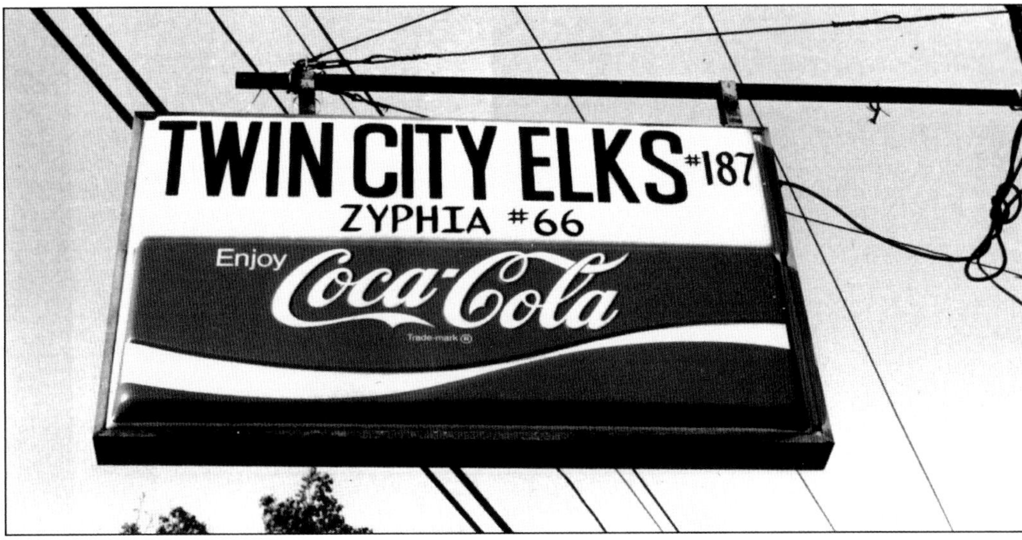

Between 1922 and 1946, under the leadership of grand exalted ruler J. Finley Wilson, the organization grew from 32,000 to 500,000 members in 1,000 lodges. The phenomenal growth of the Twin City lodge reflected this national trend, making it influential and well respected within the community. The Twin City lodge was organized in 1914 and with 700 members was recognized as the largest in the state of Pennsylvania for almost two decades. Pictured is the sign outside the site of the Twin City Elks Rest at 301 Staunton Street in 1993.

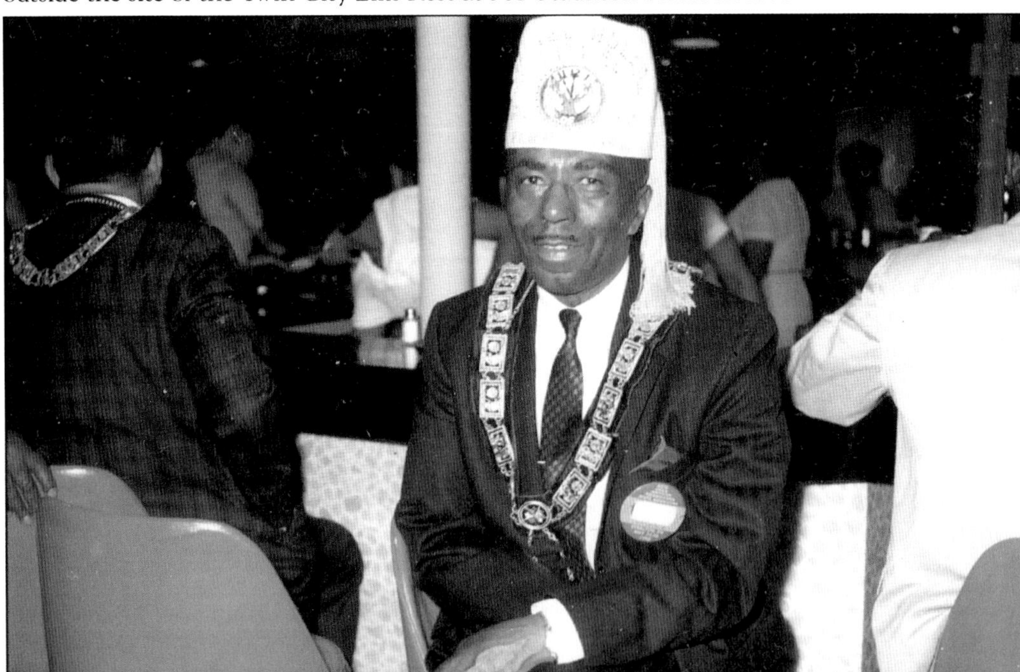

In 1934, Clarence Mitchell Sr. joined the Twin City lodge and for a decade served as athletic director and manager of sports teams. In 1944, he was appointed the Elks' state athletic director with the charge to develop sports programming. During the 1940s, Charles Vactor Sr., Harvey Satterwhite, and Clarence Mitchell Sr. realized Twin City had to invest in something before the profits got away. (Courtesy of Gerald Mitchell.)

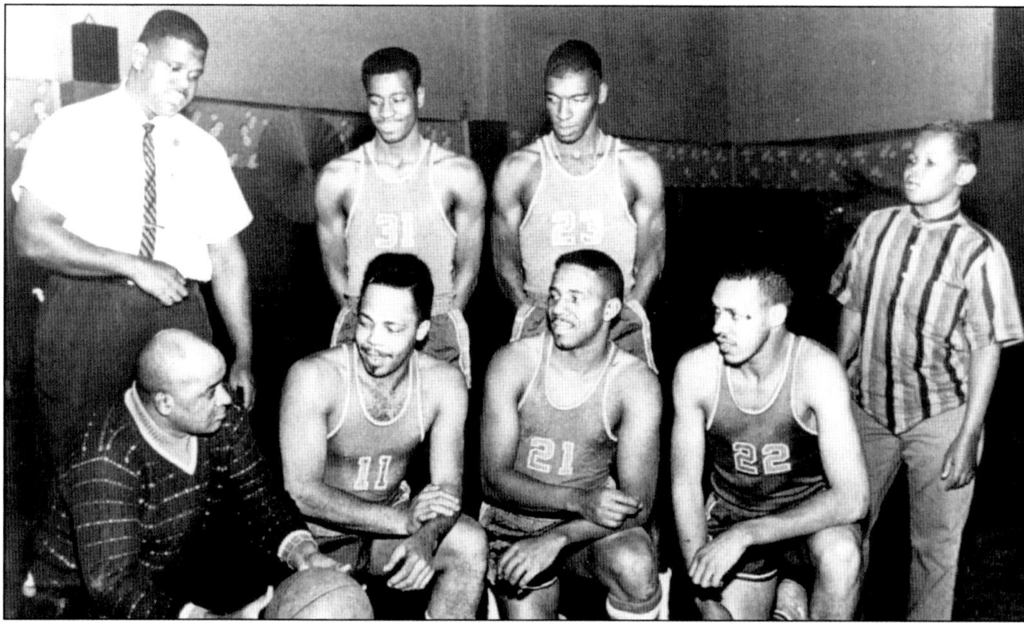

As late as the 1960s, the Twin City lodge continued to produce outstanding ballplayers. Pictured at the Twin City Elks auditorium around 1962 are the last Twin City Elks basketball team members. From left to right are (first row) coach Bobby Rapper, Hugo Washington, Charles Mitchell, Leon Ponder, and unidentified; (second row) financial officer Samuel "Bo" Satterwhite, Walter Wright, and unidentified.

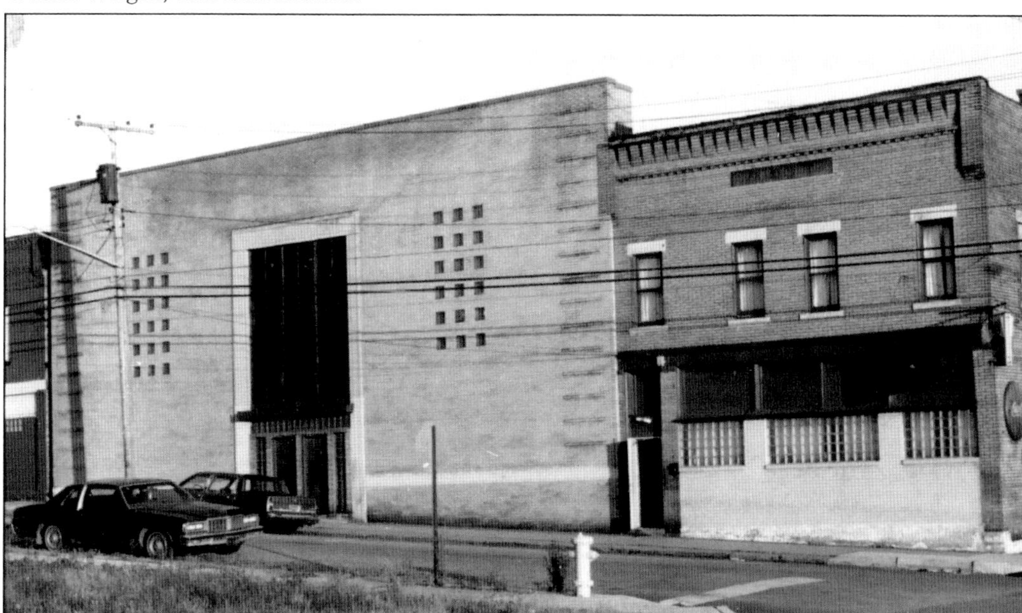

The completion of a $75,000 gymnasium was considered a great advance and was equated with racial pride in 1950. The gymnasium provided the site for recreational activities from basketball to roller-skating and got children off the street. Pictured in 1993, the site of the Twin City Elks was at 301 Staunton Street; the building to the left is the gymnasium. Thirteen years later, the building was destroyed by fire.

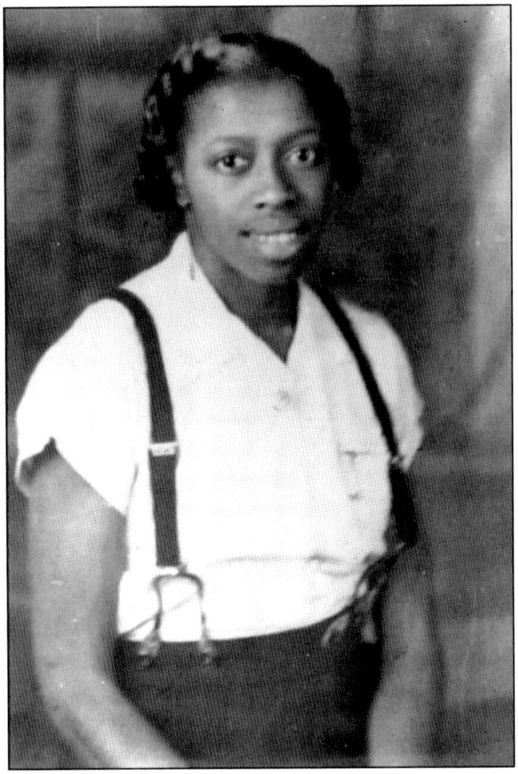

The Twin City Elks girls' basketball team had a reputation of being tough on the court. During the early 1930s, the basketball team lineup was Flozel Adams, Hannah Buchamover, Clara Capitol, Elizabeth Clayton, Elsie Gibson, Leticia Johnson, Creona Major, May McNeil, Meredith Martin, and Dorothy Steverson.

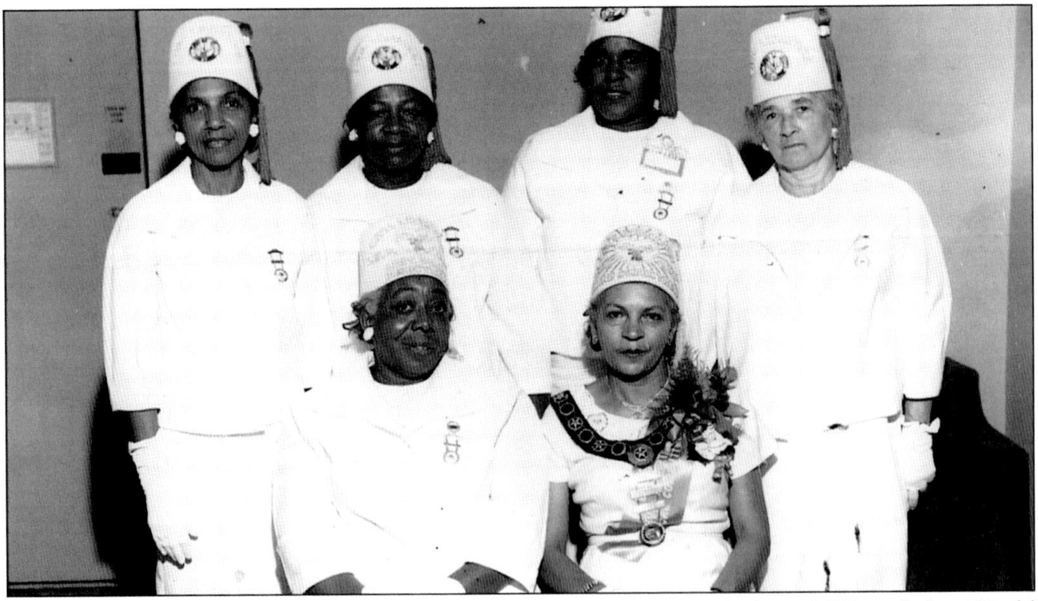

Zylphia Temple No. 66, Improved Benevolent and Protective Order of Elks of the World (IBPOEW), has many trophies to its credit, won by past drill teams. Past grand daughter rulers included Geneva English, Jeanetta Miller, Sarah Q. Anderson, Leora Davis, Janet Grear, Jeanetta S. Holloway, Geneva Jenkins, Lucille J. Parker, and Maxine M. Pulliam. Members are, from left to right, (first row) Jeannetta Miller and unidentified; (second row) Helen Wilson, unidentified, Helen Matthews, and Irene Walker. (Courtesy of Debbie Matthews Walters.)

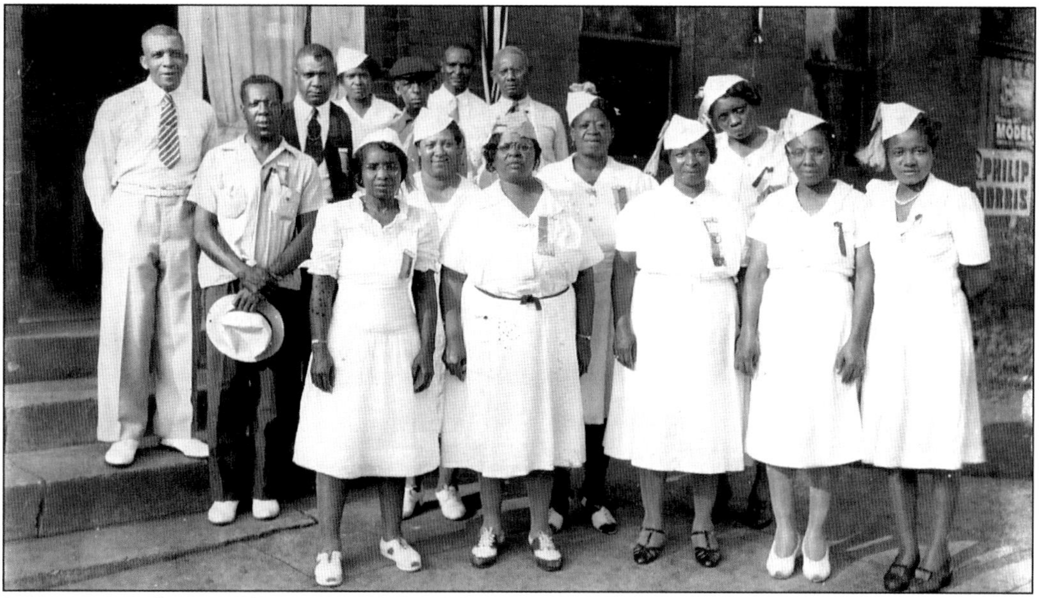

During its peak years, the membership of the Twin City Elks Lodge female auxiliary, the Zylphia Temple, reached 300. In 1915, the Zylphia Temple, named by Hilda Smith of Wheatland, was organized with regular meetings in Hess Hall on Broadway Avenue in Farrell. Zylphia Temple's organizer, Lettie A. M. Bryant Jones (1866–1962), was a former member of Western Star temple in Washington, Pennsylvania. First daughter ruler was Etta Caution Lacey. (Photograph by Lininger Photo, courtesy of Debbie Matthews Walters.)

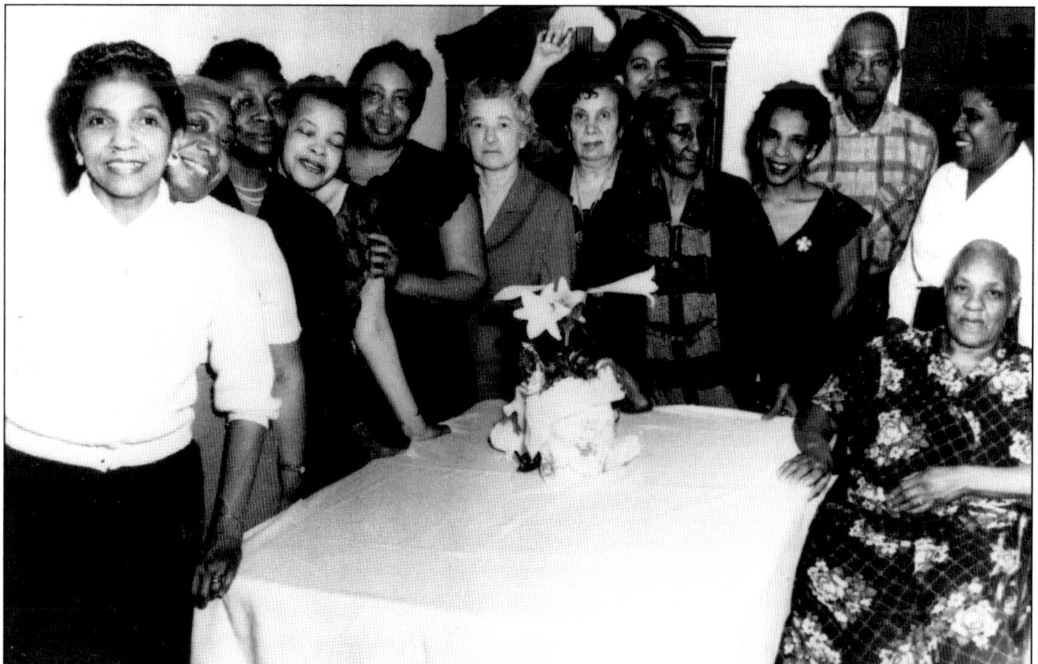

Ladies' social club gatherings at the home of Odell (standing) and Bessie (seated) Matthews on Erie Street in West Middlesex were common events around 1944. All pictured are members of the Twin City Elks and its female affiliate, Zylphia Temple. This photograph is from the mid-1940s.

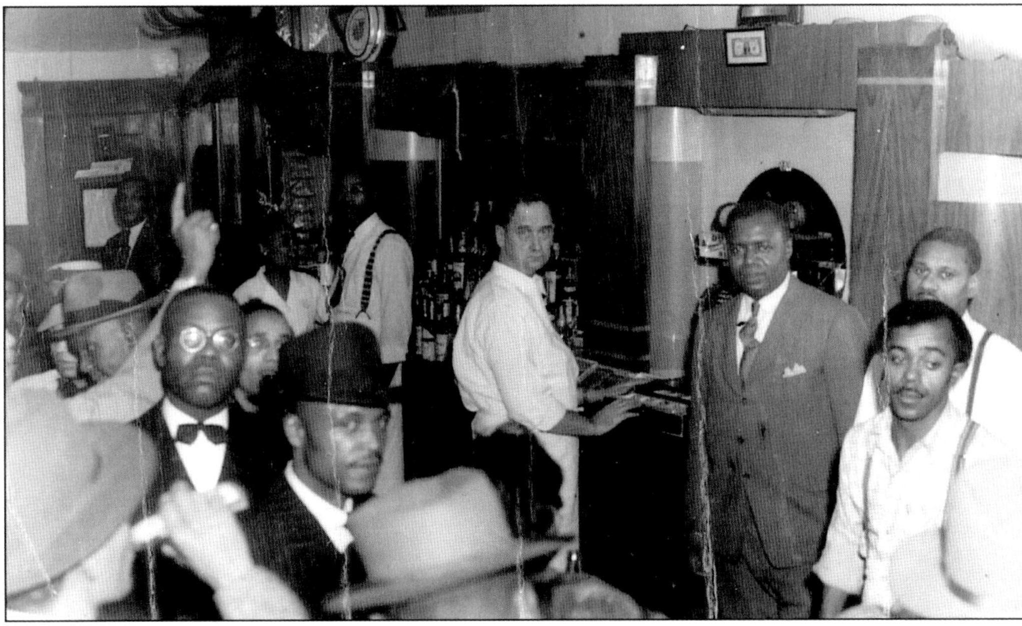

The Twin City Elks was an extraordinary organization with community-based programs and activities of wide appeal. Bands and private orchestras often performed at Twin City–sponsored events. The bar at the Twin City Elks rest is packed with people from New Castle, Youngstown, Beaver Falls, and home during the weekend. Pictured behind the bar are Roy Parker, Oscar Daniels and Odell "June" Matthews Jr. during the 1950s. (Courtesy of Debbie Matthews Walters.)

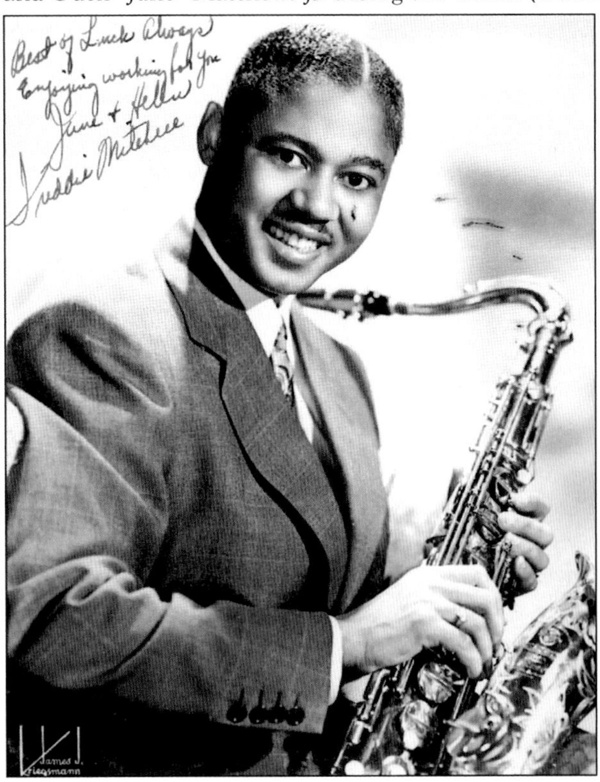

The Twin City lodge purchased a bus around 1945, arranged field trips to Pittsburgh and Cleveland, and had raffles, picnics, and cabarets. The lodge's club held floor shows and attracted celebrities like Duke Ellington, Ray Charles, Peg Leg Bates, and Jesse Owens. Guests booed Louis Armstrong off the stage when he was not playing "jumping" music. Odell "June" Matthews Jr. coordinated event planning for Freddie Mitchell's band in 1952.

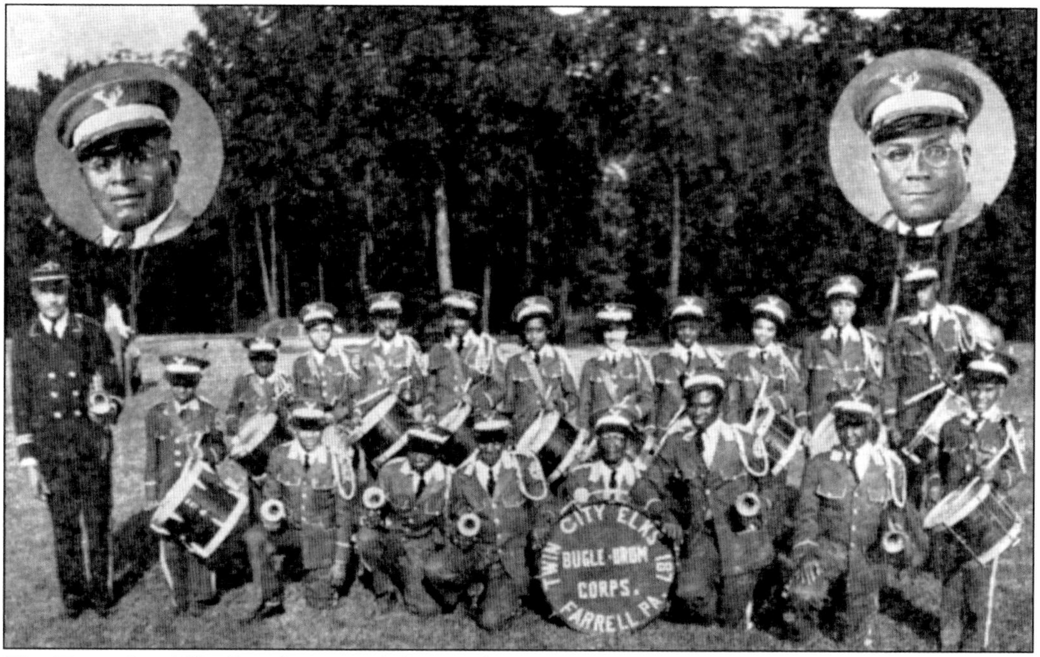

The Twin City Elks Band operated during the 1940s and 1950s. Professor Steverson was hired to provide music instruction to adults in the Twin City Elks Band in the 1940s. The Twin City Elks Band was comprised of all adults, while youth formed the Twin City Elks Bugle and Drum Corps. Edward Smith (upper right), an exalted ruler in the 1920s, and a Mr. Hyatt (upper left) were band directors for the Twin City Elks Bugle and Drum Corps.

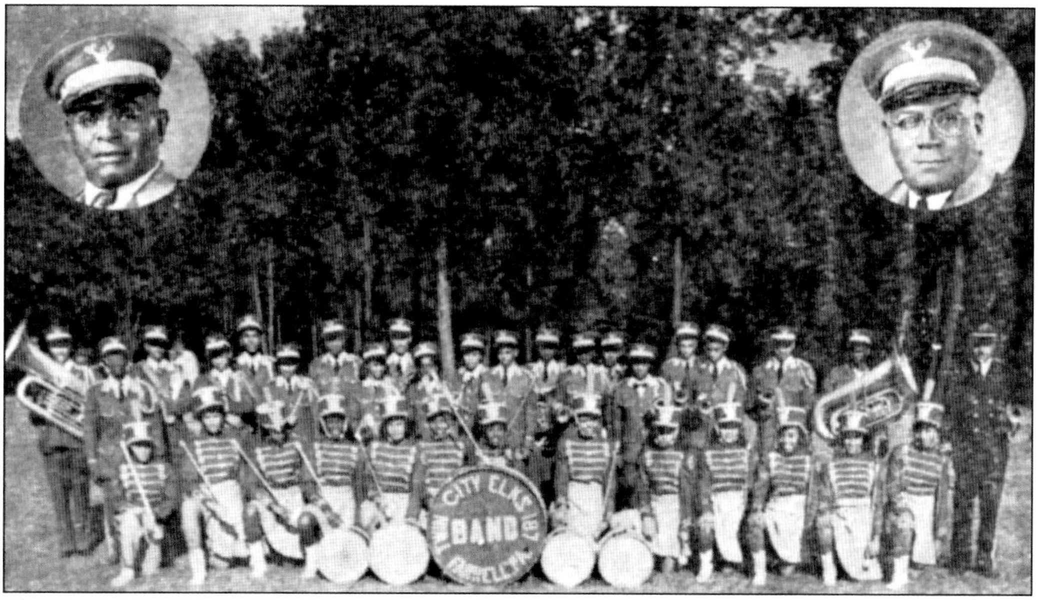

The teeming Twin City youth council provided a strategic means to bring youth into the organization. The Twin City Elks–sponsored activities for youth ranged from basketball to roller-skating. During the Christmas season, the Twin City Elks provided treats and spent several hundred dollars on charitable works in the community. Comprised of youth, the Twin City Bugle and Drum Corps was visible in the community in the 1950s.

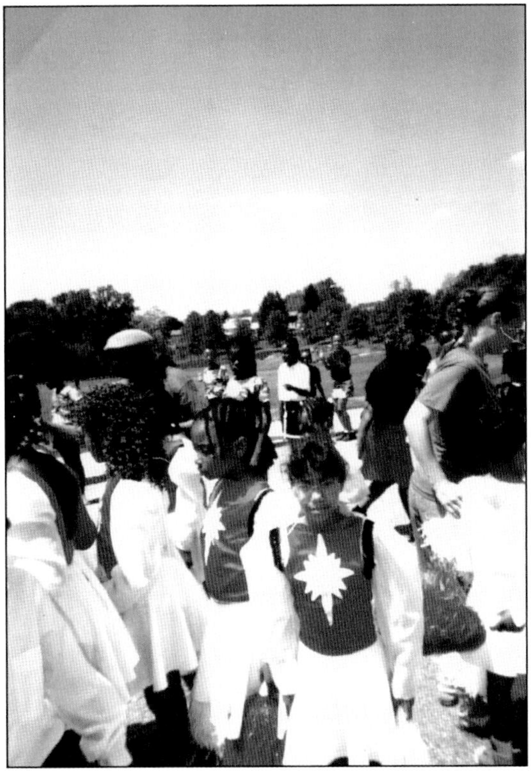

Between 1938 and 1951, exalted ruler Charles Vactor Sr. "worked with the mayor" since he was spokesman for Farrell's largest community-based African American organization. The Twin City lodge's exalted ruler became an influential person because of the organization's large membership. Dora Smith directed the majorettes during the 1940s. Chaperones included Sara Turnage Anderson and Belle Wright and her daughter Ruth Wells. The community viewed the Twin City majorettes with distinction. (Courtesy of Janet Grear.)

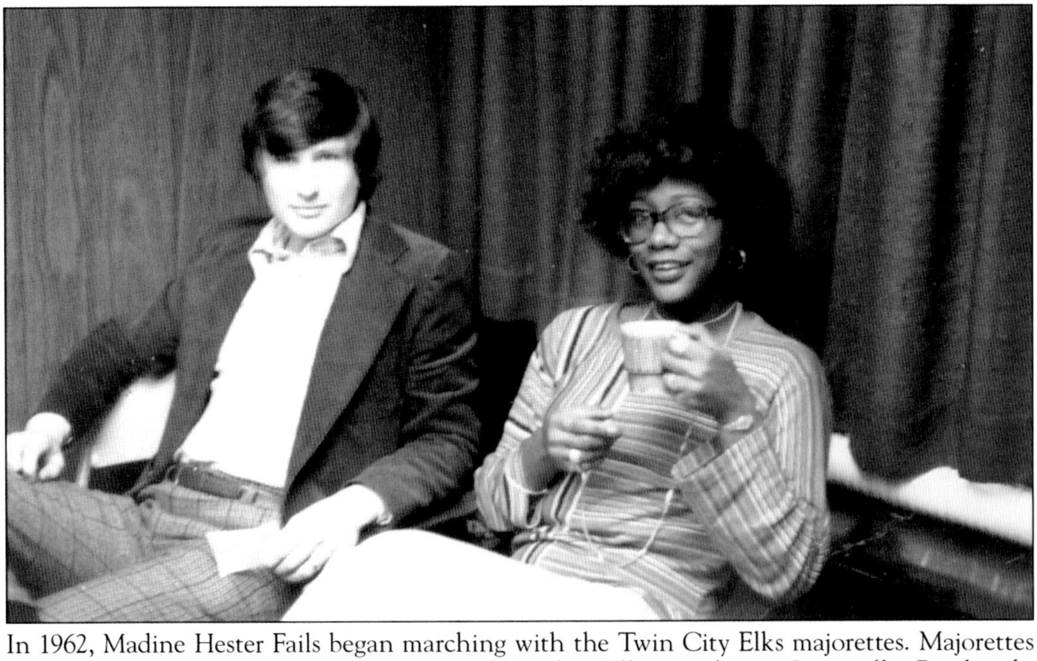

In 1962, Madine Hester Fails began marching with the Twin City Elks majorettes. Majorettes under the direction of Bernice Jacoway performed in Elks parades in Greenville, Pittsburgh, Cleveland, Ohio, and Chicago, Illinois. In 1971, she and other high school students met with Farrell administrators about the overall lack of representation of African American cheerleaders, which produced favorable results. Pictured is Fails as director of the SVUL.

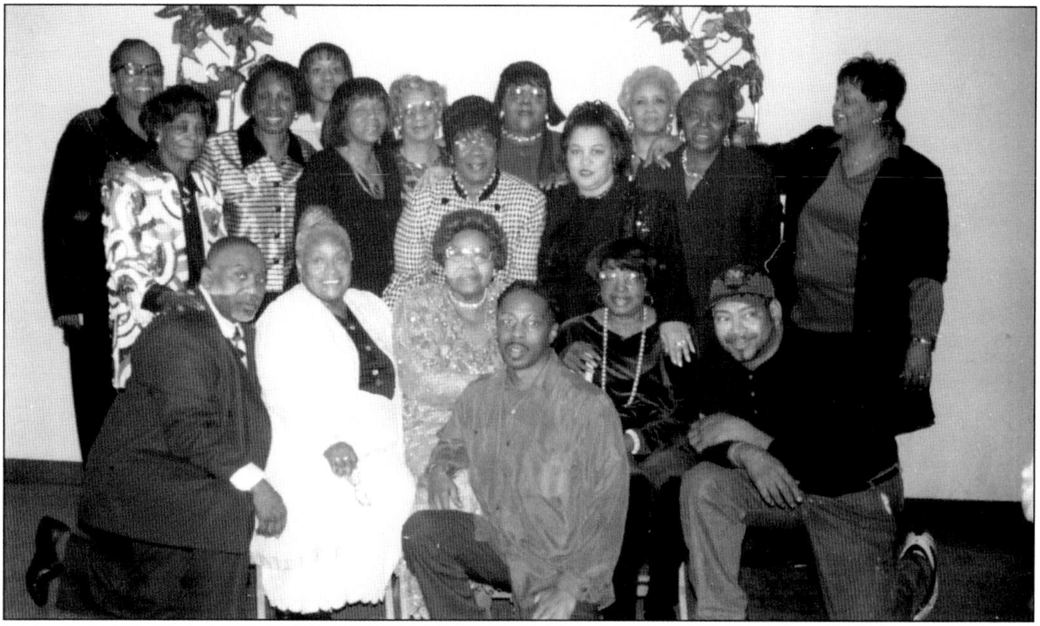

In 2001, the Twin City lodge received the Mercer County Frontiers Club Community Service Award for its years of providing service to the youth with special needs in the Shenango Valley. In 1973, the Atlanta Club of the Twin City Elks organized to promote funds to attend Elks national conventions. Sarah Quarles Anderson is president. (Photograph by George B. Thomas, courtesy of Janet Grear.)

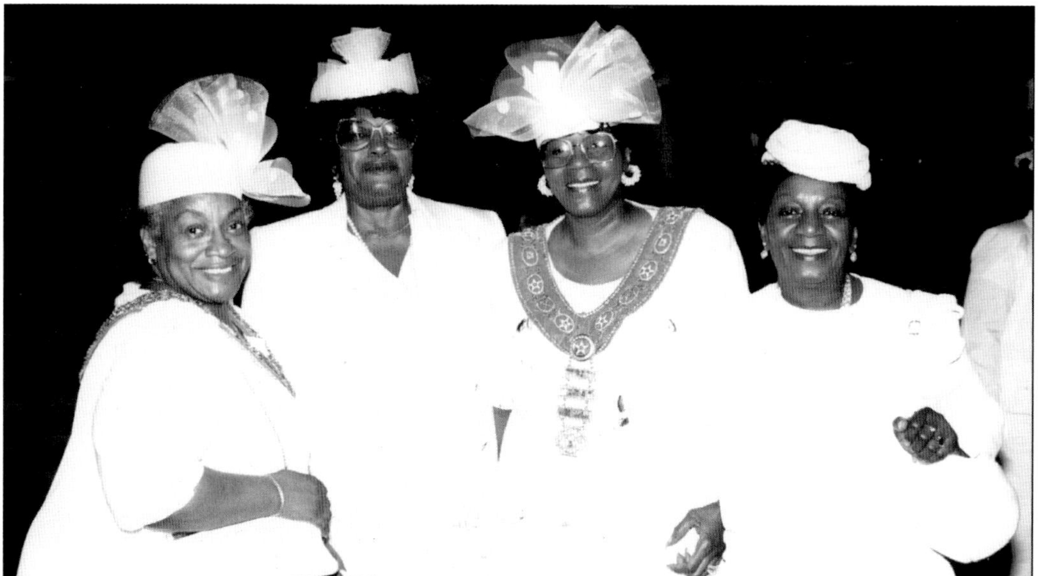

The Twin City Elks and its auxiliary have a strong presence at state and national conventions. The Twin City education department hosted the Pennsylvania Oratorical Contest, whose winners included Dorothy Height, president emeritus of the National Council of Negro Women in 1994. During the Las Vegas national convention, past grand daughter rulers are, from left to right, Jeanetta "Flossie" Holloway, Vivian Clarke, Janet Grear, and an unidentified person at the memorial service around 2001. (Courtesy of Janet Grear.)

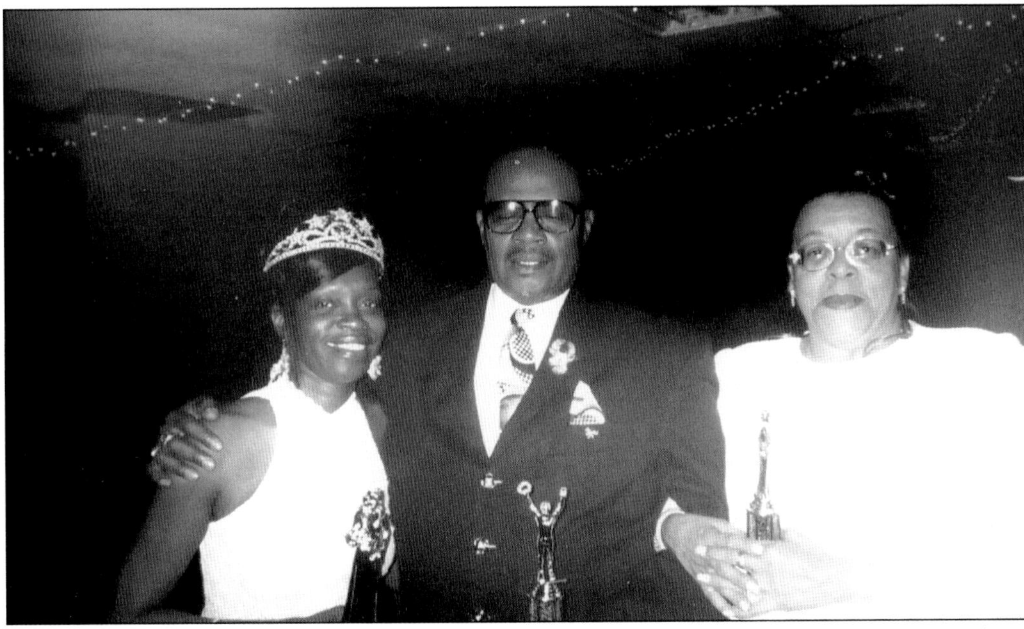

By the end of World War II, African American Elks were dismayed by the deterioration of race relations and subsequently turned inward to strengthen their own institutions. The Twin City king and queen coronation was a popular fund-raiser. Shown from left to right in 2005 are Donna Prouitt, queen of the Twin City Elks; Jimmie Smith, king of the Twin City Elks; and Sharon Owens, attendant at the Twin City Elks. (Courtesy of Janet Grear.)

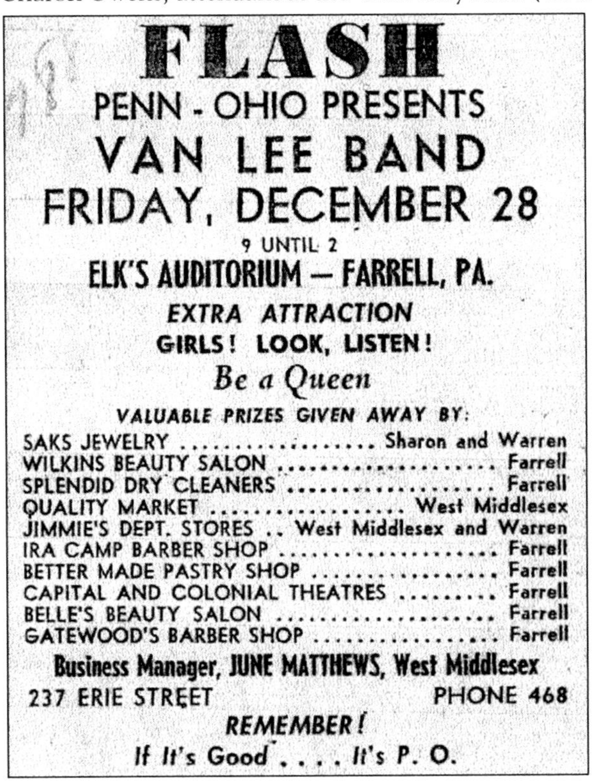

The Van Lee Band, under the direction of LeVan McKay, drew large crowds to the Twin City Elks auditorium during the 1950s. Helping to meet the aspirations of African American migrants—those from northern industrial communities as well as those from the rural South—Farrell's Twin City lodge touched the lives of many people. In 2006, the Twin City Elks auditorium was destroyed in fire.

Six

Camp Reynolds
In Service to Home and Country

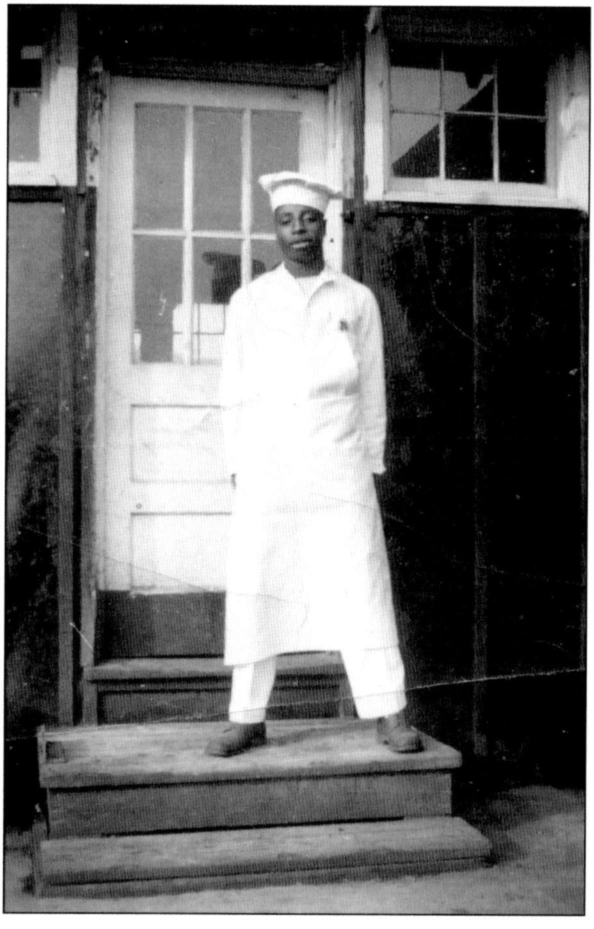

During the 1930s, while assigned to the Civilian Conservation Corps (CCC), young men from indigent families received their first exposure to segregation and a regimental lifestyle. Clyde Steverson Sr. (1920–2001) of Farrell served as the cook for Company 2312, stationed at Westford around 1938.

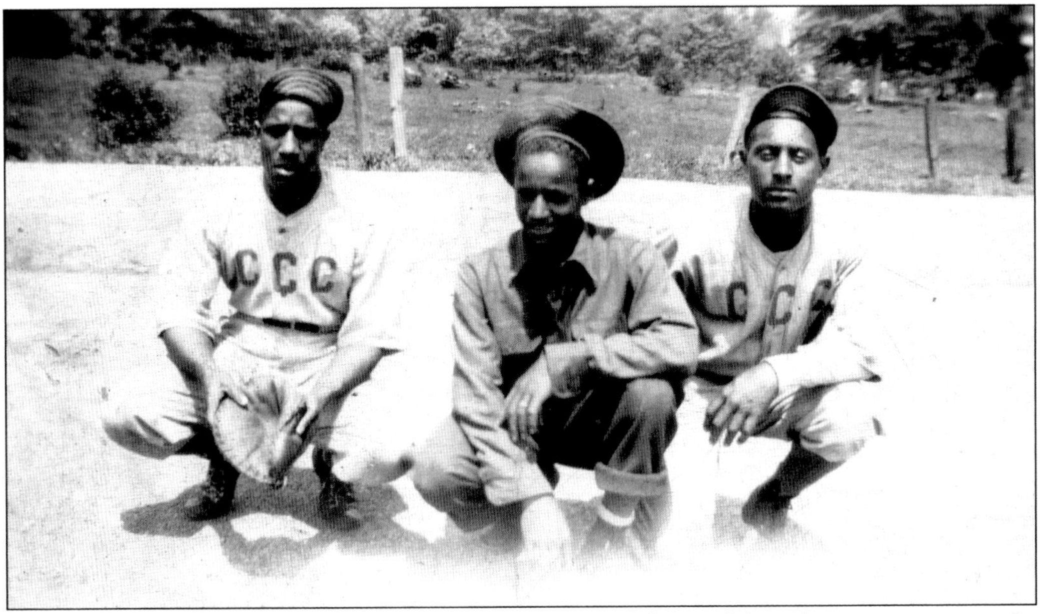

Young men, some experiencing their first time away from home, labored in construction of a dam to protect the Shenango Valley and other communities from flooding downstream. They participated in planned educational and recreational activities. William "Red" Bullock (right) played on a CCC baseball team.

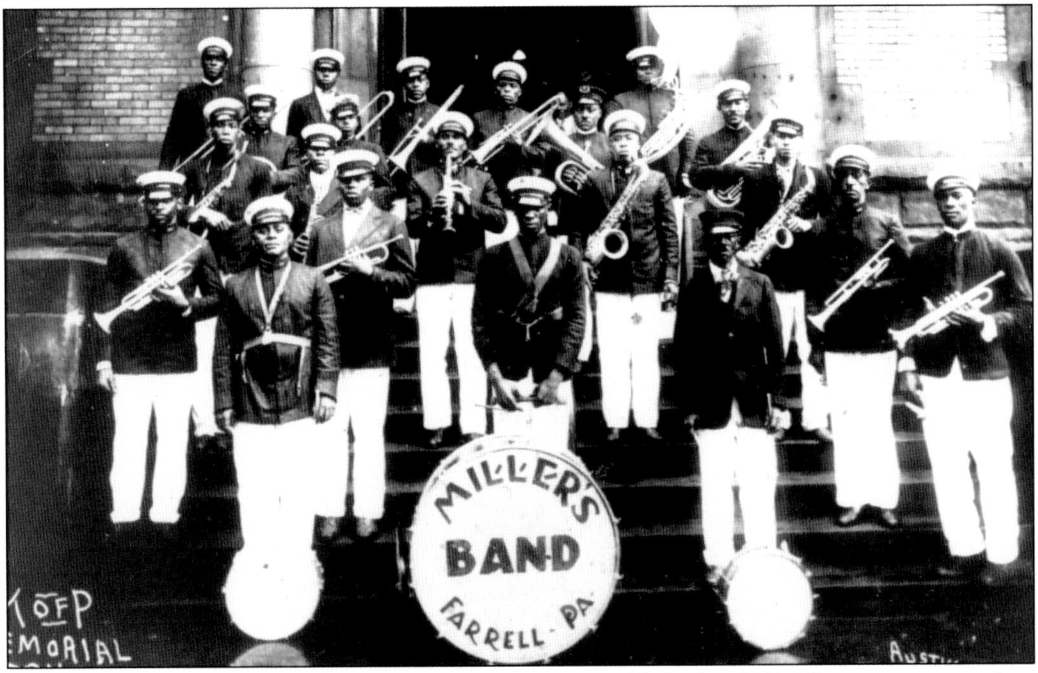

The Russell L. Chinn Post of the American Legion was established in 1921. The post commandeer was Thomas Robinson. Many African Americans worked for private families in the late 19th century. Few opportunities outside of charwoman existed for Maria Chinn, a founder of Ruth African Methodist Episcopal Zion Church. Yet beyond adversity, her family earned distinction. Pictured is Miller's Band, one of several African American bands and orchestras in the 1920s.

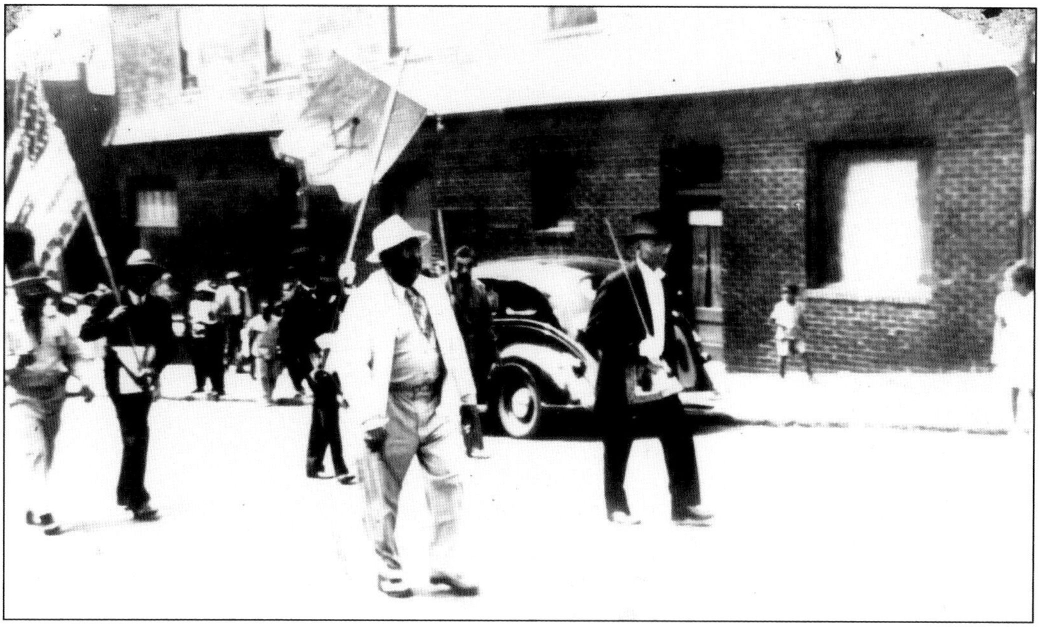

In 1917, the mills' whistles blew for 15 minutes when a group of local African American recruits set out for Camp Lee. Fred Lofton (second row, far left) appears as a flag bearer in the Masonic St. John's Day parade at the corner of Union Street and Greenfield Avenue in Farrell around 1927. The Russell L. Chinn Post of the American Legion was named in honor of the first African American soldier killed in battle during World War I.

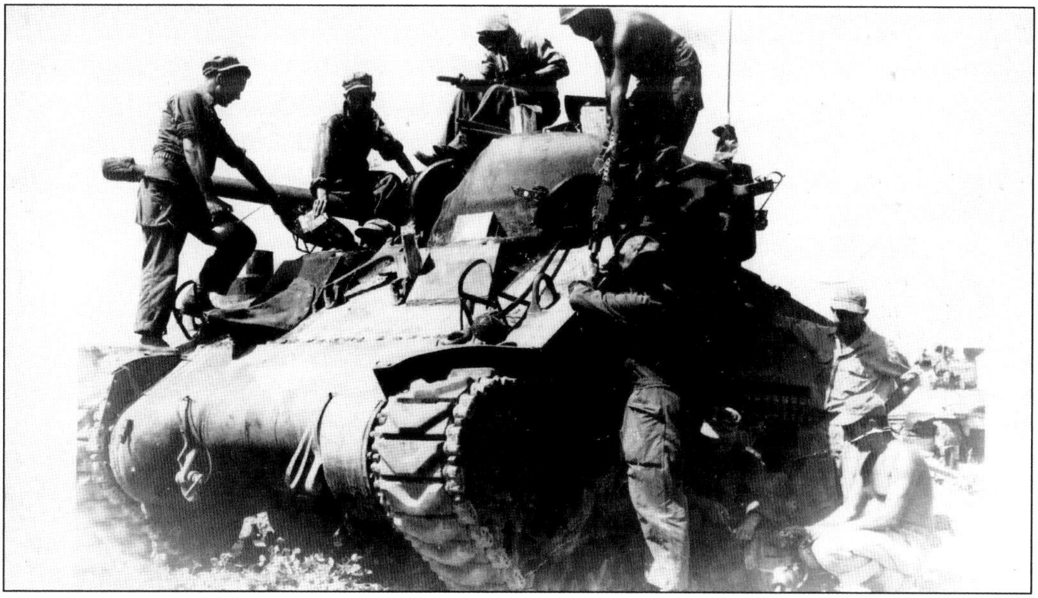

Until recently, the Tuskegee Airmen, like the 92nd and 93rd Infantry Divisions, the 366th Infantry Regiment, and the 761st Tank Battalion, were often overlooked by America. Under the direction of Col. Benjamin O. Davis Jr., four squadrons of African American fighters had one of the best records of any air force fighter group. During World War II, the airmen earned 150 Distinguished Flying Crosses. They flew 15,533 sorties and 1,578 combat missions and never lost a bomber they escorted over North Africa and Europe.

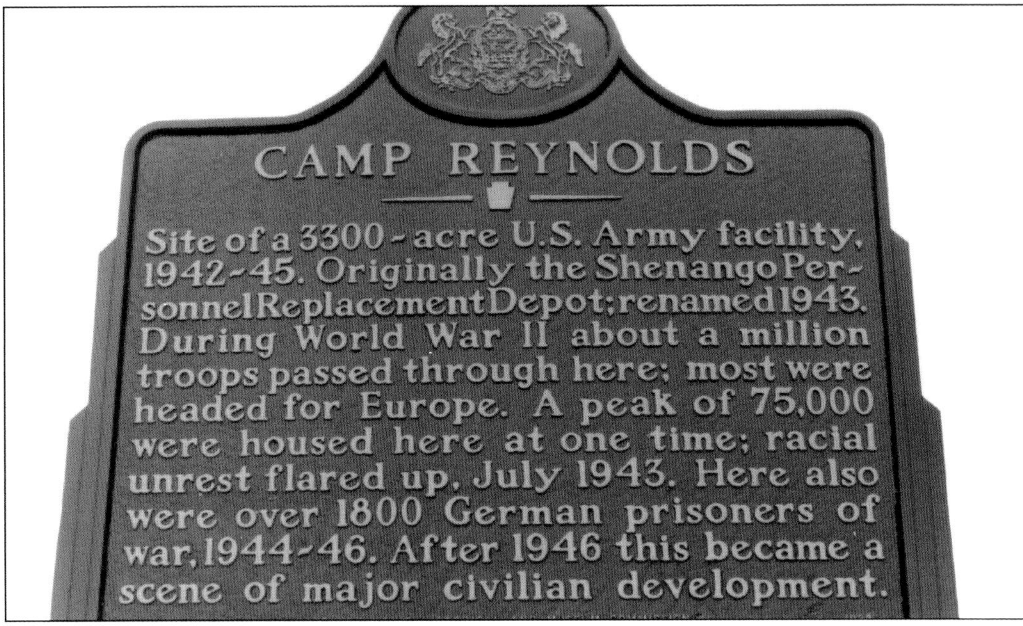

Dempsey J. Travis's *I Refuse to Learn to Fail* describes life at a U.S. Army facility where German prisoners of war received better treatment than American citizens. The existence of a segregated post exchange and theater precipitated racial tensions. Questions still exist as to the number of African American soldiers killed. Some local observers estimate six or more. A 20-year-old African American college graduate, Pvt. Norman Taylor, of Rosedale, Kansas, was killed.

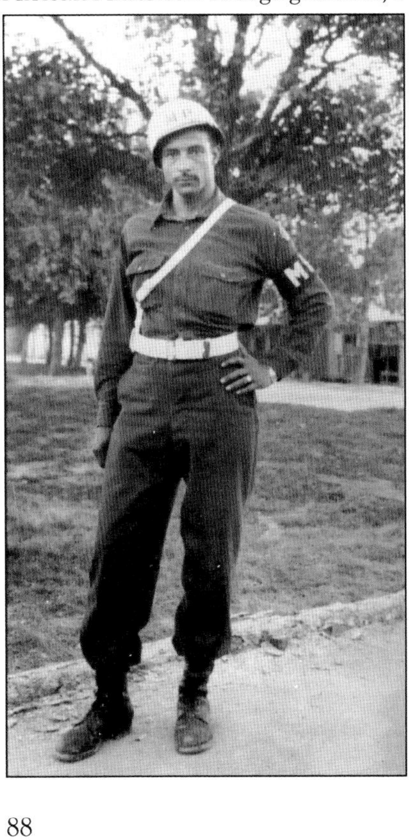

Little was known about the race riot in July 1943 at the Shenango Personnel Replacement Depot until present times. What is known is that African American soldiers were transported off base in leg irons and forced to eat outside at the nearby Blue Sky Inn in the early days. Richard McClain (1921–1987) appears in uniform around 1942.

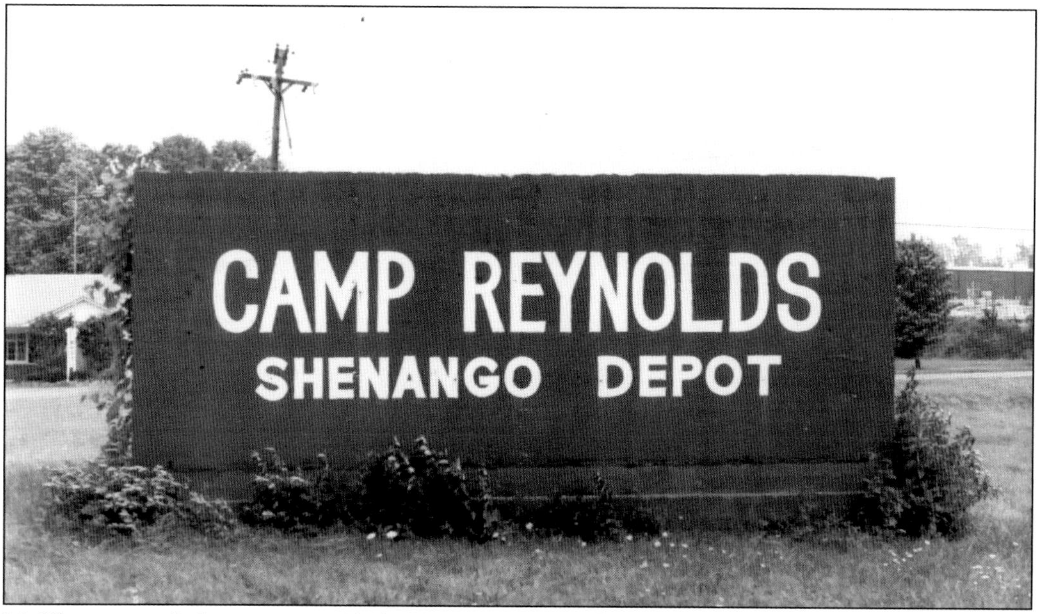

McClain joined the army in 1942. He was among the first soldiers stationed at the newly established Camp Reynolds in Mercer County, which was previously known as the Shenango Personnel Replacement Depot. McClain completed a 14-month tour of duty at Camp Reynolds, which closed at the end of World War II. The site became an area of massive suburban civilian development. The sign stands marking the military installation.

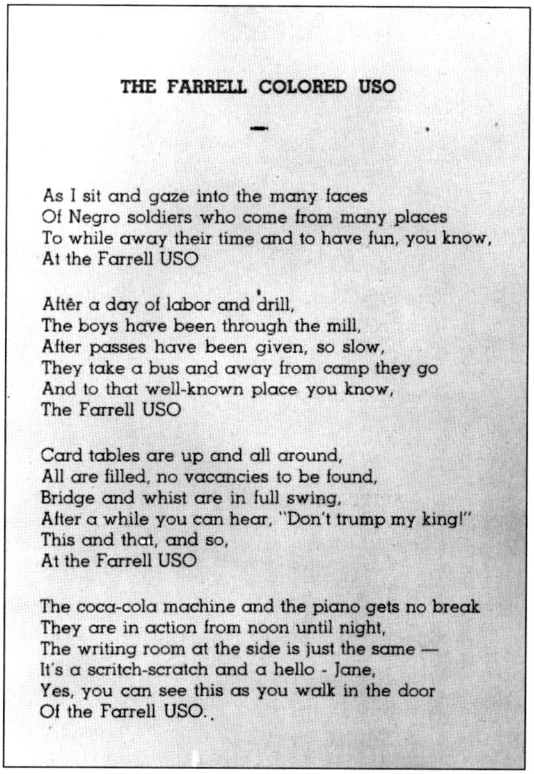

THE FARRELL COLORED USO

As I sit and gaze into the many faces
Of Negro soldiers who come from many places
To while away their time and to have fun, you know,
At the Farrell USO

Aftêr a day of labor and drill,
The boys have been through the mill,
After passes have been given, so slow,
They take a bus and away from camp they go
And to that well-known place you know,
The Farrell USO

Card tables are up and all around,
All are filled, no vacancies to be found,
Bridge and whist are in full swing,
After a while you can hear, "Don't trump my king!"
This and that, and so,
At the Farrell USO

The coca-cola machine and the piano gets no break
They are in action from noon until night,
The writing room at the side is just the same —
It's a scritch-scratch and a hello - Jane,
Yes, you can see this as you walk in the door
Of the Farrell USO.

On September 26, 1943, the Farrell Colored United Service Organizations (USO) Club was officially opened with appropriate ceremonies. The national USO spent approximately $6,000 in renovations and furnishings for this club. Two separate USO clubs existed for white servicemen in the vicinity—one in Greenville costing $86,000 and the other at the Buhl Club in Sharon. The poem appears in the Farrell USO souvenir book in 1945.

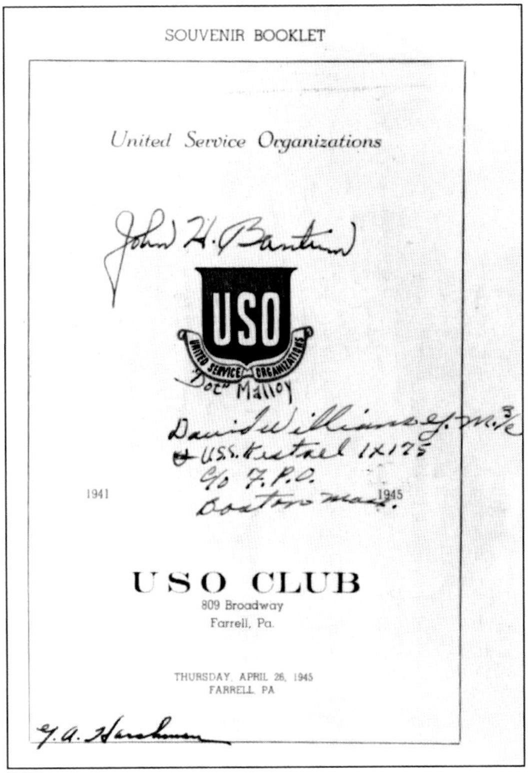

In 1943, the Farrell Colored USO was located in the F. H. Buhl Memorial Center, later known as the Carver Community Center. African American women from Farrell provided numerous volunteer hours. Hostess groups also were organized in New Castle and Youngstown, Ohio. The Farrell USO Club souvenir booklet belonged to Dorothy Steverson Malloy (1915–1996), who served as a junior hostess from September 1943 to the end of World War II.

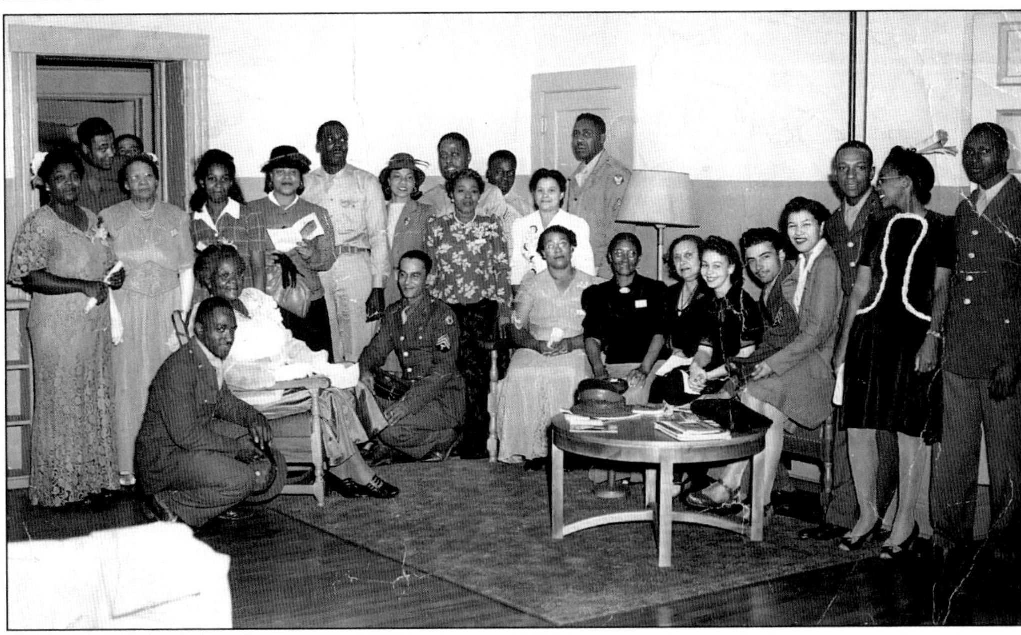

Servicemen often said that the Farrell Colored USO certainly was "a home away from home." They frequently commented that it was "most hospitable" and one of the nicest organizations they had seen since entering the service. The site was at 809 Broadway Avenue in Farrell. Richard McClain is pictured fifth from the right, and Silas Askerneese (1916–2000) is in front of the door at center. (Courtesy of the Farrell Colored USO.)

Lucille Satterwhite (1905–1972) was director of the junior and senior hostesses at the USO. The hostesses took turns in preparing and serving at the snack bar. The young women participated in dances at the camp each Friday night. Harvey Satterwhite, a prominent barber, and Lucille Satterwhite are pictured at home in Farrell. (Courtesy of Darlynna Thompson.)

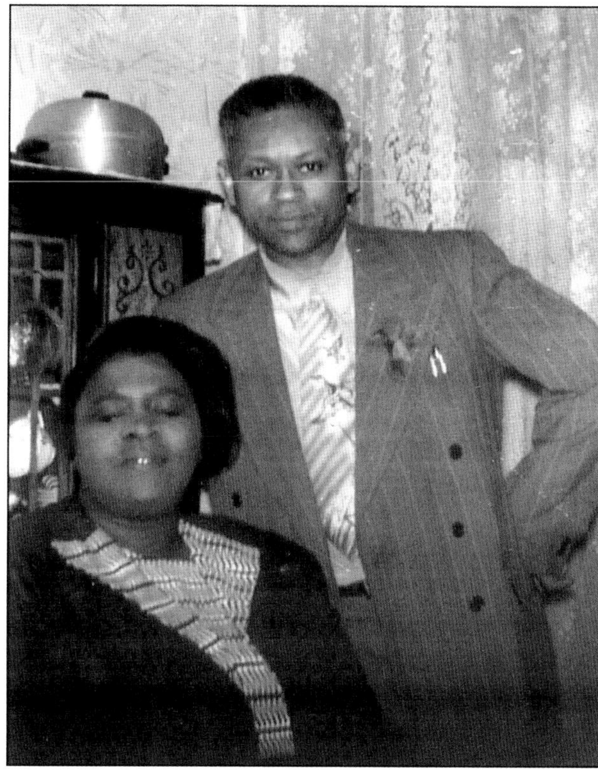

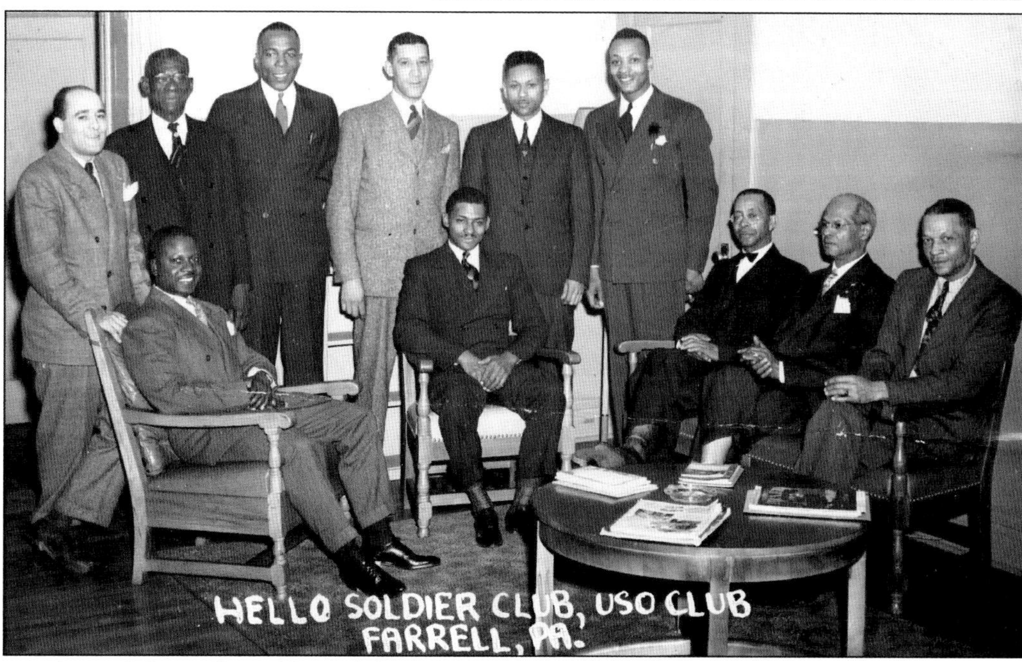

Members of the Hello Soldier Club of the Farrell Colored USO are pictured. From left to right are (first row) Henry McCall, two unidentified men, Thomas Dillard, and unidentified; (second row) George Mears, Herbert Paige, Raymond Johnson Sr. (1916–2000), Elmore Patterson, Harvey Satterwhite, and Lonnie Crawford. (Courtesy of Renea Ingram.)

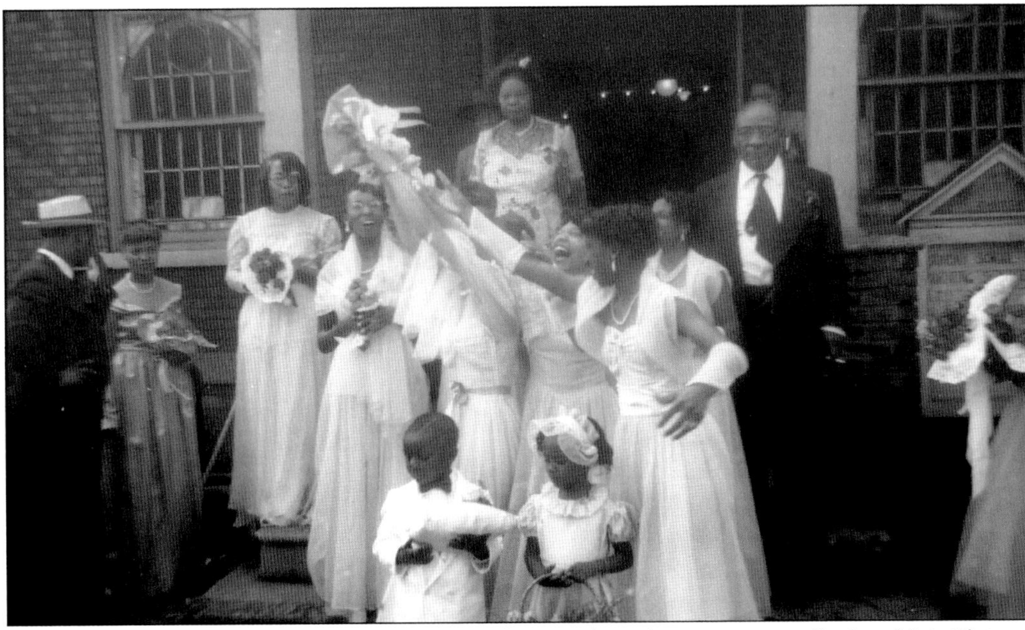

At the Farrell Colored USO, a few lucky girls met their future spouses. Richard McClain, a soldier, married Ethel Jackson of Wheatland on July 4, 1943. The wedding party of Henry K. Sanders and Martha Jane Wiley are in front of the Second Baptist Church at 1116 Market Avenue on June 31, 1951. The party includes father of the bride James Wiley (far right) and Alice Scott (top center). (Courtesy of Selma Sanders-West.)

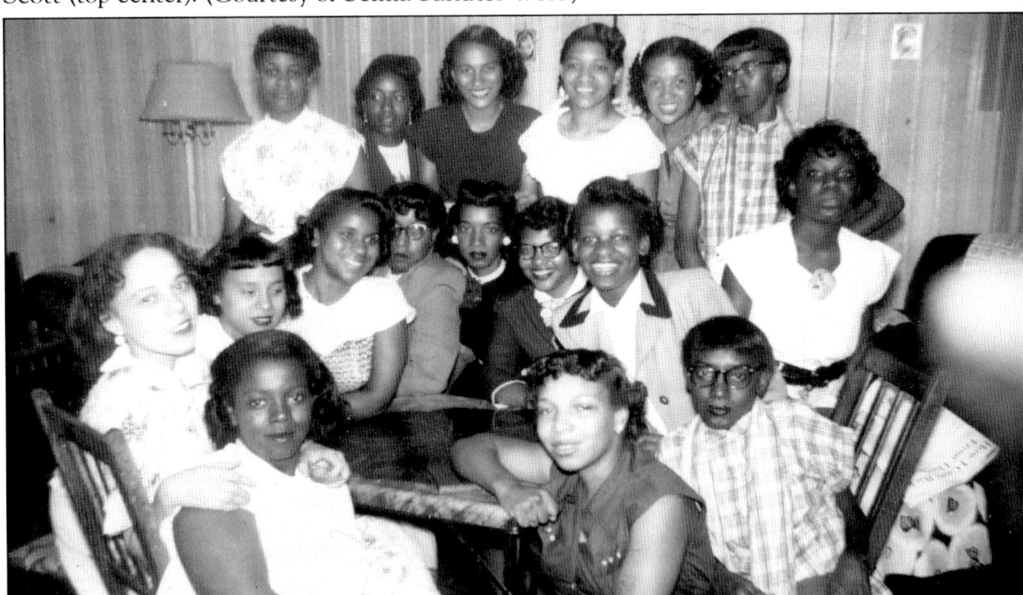

The USO offered to young women an opportunity to join an organization that had standards for acceptance. Regular dances were held in the club each Saturday night, movies were each Sunday, and finger painting, bingo, pokeno, an art colony, and special educational programs were presented at regular intervals. In this image from the Farrell USO souvenir book, Martha Jane Wiley and her girlfriends are at a bridal shower. (Courtesy of Selma Sanders-West.)

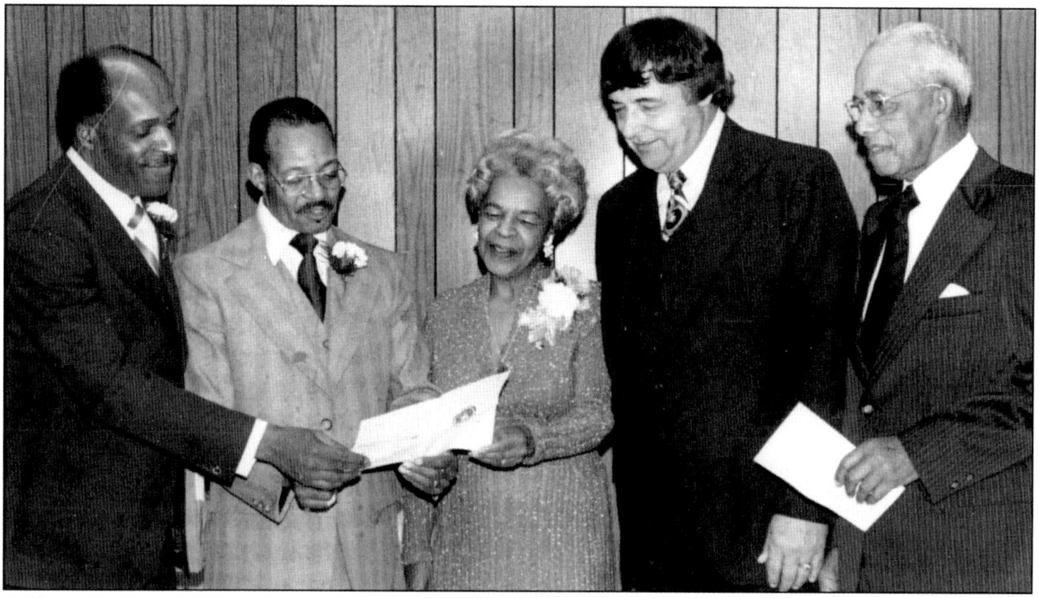

Although World War II signaled changed roles for minorities, some African Americans felt invisible during the war. At this time, Sara Dillard Austin and Helen Singletary moved from Farrell to Washington, D.C., where they worked in the federal government. Austin recalled the excitement of the times and expressed a tinge of anger over segregated theaters and restaurants in the nation's capital. Pictured are, from left to right, speaker Nathaniel Jones, Esq., Ras Tapari Hailstock, Sara Dillard Austin, Richard McClain, and Rev. Ira B. Lavigne.

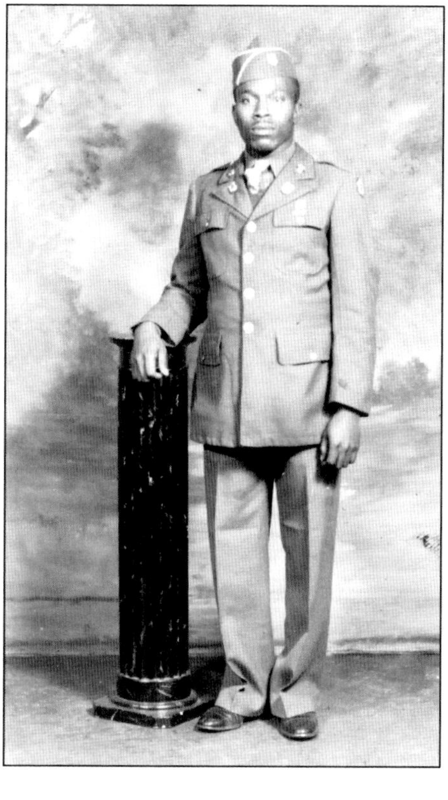

After World War II, Dillard Fielder (1915–1988) moved from Douglasville, Georgia, to Farrell for economic opportunity. Fielder served in a segregated unit where he survived sniper fire in the Philippines around 1943. At Sharon Steel, he suffered contusions and abrasions when a three-and-a-half-ton plate fell 50 feet down into the blast furnace where he worked. He witnessed Graham Matthews and Gardner Birch being killed. It was a sight Fielder never forgot.

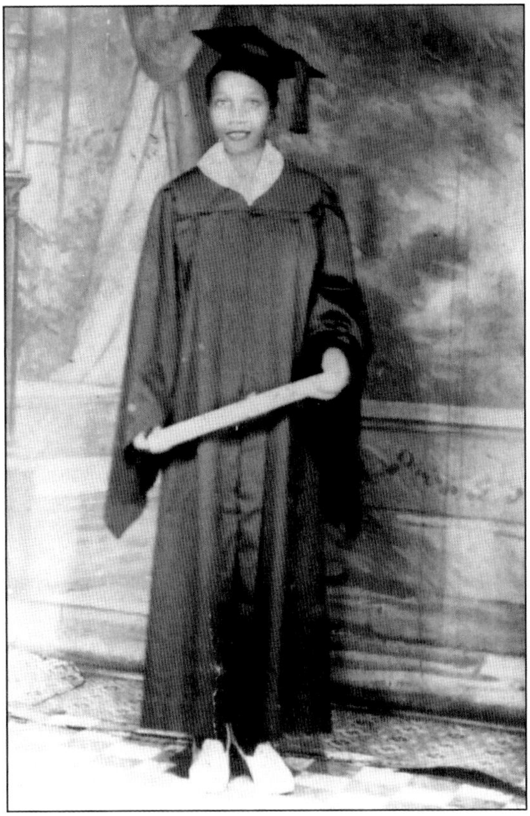

Women wore work uniforms and entered steel mills and factories. During World War II, Anna Steverson (1918–1982), a 1937 Farrell High School graduate, worked boring holes for armor at the Carnegie-Illinois Steel Corporation. As a result of correspondence with 58-year-old James Elmer Matthews, the secretary of the United Citizens Committee, Fair Employment Practice Commission (FEPC) examiner James Fleming visited the Farrell Works, which had been charged with discrimination against African American women, and resolved that the case reported "a correction of [the] original complaint." Steverson later worked at Ellwood Textiles where she sewed girdles. She married soldier Clarence Hall Sr. (1926–1979), and the couple raised a family in Sharon. Steverson is one of two African Americans in her elementary class in Farrell around 1924.

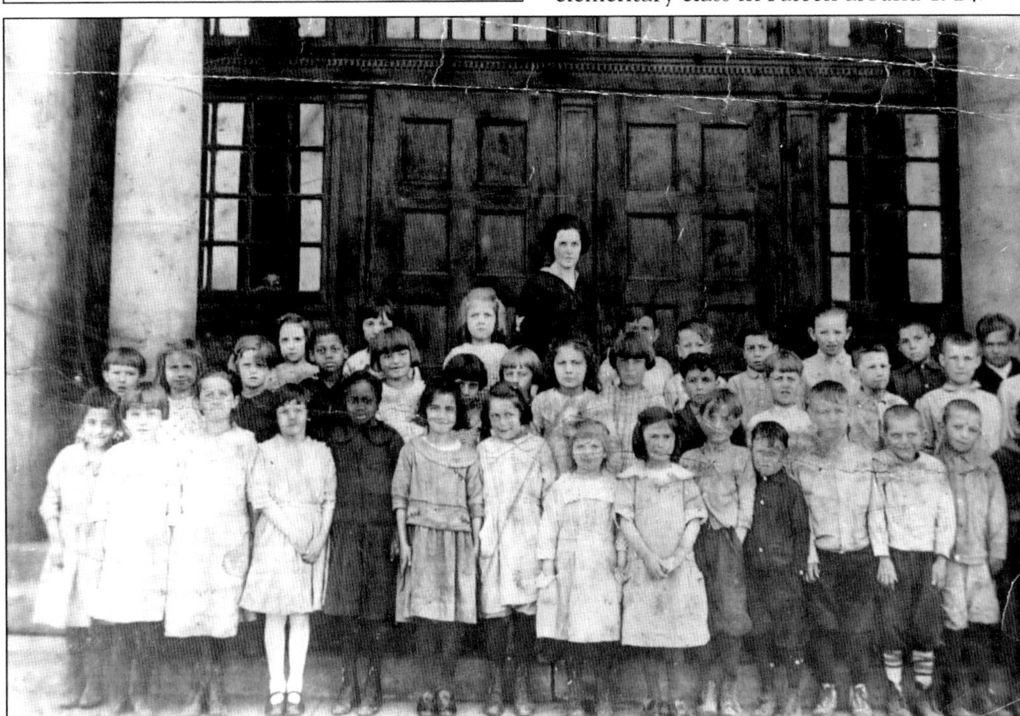

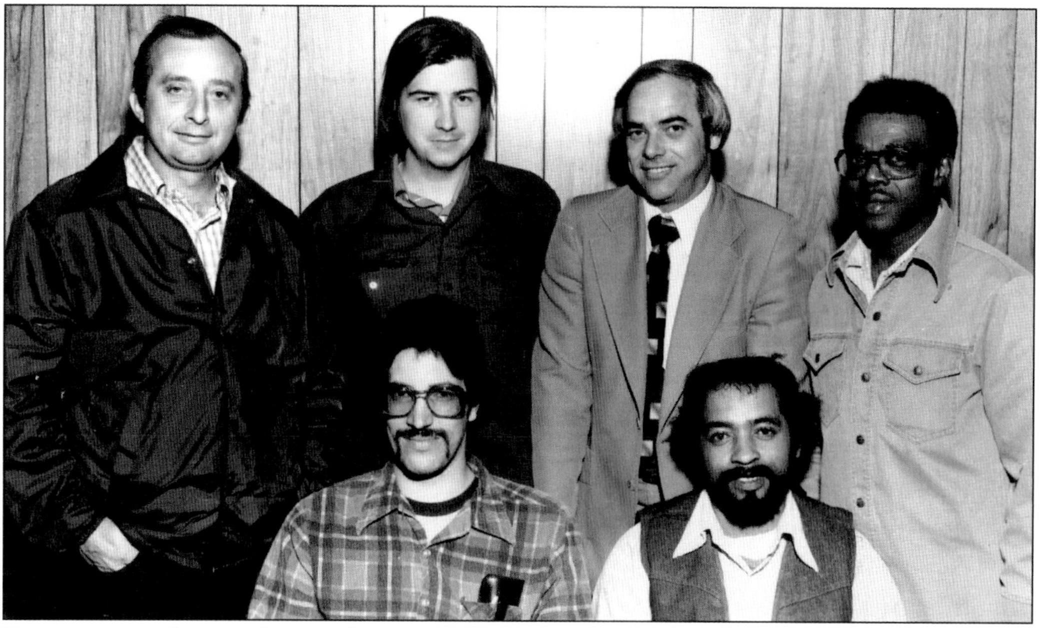

For protection from unfair employment practices and to make a better life for their families, African Americans joined labor unions. African Americans began to assume more responsible leadership positions in union locals during the 1960s. Larry Austin (first row, right) served as president of Union Local 1477 of the United Steelworkers of America, and Clarence Hall Sr. (second row, far right) was chairman of the Grievance Committeemen in the 1970s.

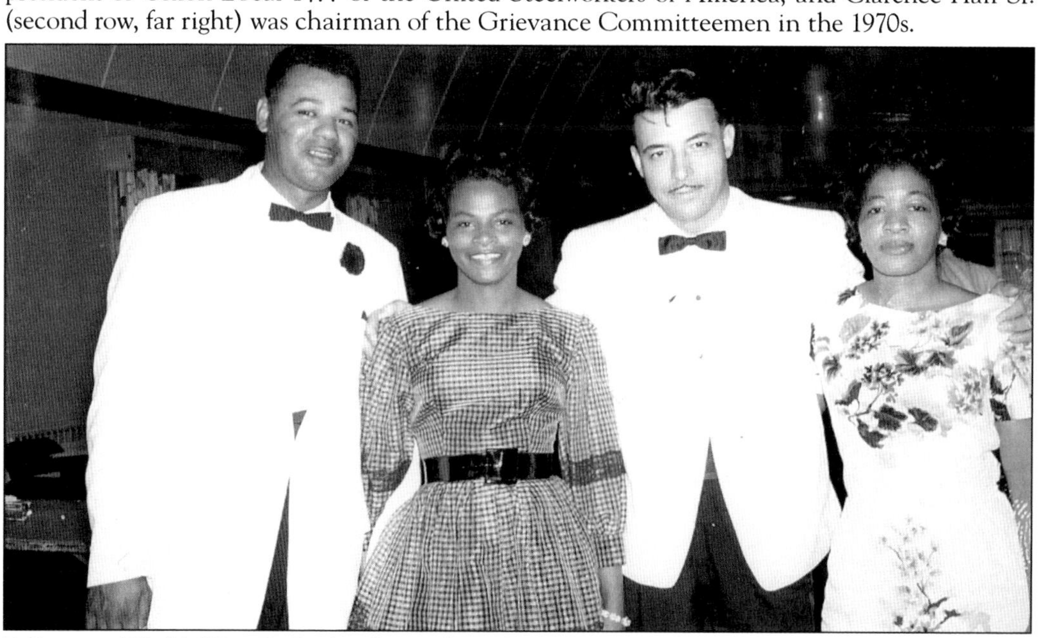

Following World War II, Richard McClain (1921–1987) found employment at Sharon Steel and served on the board of directors of the Mercer County branch of the NAACP. He was an elected constable in Farrell. Pictured from left to right are Ernie and Sallie Saunders and Richard and Ethel McClain at the Masonic ball in Sharon. Sallie Saunders was a long-serving registered nurse at Sharon General Hospital; Ernie Saunders was a Farrell policeman. (Courtesy of Ethel McClain.)

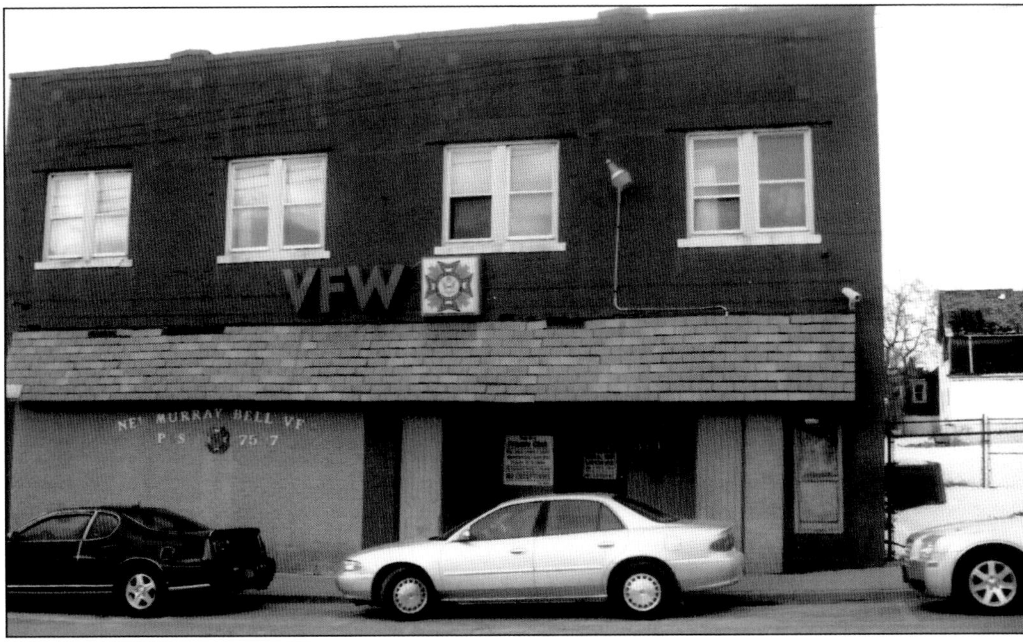

In 1913, William Hayes was appointed the first African American policeman in Farrell. Hayes made several significant arrests and purchased substantial residential property in Farrell. James Gillespie Jr. was the first African American chief of police in Farrell. In Wheatland, William Hosey, Willie T. James, and Fred Jarrett were policemen. Pictured is the New Murray Bell Post No. 7597, VFW.

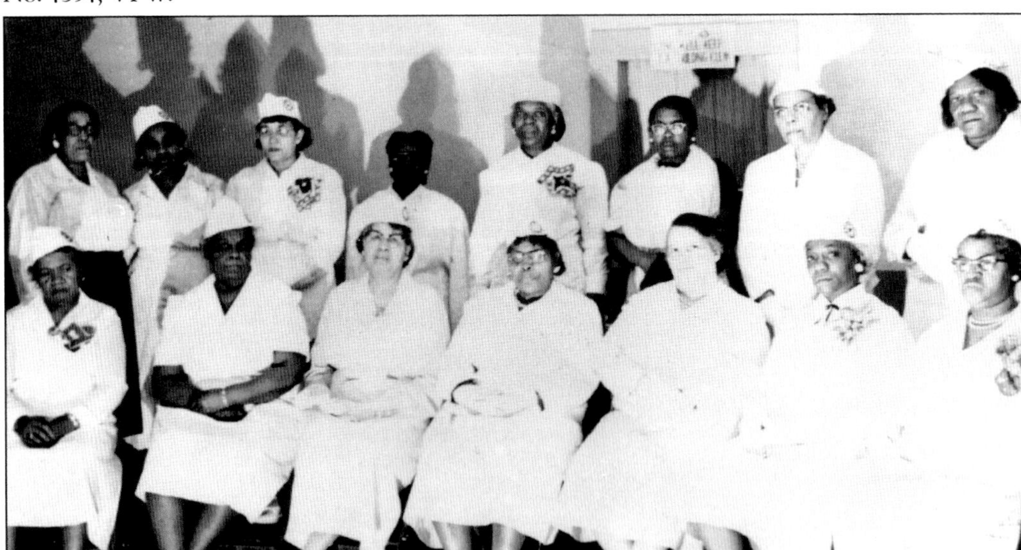

During the 1940s, the Carver Community Center was a hub of cultural life. Membership peaked at 1,000 in 1950. Pictured in 1946, charter members of Crowder-Stewart No. 63 Blue Star Mothers are, from left to right, (first row) Francis Hamm, Florence Stitt, Ruth Crowder, Della Farrow Stewart (1898–1990), Maude Hobbs, Onnie Alston, and Ocy Adkins Daniels (1888–1973); (second row) Henrietta Bowman (1904–1970), Lucretia Norman, Lorena Canty Hill (1897–1979), Myrtle Preston, Dora Pegues, Mary Lee Edwards (born in 1902), Willie Hatwood, and Genetta Keys.

In the 1940s, Edward A. Johnson (1915–2002) coached the Carver Community Center basketball team. Edward A. Johnson, the first African American Buhl Day honoree in 1984, served as executive secretary of the F. H. Buhl Memorial Center, later known as the Carver Community Center. He was the first African American school board director in Sharon. Martha Martin was the Pennsylvania department president of the Blue Star Mothers in the 1980s. (Courtesy of Martha Martin.)

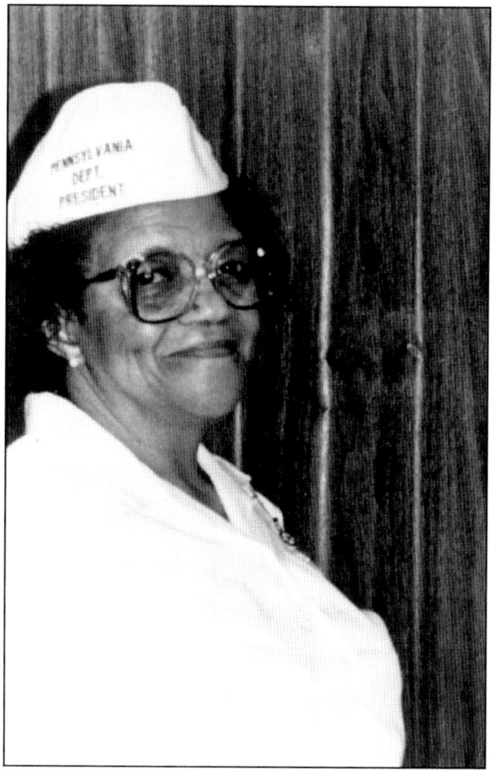

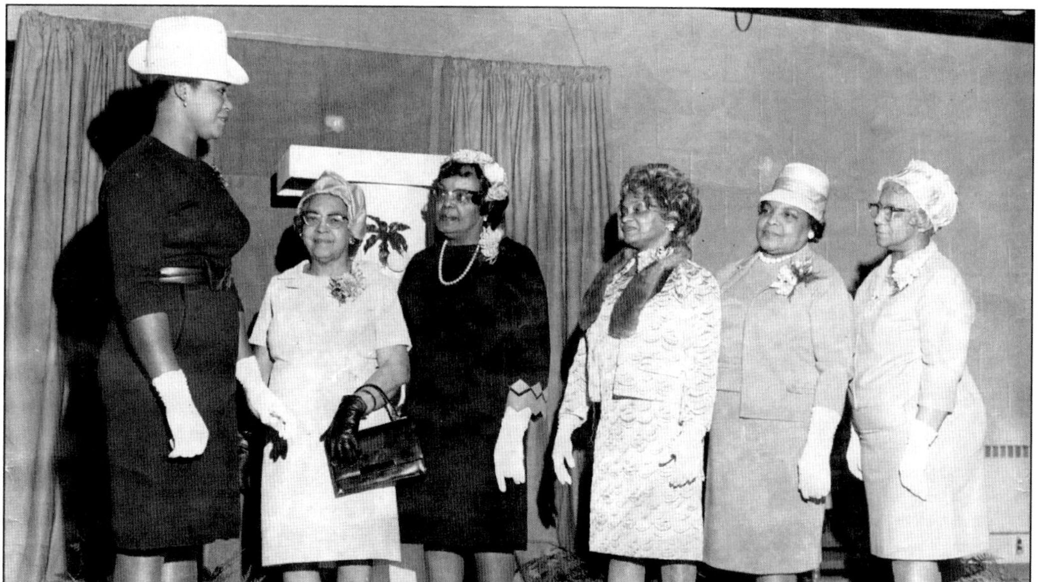

On April 8, 1964, Wilma Mitchell founded the Altruist Club, which provided scholarships for African American students. African American women recognized that education was the key to the future success of their children. The Willing Worker's Style and Hat Show was held at the Carver Community Center in Farrell in 1962. From left to right are unidentified, Grace Brown James (1897–1971), Catherine Matthews, Mary Johnson, Wilma Mitchell, and Freda Palm. (Courtesy of Ulysses and Frances Flemon Ward.)

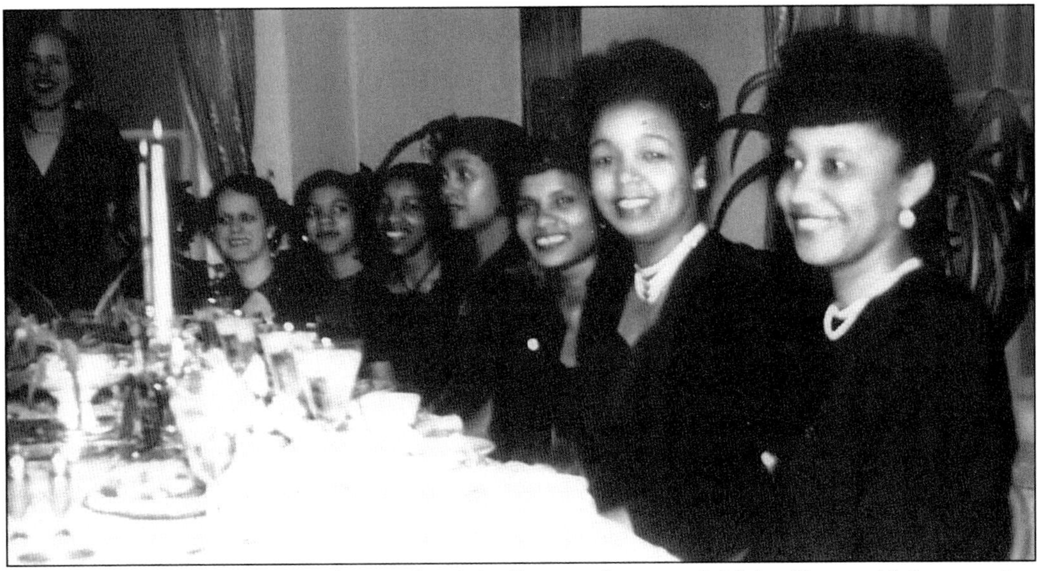

Pictured in September 1955, the Epsilon Mu Omega chapter of Alpha Kappa Alpha sorority, chartered in Youngstown, Ohio, on May 21, 1949, promotes education and service. The chapter has a life membership in the Mercer County branch of the NAACP. Charter founders include Gertrude Guilford, Arcelean Hampton, Winifred Johnson, Ethel Love, Etherine Paige, Carolyn Patton, Lucile Ruff, Lillian Jackson, Evelyn Staton, and Mary E. Lovett Belton. (Courtesy of Theresa L. Yarboro.)

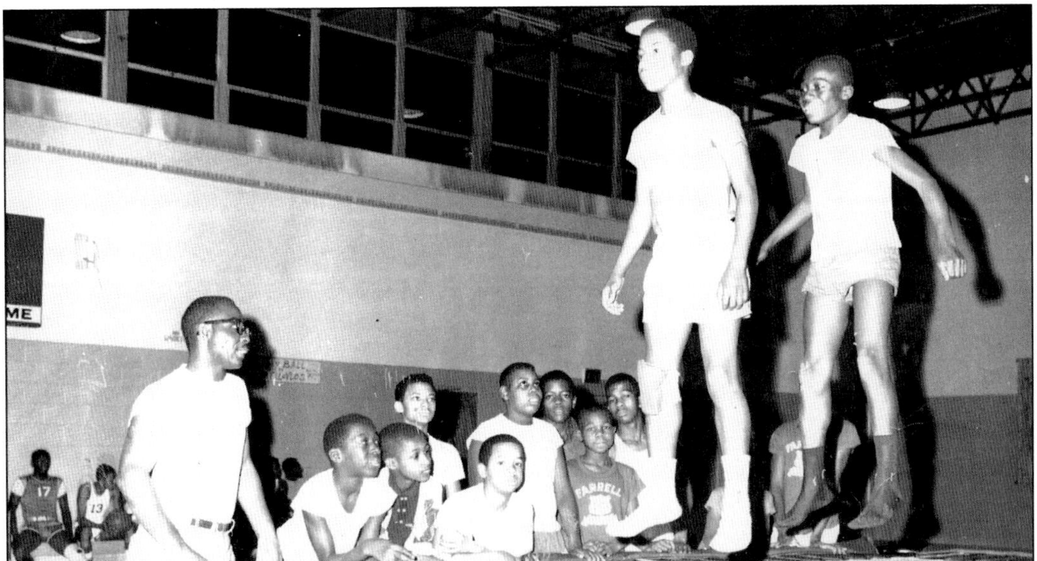

Ulysses Ward, the 1994 Buhl Day honoree, served in the first service outfit and was awarded a presidential citation during World War II. He earned four battle stars along with a Good Conduct Medal. In civilian life, he was a youth advocate and sports booster. As a physical education director, he gives supervision to Robert Smith and Michael Smith on a trampoline at the F. H. Buhl Memorial Center around 1980. On May 21, 2005, Ward Field, a baseball park in Brookfield, Ohio, was named in honor of Ulysses Ward for a "lifetime commitment to serving his community and for his involvement in youth baseball." (Courtesy of Ulysses Ward.)

In 1954, Russell C. Phillips became the first African American teacher hired in Mercer County when he began teaching physical education. He became the first African American head track coach, high school principal, and school administrator in the Farrell Area School District. In the 1940s, the Carver Community Center basketball team, coached by Edward Johnson, includes, from left to right, Levon McKay, Maurice Phillips, Walter Lee Wright, Russell C. Phillips, William Satterwhite, and Robert Peyton.

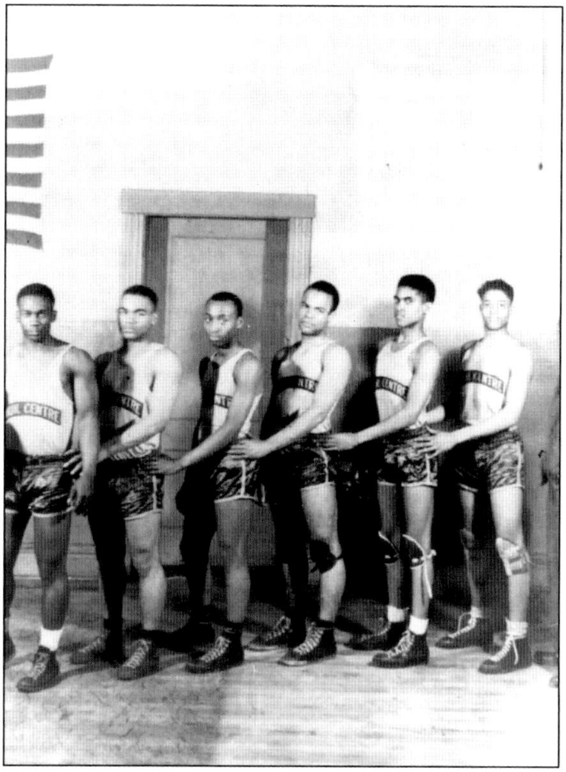

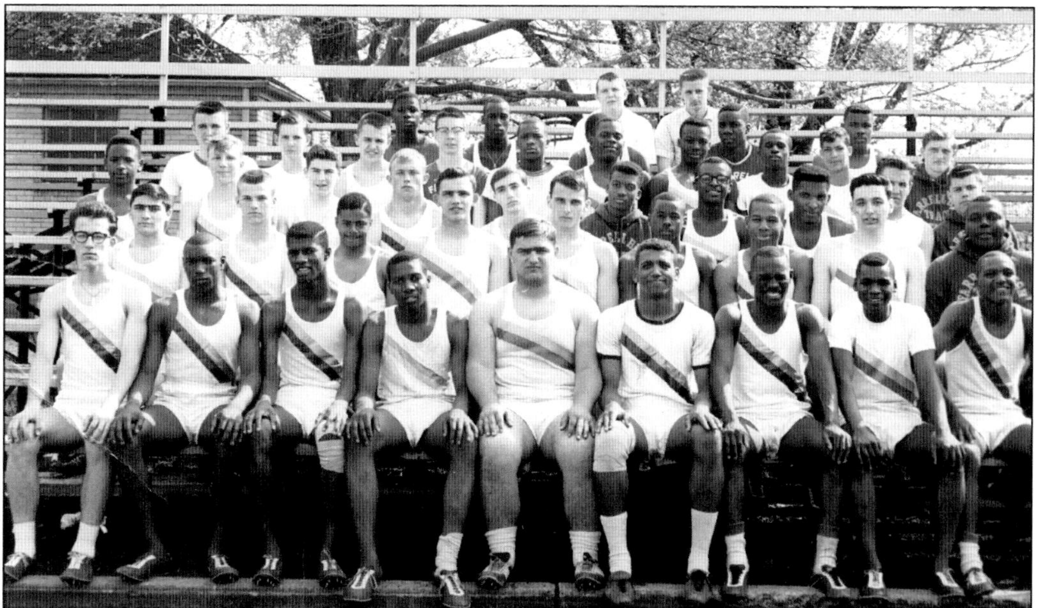

African American educators and health care providers played a significant role. In 1964, Phillips had an outstanding track team at Farrell High School. In 1996, the first recipient of the Russell C. Phillips Educational Award established by the Tri-County Affiliate of the Pennsylvania Conference on Black Basic Education (COBBE) was Constance J. Langley, who was the second African American hired by the Farrell Area School District.

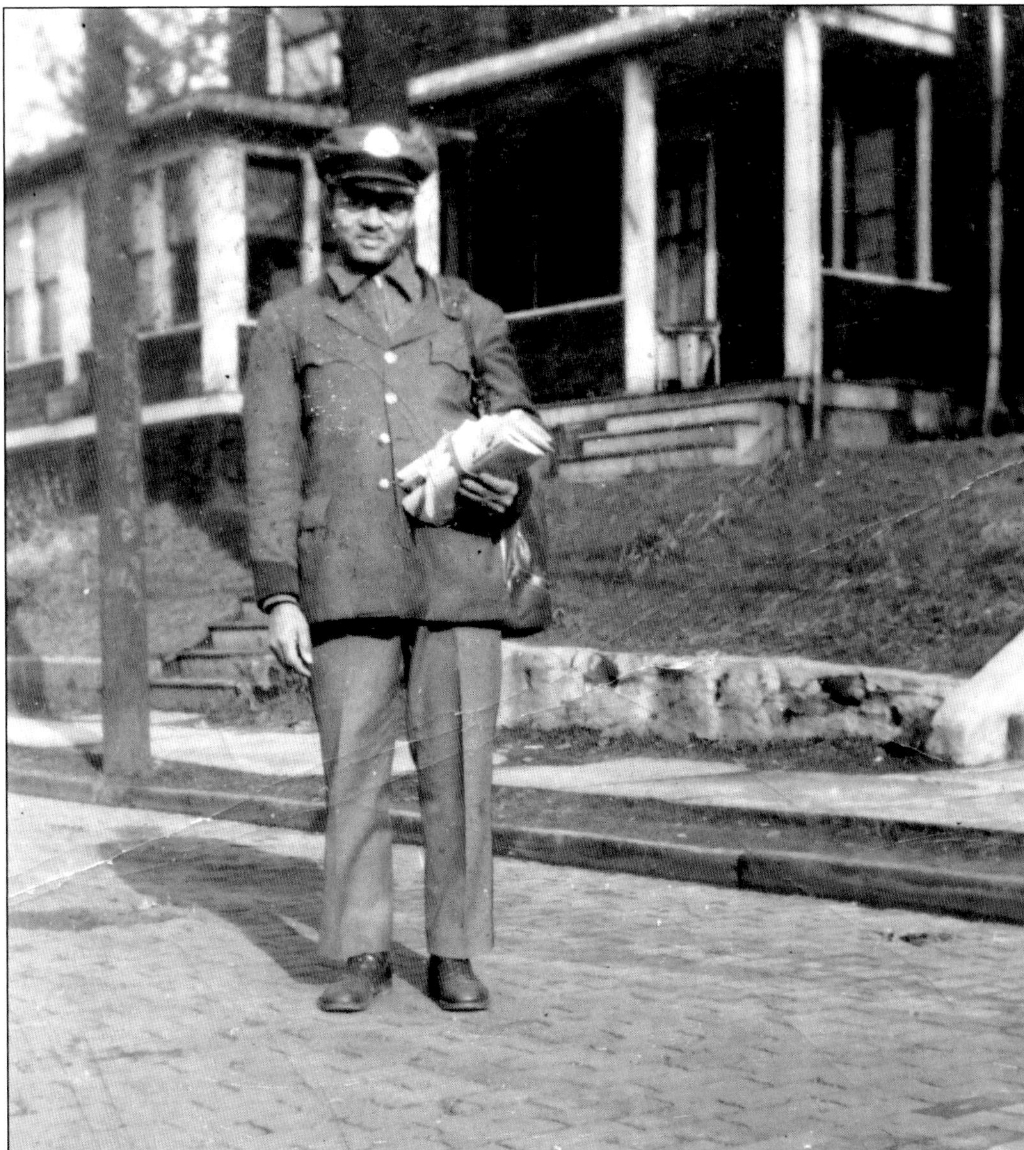

Dr. Maceo Patterson and wife Mildred Patterson served on the Farrell Colored USO Council. In the 1970s, the Mercer County Housing Authority named a public housing site on the corner of Wallis Avenue and French Street, Farrell, in honor of Dr. Maceo Patterson. In 1911, Dr. William Morgan Writt (born in 1888) graduated the first African Americans from the University of Pittsburgh's School of Medicine. In 1915, he moved to Farrell and was elected president of the Farrell Board of Health and police surgeon. In 1918, Writt was instrumental in organizing the Mercer County branch of the NAACP. His sister Sara B. Writt Dunston was the membership chair for the Pittsburgh branch of the NAACP. Prior to 1919, the association's executive secretary John R. Shillady commended the Mercer County branch of the NAACP for its firm stand against racial prejudice. The FEPC was given the authority to investigate defense-related employers when Pres. Franklin D. Roosevelt issued Executive Order 9346, which opened doors to local defense industries. James Mendez Matthews, a postal carrier and past president of the Mercer County branch of the NAACP, delivers mail in Farrell.

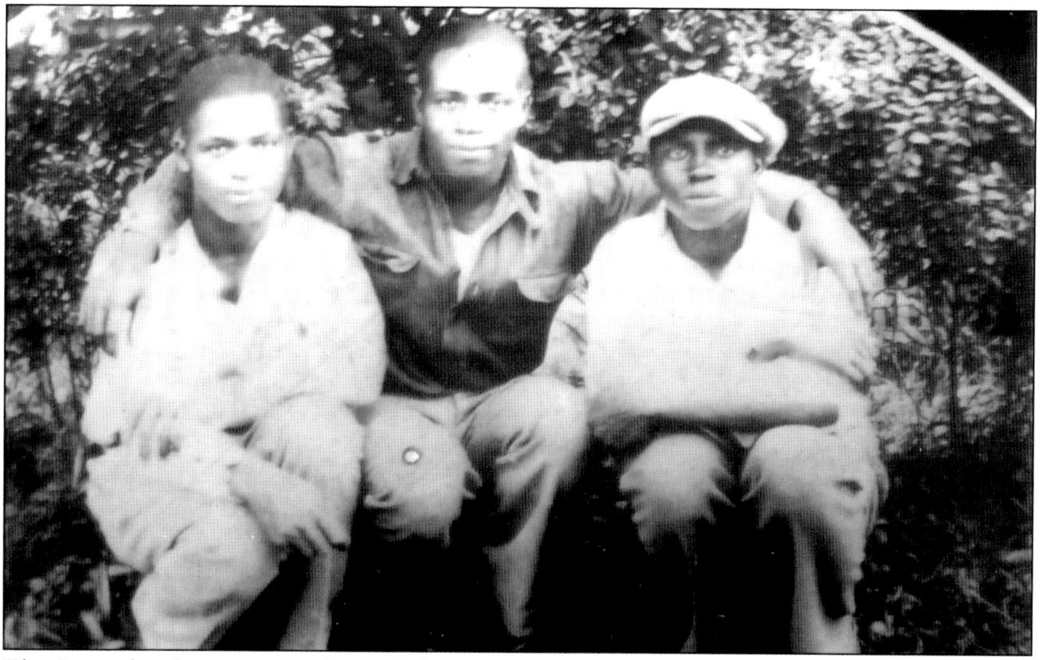

The James brothers are members of the enterprising Adair-James-Jarrett family. David James (1906–1967) owned and operated the David James Hotel for 20 years in Farrell. Pictured from left to right are John James, William James, and David James in the 1930s. (Courtesy of Donna Marie Lee.)

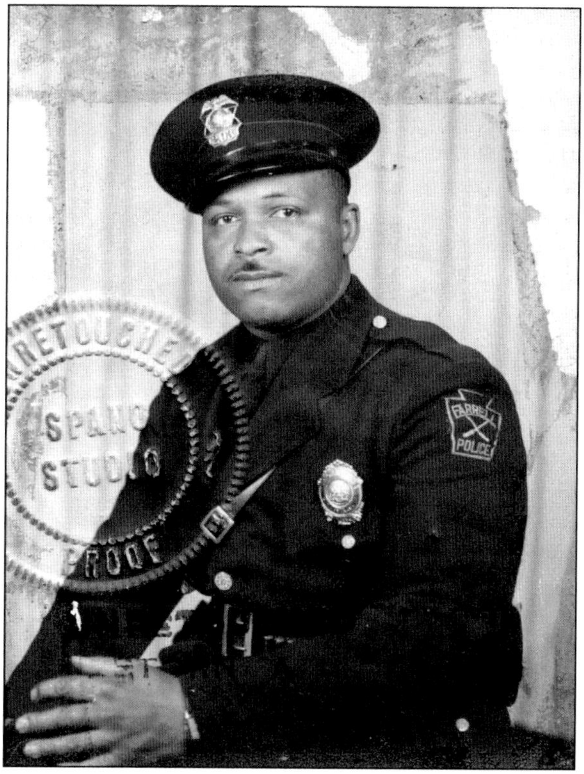

Pictured is Capt. John James (1910–1982), who joined the Farrell police in 1942. He provided distinguished service for 32 years. In 1981, he was honored with a proclamation by the Joseph Volansky Memorial Lodge No. 34, Fraternal Order of Police, at Farrell's homecoming day. Other Farrell policemen included George Pulliam, Edward Smith, Ernie Saunders, Sam Lampkins, and Chief Riley Smoot. (Photograph by Spano Studio, courtesy of Donna Marie Lee.)

Congratulations from

PORTER'S BARBER SHOP

Looking for A Good Hair Cut?

See . . . BEN PORTER

266 Vine Avenue Sharon, Pa.

Congratulations from

ATWATER'S SCHOOL OF BEAUTY CULTURE

Our Rates are Reasonable

Our Motto: "HELP THE PUBLIC"

Phone 21574

168 Vine Avenue Sharon, Pa.

During World War II, Sarah Atwater, principal and dean of Atwater's School of Beauty Culture, identified a critical "need of a future for the women of the Shenango Valley." In spite of financial challenges, she established a cosmetology school and improved the status of African American women. The first three years her school ran at a loss of more than $3,000. Yet she persisted to operate the school and had more than 300 graduates. The first teacher was Celia Frances Williams of Canton, Ohio. Well into the 20th century, those in the field of cosmetology continued to be civic leaders. Advertisements for Porter's Barber Shop, owned and operated by Ben Porter, and Atwater's School of Beauty Culture appear in the 1953 First Baptist Church mortgage burning booklet.

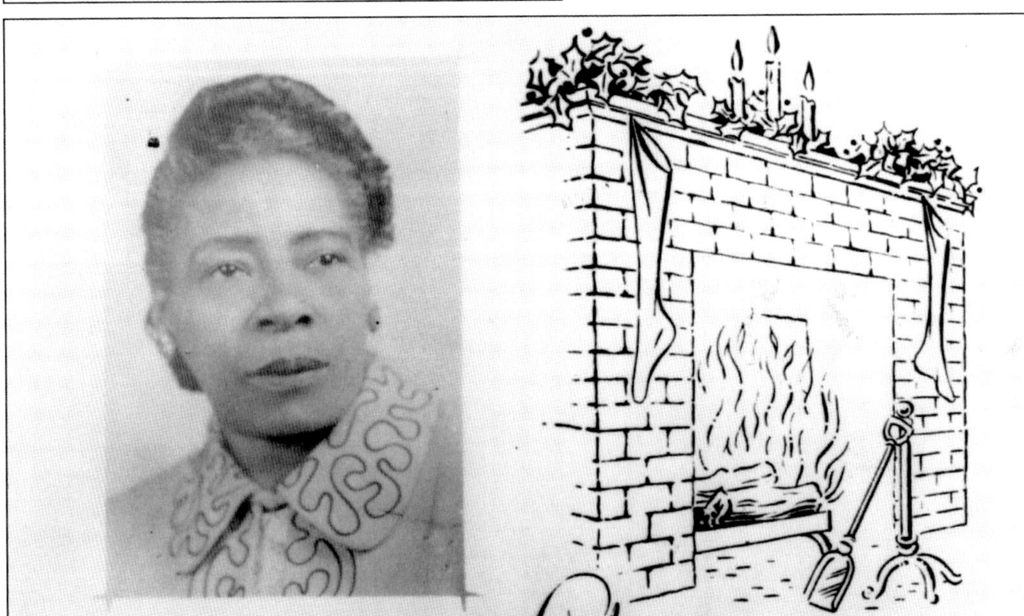

Self-employment placed Sara Atwater (1894–1967) among the ranks of the elite during a time when employment for African American women was limited to domestic work. She established Atwater's School of Beauty Culture at 178 and 180 Vine Avenue in Sharon on September 10, 1945. She operated the beauty school at her home for about 26 years. Atwater's School of Beauty Culture graduates include Gladys Cannon, Martha Richards, and Lila Savage.

Seven

WEST MIDDLESEX
ZION'S HILL BUILDING

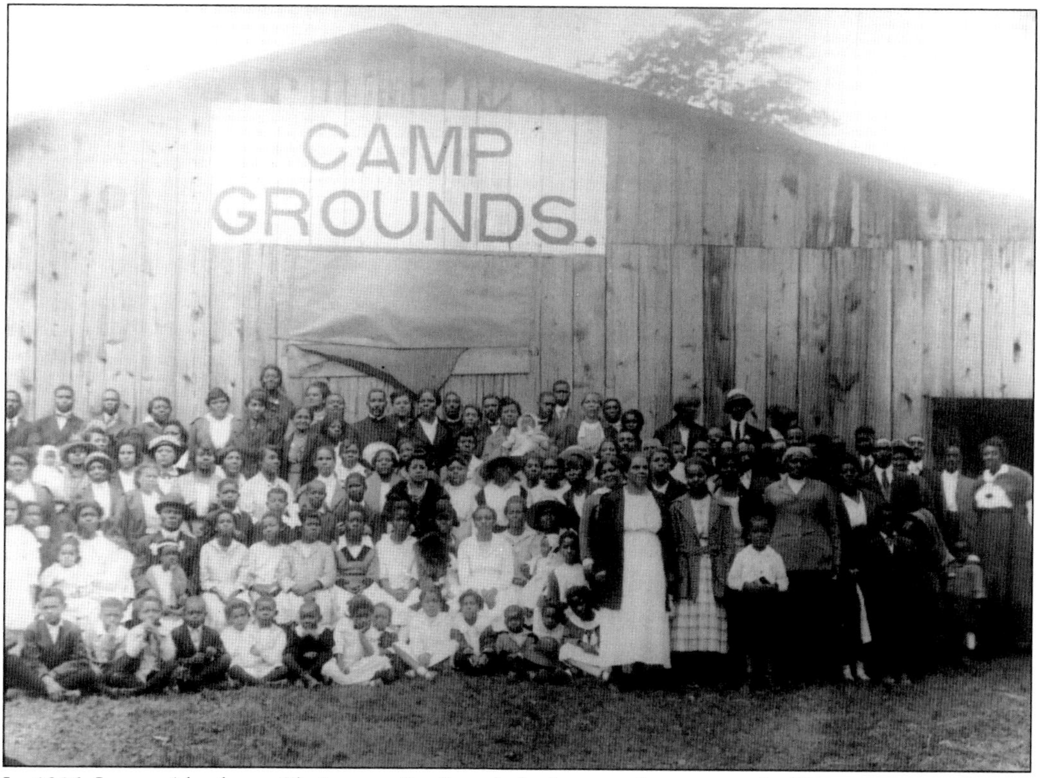

In 1916, James Abraham Christman Sr. founded what was known as the Western Pennsylvania and Eastern Ohio Camp Ground Association in West Middlesex. The camp meeting provided southern migrants an opportunity to maintain a rural tradition. (Courtesy of the National Association of the Church of God.)

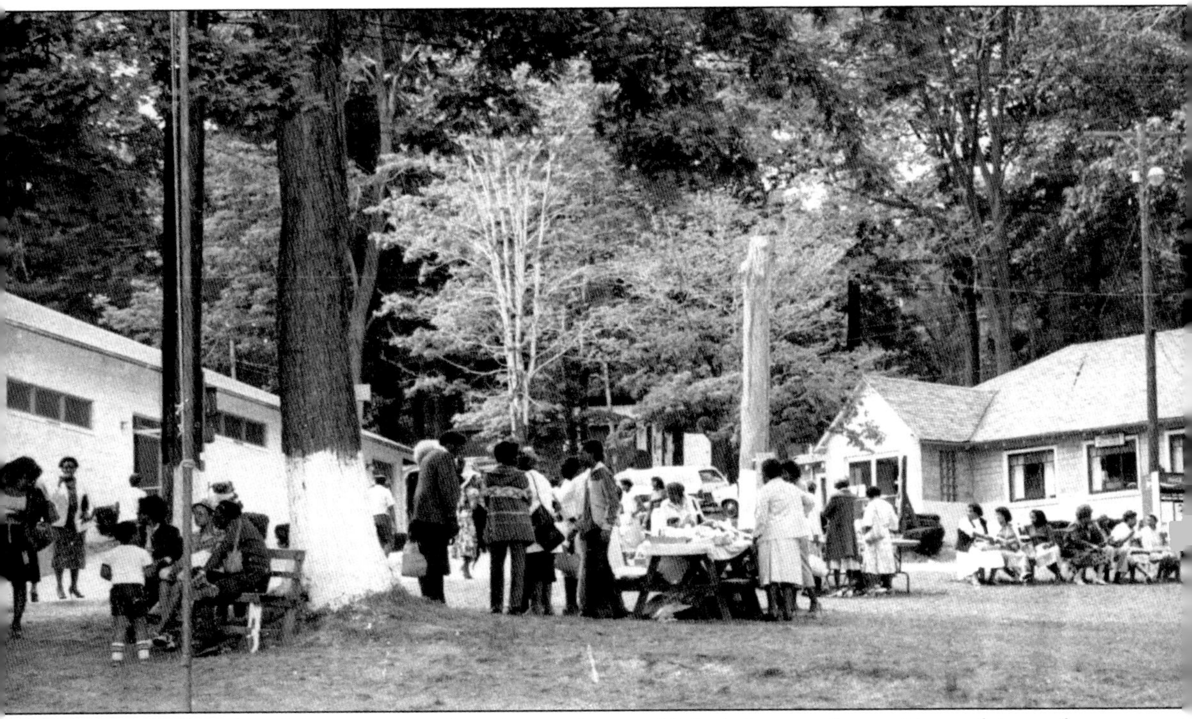

Campground builders mortgaged and sometimes sold their homes. James Crosswhite, a former campground manager, recalled, "Sharon, Pennsylvania, produced the Christmans, Phillips, Mitchells, McClendons, Redferns, Smoots, Moores, Waynes and many others who played a great part in its development and maintenance with very little compensation, if any." Records at the Mercer County Courthouse, filed on May 10, 1917, show Littleton P. White, H. Russell Wayne,

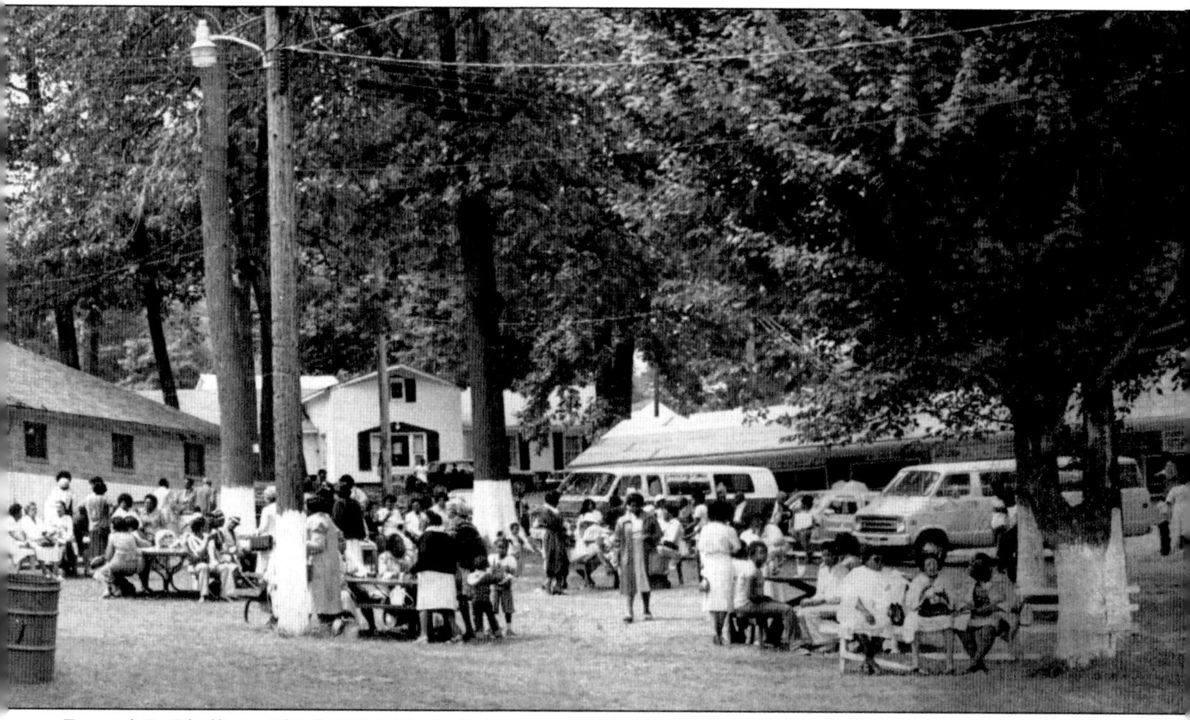

Daniel S. Phillips, Elijah W. Wimbish, Raymond H. Pryor, Roy E. Roddy, and James Abraham Christman Sr. as campground trustees who entered into an agreement to purchase the Leslie farm in West Middlesex for $5,500. The Cedar Avenue Church of God had its origins in the Christian witness of the "brothers and sisters of love." (Courtesy of Shirley Matthews Williams.)

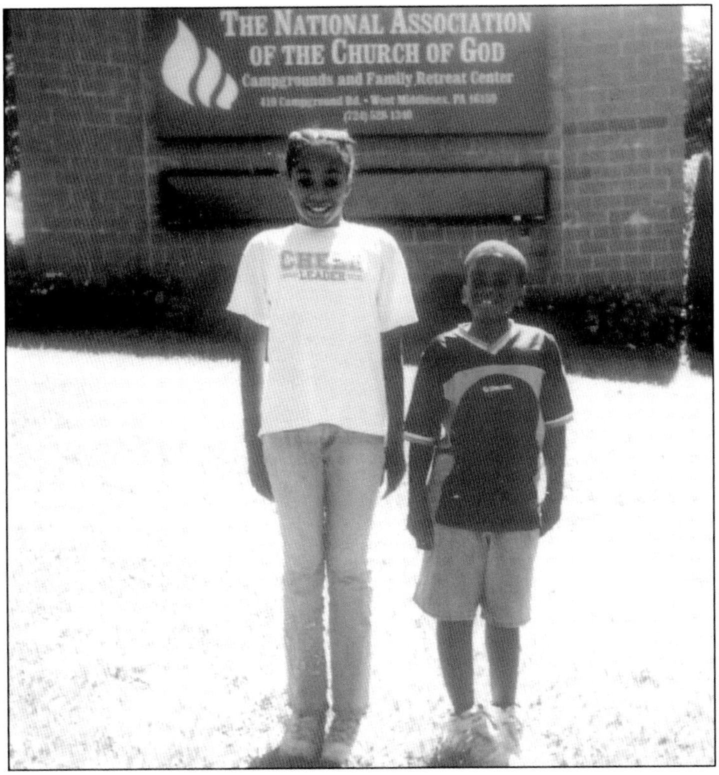

In 1919, Daniel S. Phillips and H. Russell Wayne and his brother Charles Wayne worked their way up to the position of roller in the American Sheet and Tin Plate Company mill. The three shifts at the mill were supervised by African American rollers to avoid any disruption. Shown is the sign at the National Association of the Church of God Campgrounds and Family Retreat Center, 410 Campground Road, West Middlesex, in 2006.

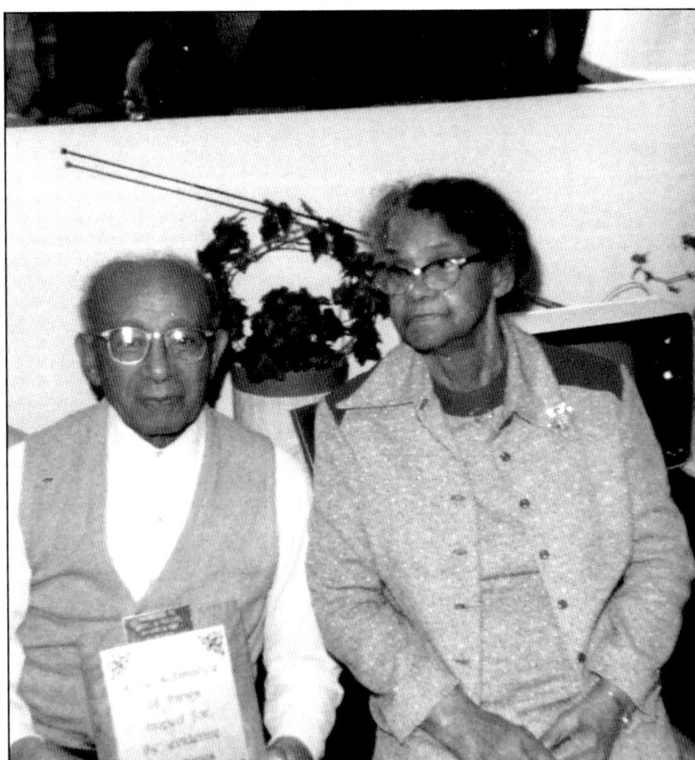

Shared work and responsibility fostered camaraderie. Phillips named one of his sons Russell in honor of H. Russell Wayne. Close bonds between Daniel S. Phillips and H. Russell Wayne, both men campground trustees, existed. At the campground, the men worked together on building projects after work and on weekends. Shown are Daniel S. Phillips and wife Roxie at home in Shenango Township outside West Middlesex. (Courtesy of Russell C. Phillips.)

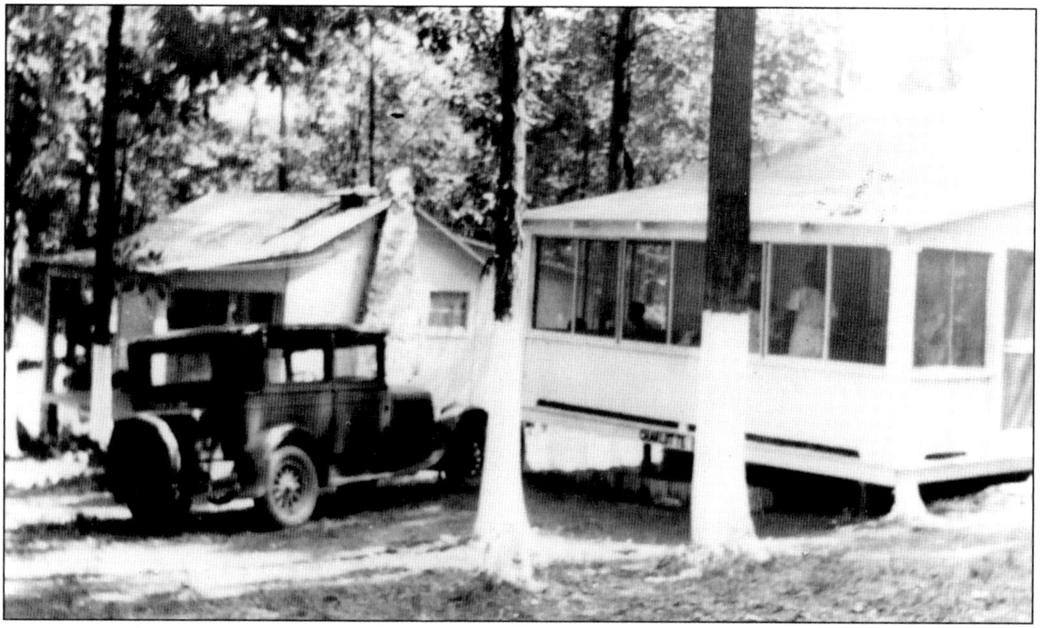

In 1940, Esther B. Culp (1899–1970) of Sharon was the first president of the National Ushers Fellowship, upon recommendation of Phillips and Rev. L. M. Turner. She served over 25 years. A leadership award was named in her honor. Her funeral was held at the National Campground tabernacle in 1970. Shown is the Phillips Cottage on the campground in West Middlesex in the 1940s. (Courtesy of Russell C. Phillips.)

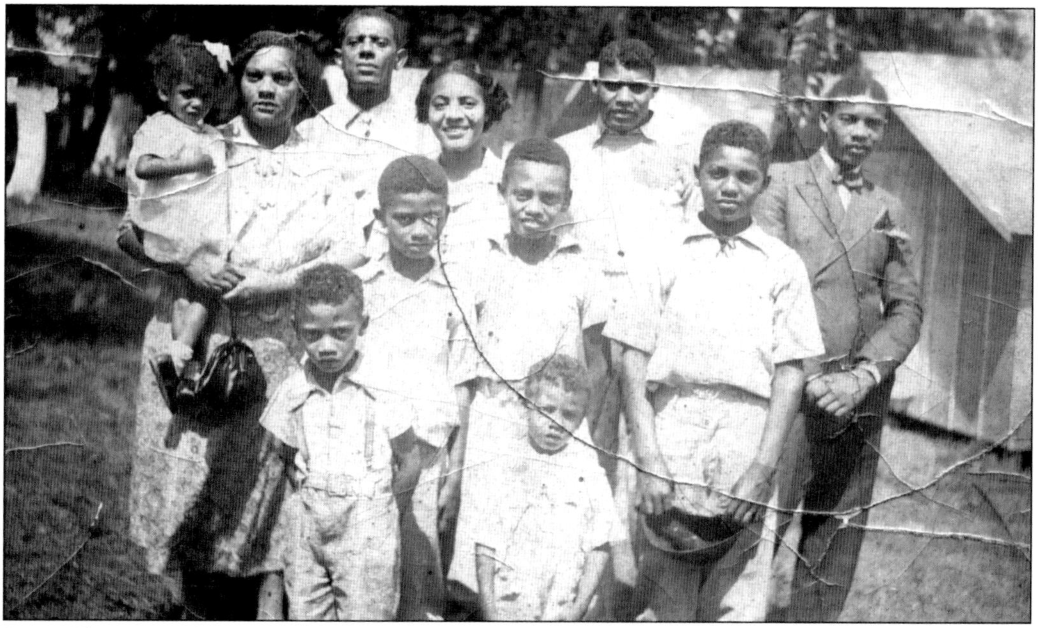

James Elmer Matthews and his family visit the campgrounds around 1936. Family members are, from left to right, (first row) Roy and Carl; (second row) Kenneth, Elmer, and William Frank; (third row) Shirley (being held by her mother), Sadie, James Elmer, Gertrude, Harold, and Shelton. The tin roof cabins, which became quite warm in the summer, were situated along what was known as Tin Row and are visible in the background. (Courtesy of Shirley Matthews Williams.)

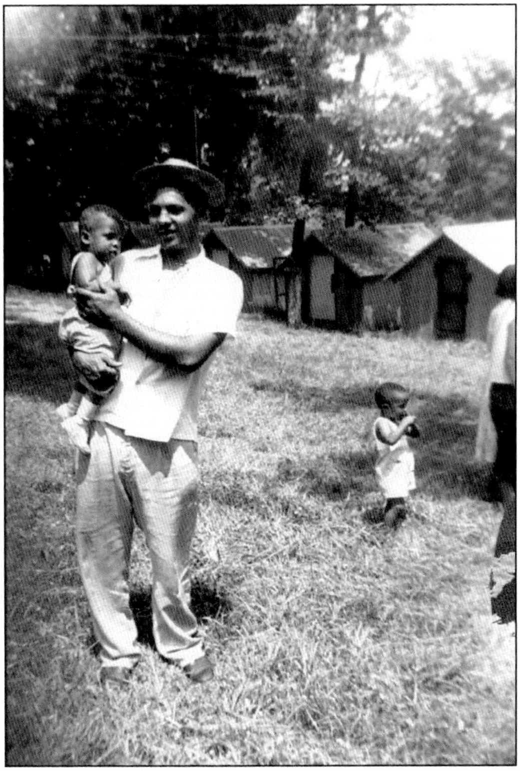

Cedar Avenue Church of God served in numerous leadership roles throughout the development of the campground. In 1917, D. C. Copeland, Norton Minor, and Elisha Wimbish served on the first trustee board. Charlotte Copeland was secretary for the trustee board. George S. Barbour, Fred Jaggers, R. M. Pryor, A. Moorehead, and L. B. White were on the first grounds committee. James Abraham Christman Jr., inventor, installed a generator to provide lights for evening services and set up steam tables to heat food in the cafeteria. During the 1920s, Joseph S. McClendon and his wife, Mary Steverson McClendon, and Wilson Steverson were caretakers there. Rev. William Frank Matthews holds son Shelton Emery at the campground around 1953. In the background are the cabins pilgrims occupied during their 10-day stay. (Courtesy of Shirley Matthews Williams.)

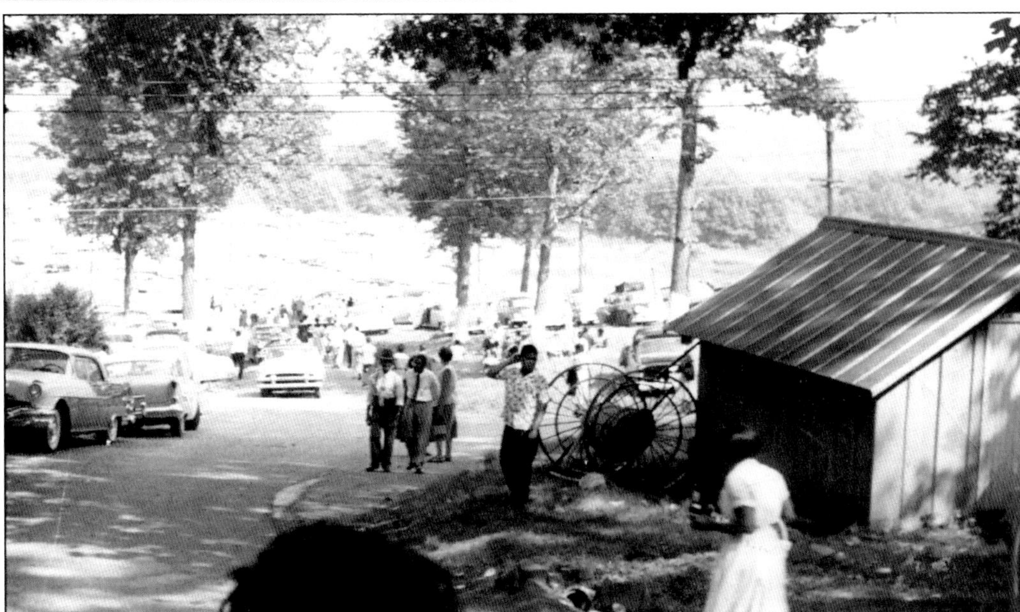

The expansive facility has undergone numerous building stages. According to the January 25, 1964, *Sharon Herald*, for 40 years, campground manager Joseph Crosswhite designed "seven large buildings, three reservoirs that supply . . . running water, the sewage system . . . and fifty out of the one hundred and seventy five cabins." Shown is a view from the top of the hill looking down on the parking lot in the 1950s. (Courtesy of Josephine Gibbs.)

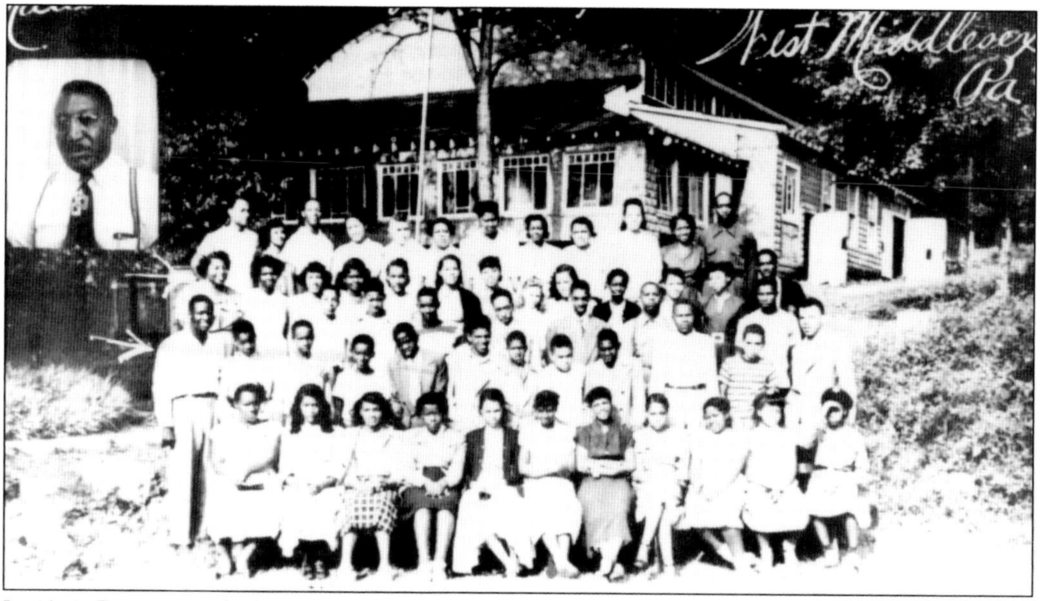

In 1949, Emery Wimbish (upper right), the first youth camp director, holds the first youth camp. The old tabernacle is seen in the background. In 1959, Russell C. Phillips, director of Youth Camp Middlesex, drafted plans for a youth campsite away from the main campgrounds with an all-purpose building, six cabins, and a bathhouse. During the 1970s, completion of the all-purpose Wimbish-Phillips Building, named in honor of the first two youth directors, occurred. (Courtesy of Russell C. Phillips.)

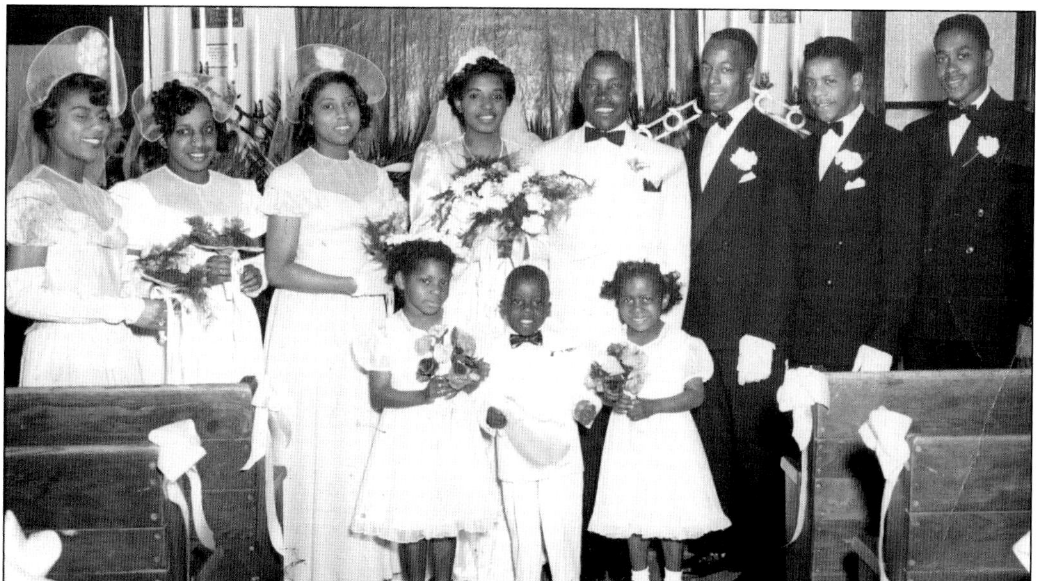

Benjamin and Josephine Lawson Gibbs bonded with three other married couples. They formed a social group called the '49ers. The couples—all married in 1949—were Wilby and Dorothy Askerneese, Rev. William Frank and Dorothy Matthews, and James and Helen Mitchell. The wedding ceremony of Benjamin and Josephine Lawson Gibbs (descendant of Underground Railroad operators) was held at the Church of God in Franklin on Easter Sunday, April 17, 1949. (Courtesy of Josephine Gibbs.)

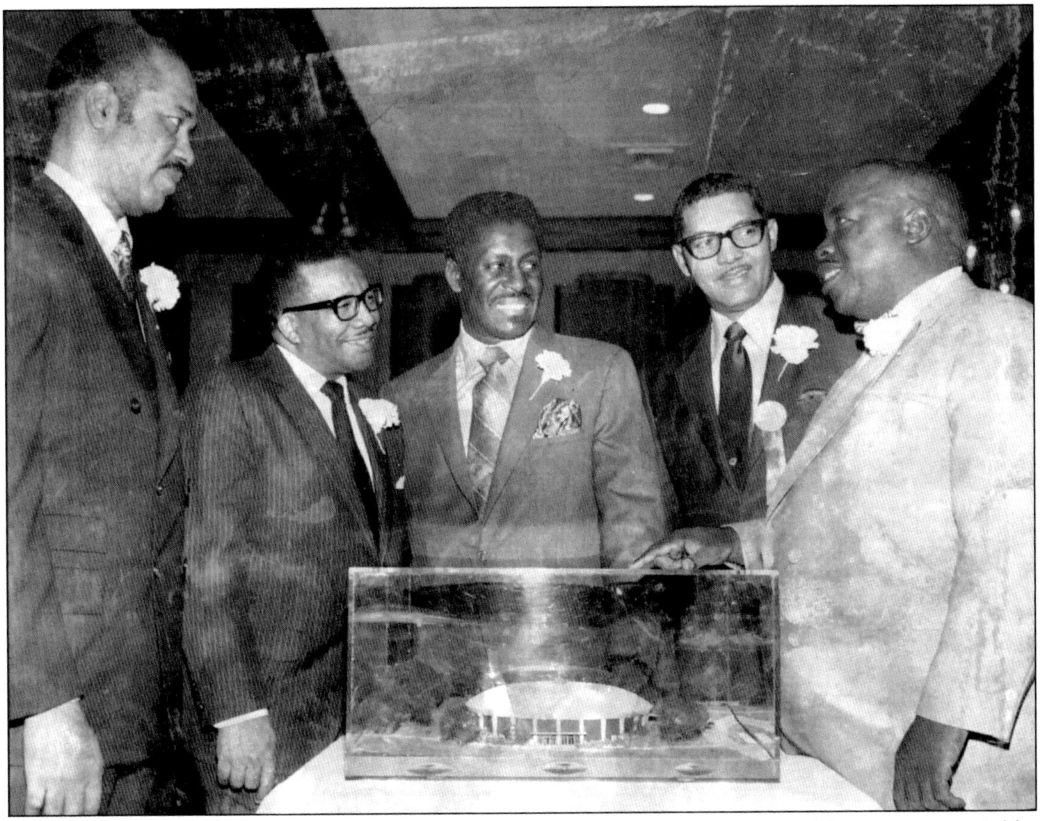

During the 1970s, several plans for a new, larger tabernacle were on the table. Benjamin Gibbs Sr. (1925–1987) served as campground manager. Pictured in 1972, campground boosters are, from left to right, Rev. Leonard Roache, Rev. Noah White, Wilby Askerneese, Rev. William Frank Matthews, and Gibbs. The men exhibit a proposed model for a tabernacle to be constructed down the hill from the current site. (Courtesy of Shirley Matthews Williams.)

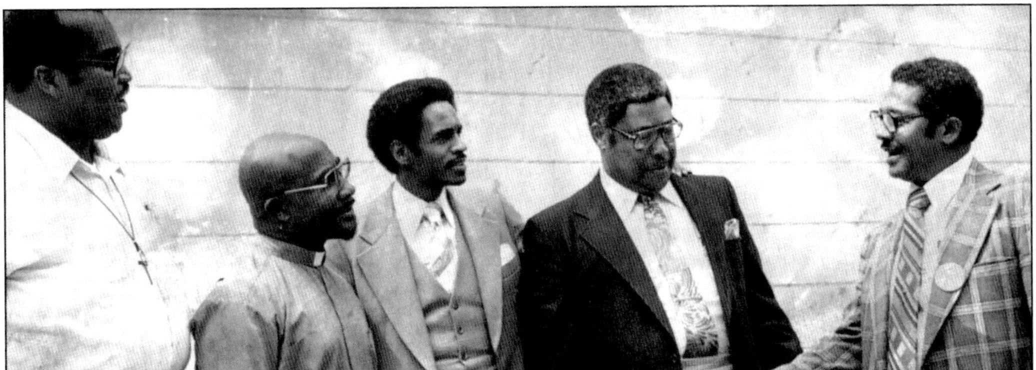

During the 1970s, Rev. William Frank Matthews was executive secretary of the National Association of the Church of God. Wilby Askerneese of Sharon invented an electrical remote transmitter. Gibbs, owner of Gibbs Demolition and Paving in Hermitage, served as campground manager and the chairman of the executive board of the national association from 1963 to 1971. Executive committee members are Rev. Benjamin Reid, Rev. Horace Shephard, Rev. Robert Culp, Rev. L. Wyatt, and Rev. William Frank Matthews.

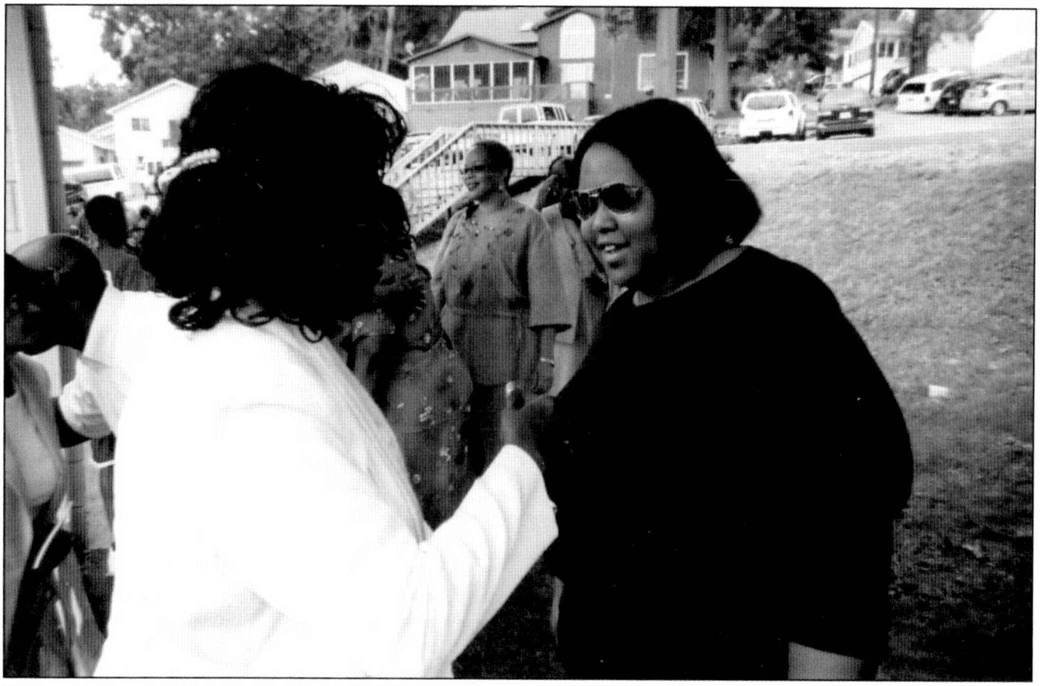

The campground has provided a location for many to rekindle friendships, hold celebrations, and host family gatherings. Congregants converse on a courtyard outside the tabernacle following service around 2007. In the background is Bishop Robert Davis's cottage.

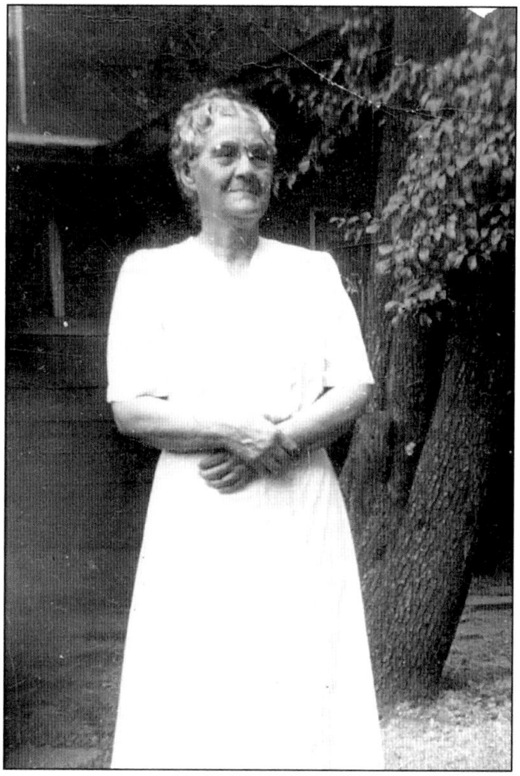

The dining hall, named in honor of Mary Belle Truman Terrell (1873–1960), is a center of fellowship. In 1917, Terrell was treasurer of the commissary committee for the first campground. At the same time, Matilda Derry Matthews (1842–1938) served as chairperson of the commissary committee for the first campground. Commissary committee members included secretary Elizabeth H. White and Laura Spraul Moore. Pictured is Terrell at her home. (Courtesy of Russell C. Phillips.)

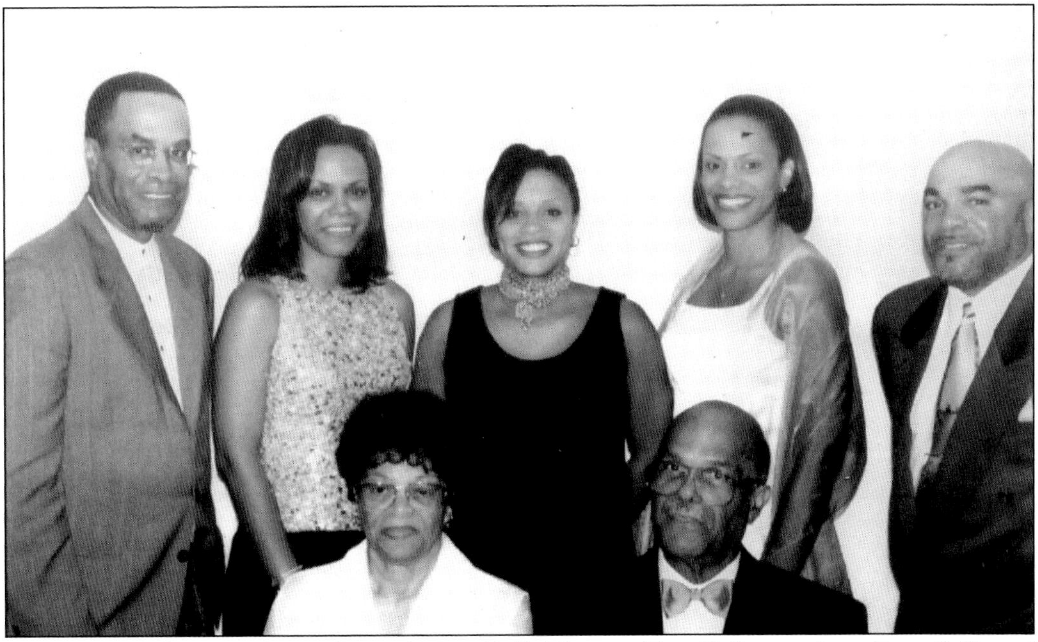

Russell C. Phillips is a descendant of Mary Belle Truman Terrell. Pictured are Russell C. and Mary Phillips and their adult children at their 50th wedding anniversary. The celebration was held at the Mary B. Terrell Dining Hall on the campground. (Courtesy of Russell C. Phillips.)

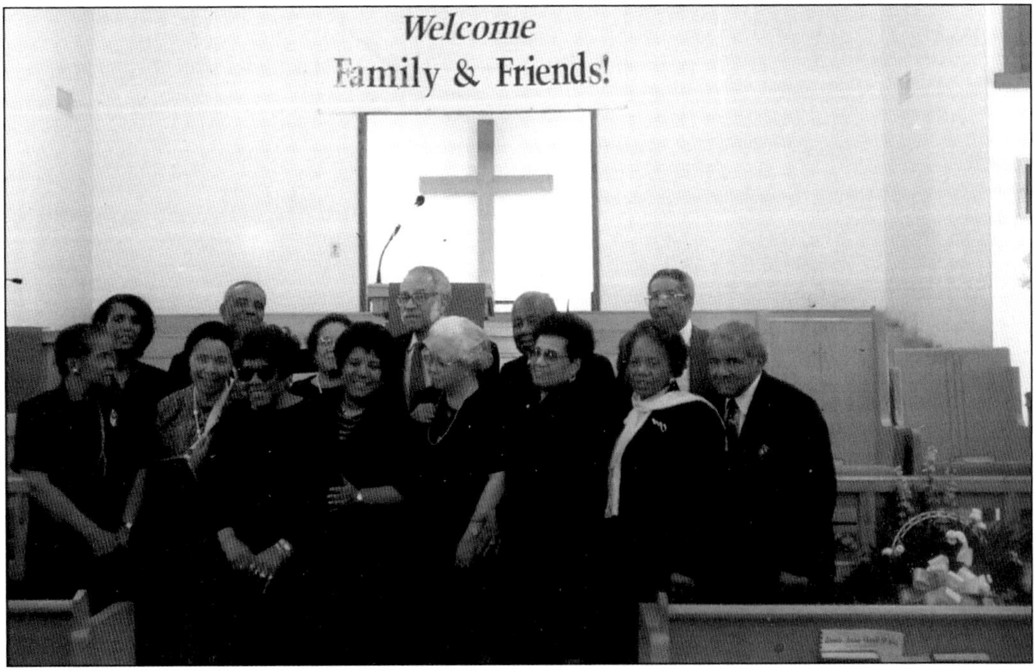

The Mitchell family, descendants of founder James Abraham Christman Sr., gathers for worship in Pittsburgh. Rev. Isaac Mitchell of Sharon served in various capacities for the national association. Robert Lee Mitchell and Charles R. Mitchell were recipients of the Esther B. Culp Distinguished Christian Service Award. Dr. Joyce Mitchell, former Sharon High School valedictorian, was recognized as one of the greatest thinkers in the nation. (Courtesy of Darlynna Thompson.)

Eight

Hermitage and Farrell
Frontiers after the 1960s

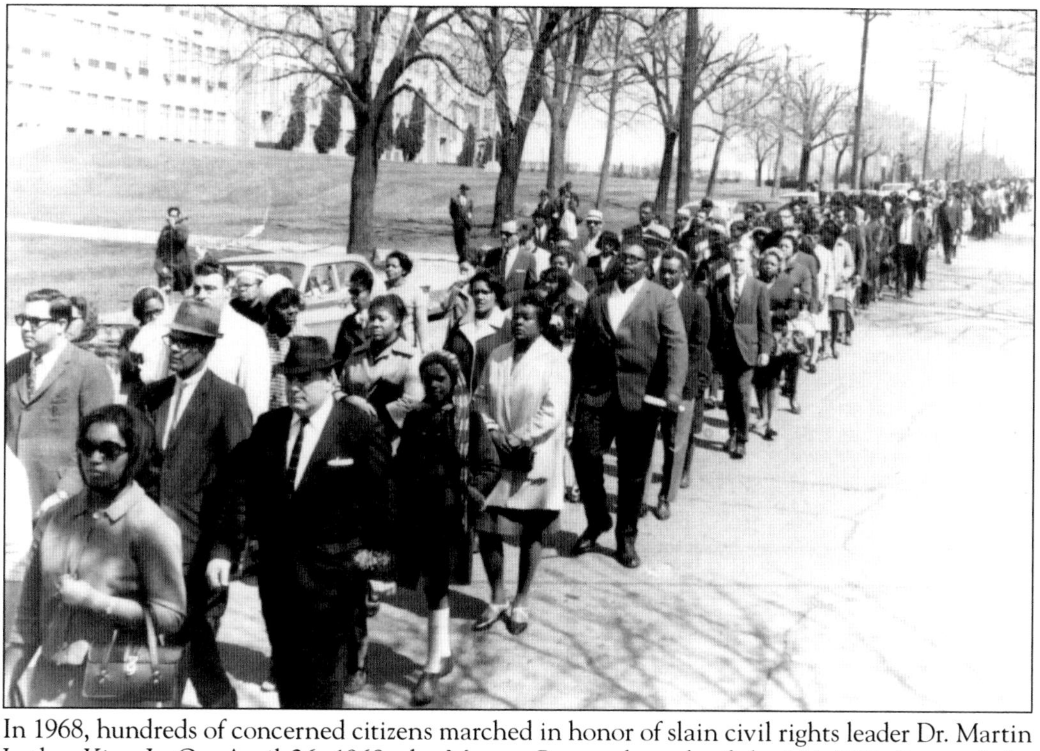

In 1968, hundreds of concerned citizens marched in honor of slain civil rights leader Dr. Martin Luther King Jr. On April 26, 1968, the Mercer County branch of the NAACP discussed the need for a local urban league. (Courtesy of Russell C. Phillips.)

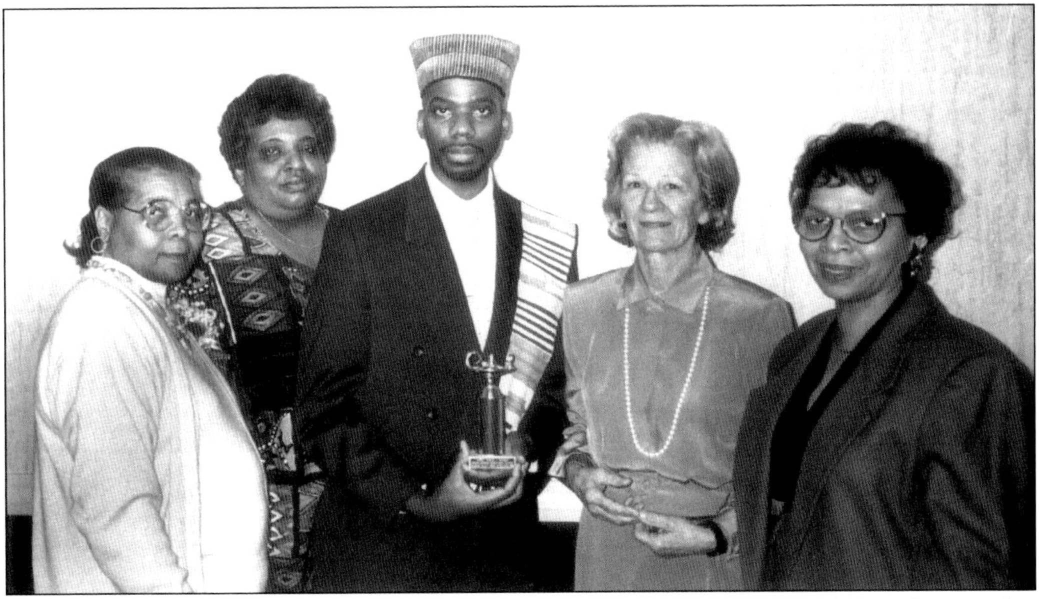

The SVUL, also known as the Instant Urban League, became operational in eight months. Pictured are, from left to right, Deanna M. R. Yarboro, Rose Mary Talbert, speaker Roland Barksdale-Hall, Donna Mort, and Mariam Sanders at the SVUL Guild's 20th annual African American history luncheon at Vellente's Restaurant in Hermitage in 1994. Barksdale-Hall holds the Learning Lamp that youths receive for essays. (Photograph by Bill Vidonic, courtesy of the Sharon Herald.)

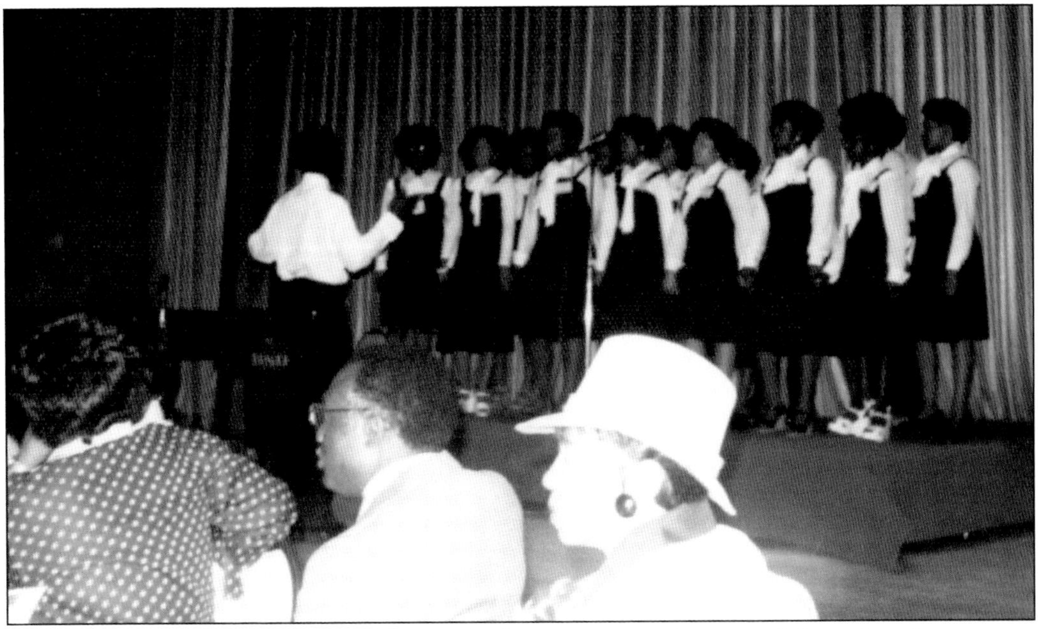

At the 1973 Hermitage banquet, Vernon Jordan, executive director of the urban league, was impressed with the SVUL youth choir performance. He invited the choir to perform at the annual National Urban League convention the following year. The SVUL youth choir, under the direction of Milton Blue, performs at the National Urban League convention in Boston in 1974. (Courtesy of Teresa Jefferson.)

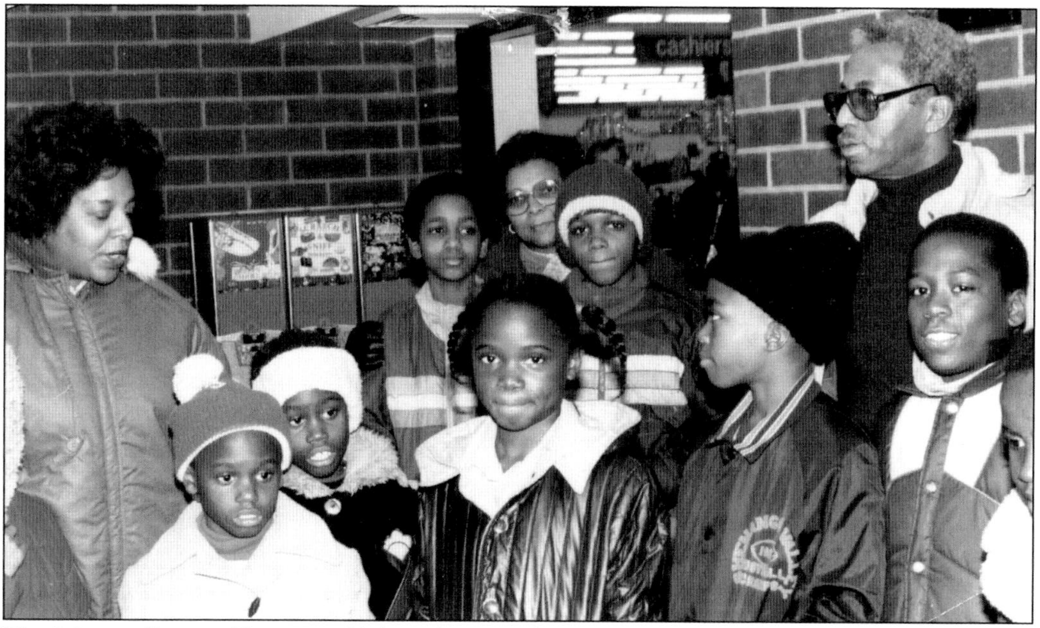

The Mercer County Frontiers Club and its auxiliary coordinating council take children on a shopping spree at Hill's Department Store in Hermitage around 1970. Gerald Mitchell, club president (back, right), Deanna M. R. Yarboro (back, center), and Mitchell's wife, Shirley (back, left), act as chaperones on the first of what became an annual event. Gerald Mitchell is a charter member of the Mercer County Frontiers Club. (Courtesy of Mercer County Frontiers Club.)

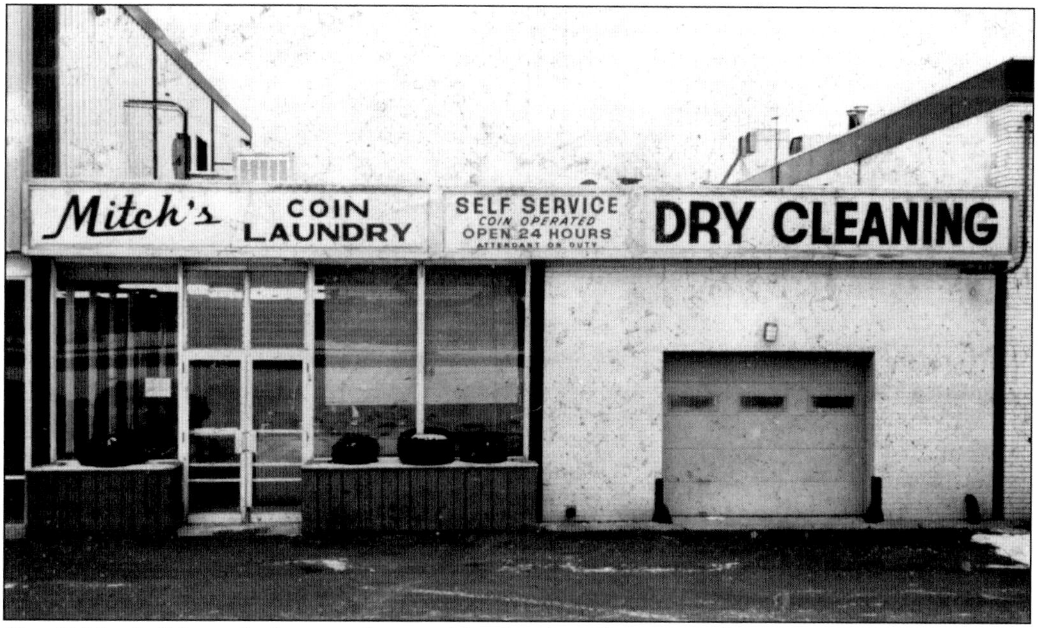

Gerald Mitchell branched out and opened his first laundry in Farrell in 1964. Four years later, he opened his second laundry in Sharon. He opened a full-service laundry, which provided drop-off and self-serve laundry at the cross section of two arteries in a major commercial corridor. He operated Mitch's Coin Laundry and Dry Cleaning at 3340 East State Street in Hermitage in the 1970s. (Courtesy of Gerald Mitchell.)

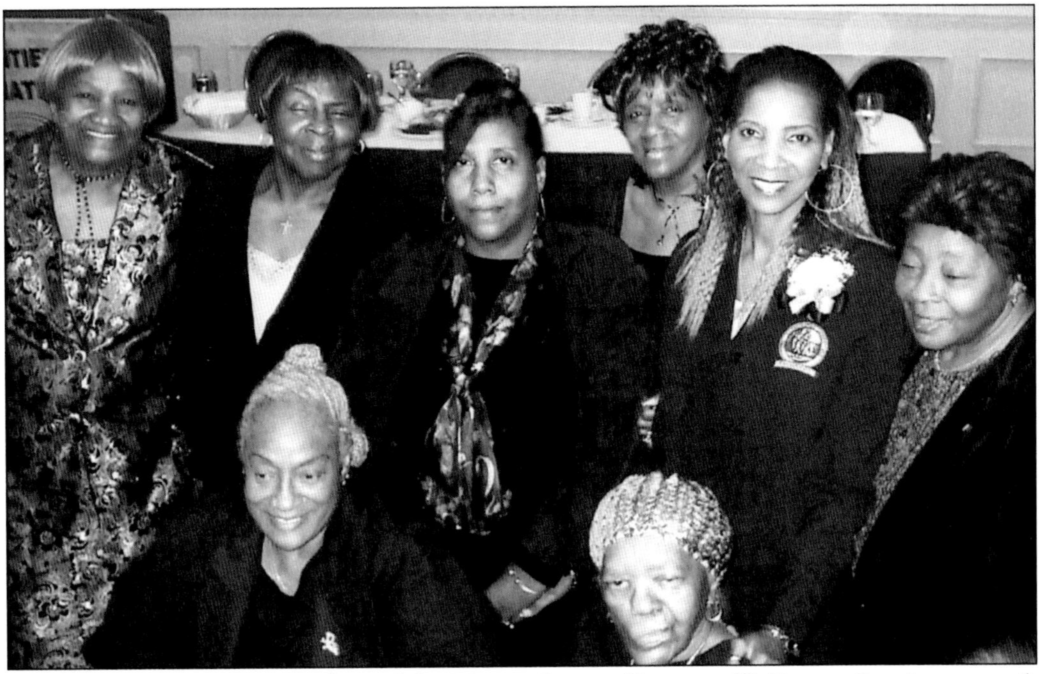

Ruth Jefferson, national president of the Mercer County Frontiers Club's coordinating council, receives a hearty welcome at the Mercer County Frontiers Club's 33rd annual awards program. Pictured at the Radisson Hotel in West Middlesex in 2007, council members are, from left to right, (first row) Jeanetta "Flossie" Holloway and Annie McMillan; (second row) Leila Bridges, Karen Weston, Angela Askerneese-Chavers, Janet Grear, ? Jefferson, and Senator McIntire. (Courtesy of Mercer County Frontiers Club Coordinating Council.)

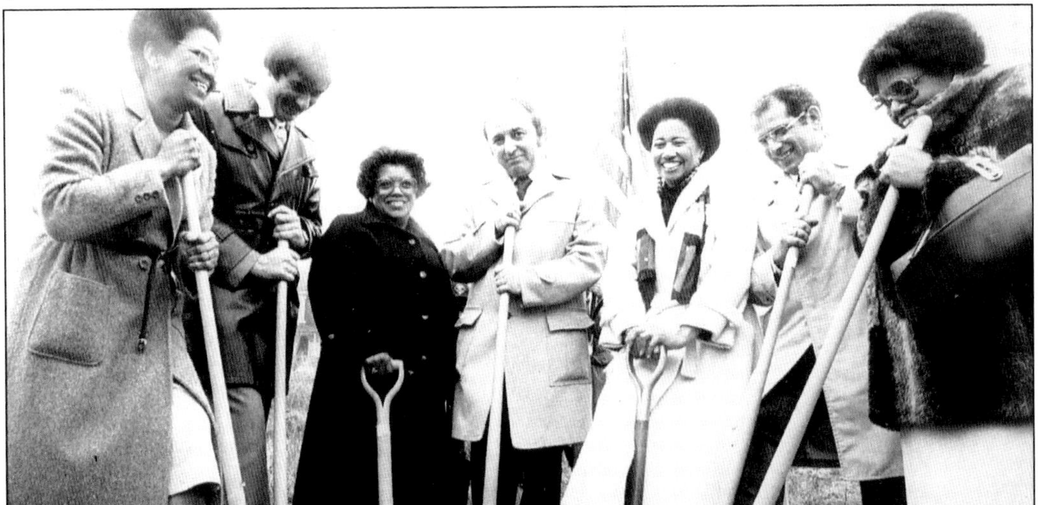

Southwest Gardens benefited from the leadership of Martha Alfred Richards (far left), Rosetta Satterwhite Ragster (third from left), and Mary Bruce Harvey (far right), who, along with Vera Smith, Nellion Ponder, attorney John Evans, and others, played a major role in the rehabilitation of a community. A milestone was the construction of the Henry W. Richards Southwest Gardens Memorial Center at 500 Darr Avenue in Farrell around 1980. (Courtesy of Martha Alfred Richards.)

In 1981, syndicated cartoonist Bill Murray began drawing *Sonny Boy* for the Sengstacke newspapers. He participated in a collective protest, organized by about 10 syndicated African American artists in 2008, which was in direct response to the majority of newspapers editors' perceived views of African American cartoonists' work as esoteric and easily replaceable. Today his editorial cartoons *Jet News* and *The Golden Years* appear in over 1,100 newspapers worldwide. (Courtesy of Bill Murray.)

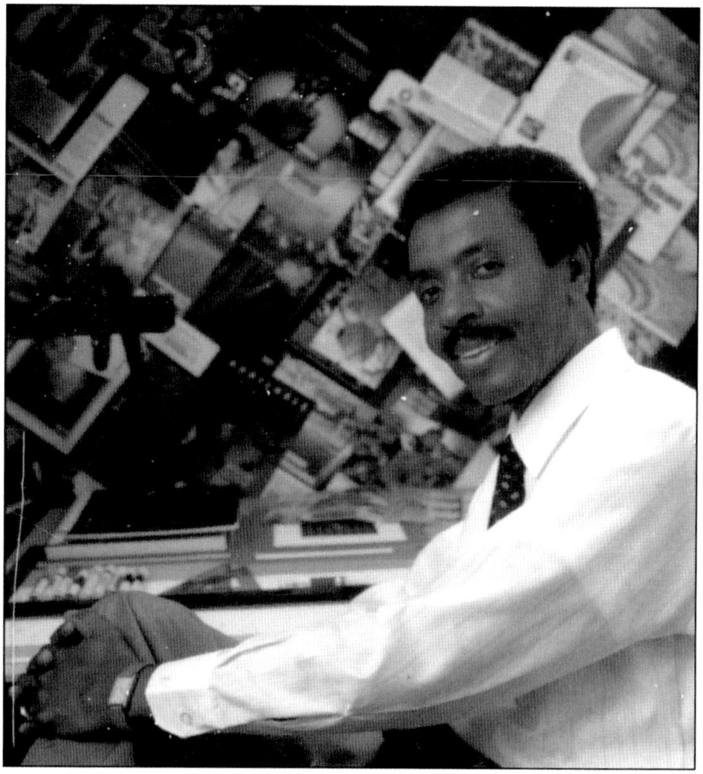

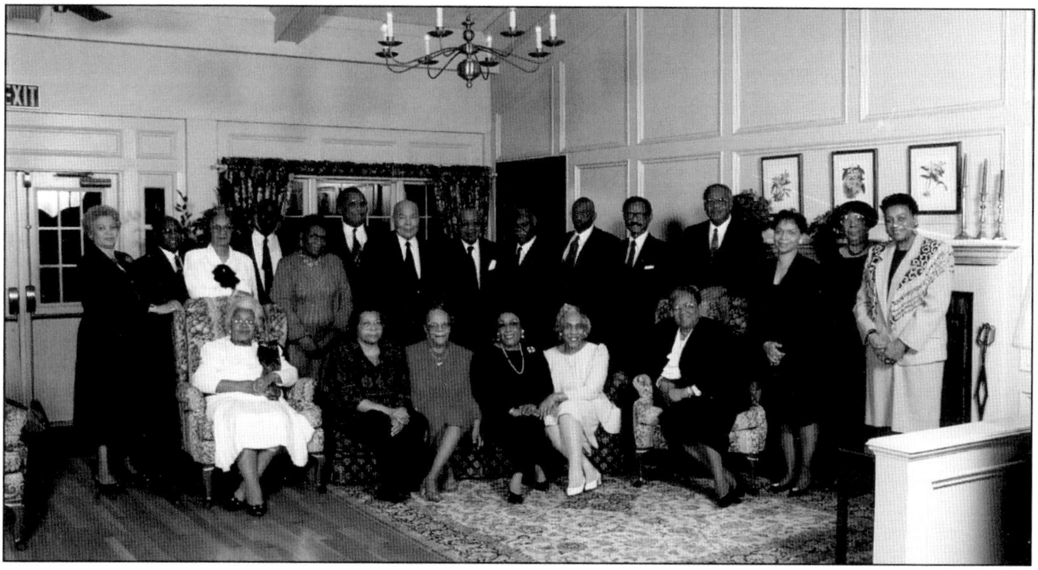

Stockholders of the Shenango Valley Services Investment and their guests are, from left to right, (first row) Bea Robinson, Deanna M. R. Yarboro, Donna Marie Lee, Cleo Lowe, Vivian Baker, and Martha Richards; (second row) Shirley Matthews Williams, Malloy Sanders, Ruth Ousley, Allen Williams, Bertha Robinson, L. Steven Robinson Sr., Lester Robinson Sr., Bennie Ousley, Dr. Theodore L. Yarboro, John L. Lee, George E. Lowe, D.D.S., Wilbert Shannon Sr., Mariam Sanders, Bernice Shannon, and Betty Marshall. This picture was taken on March 16, 1996, at the Avalon Inn in Warren, Ohio. (Courtesy of Dr. Theodore L. Yarboro.)

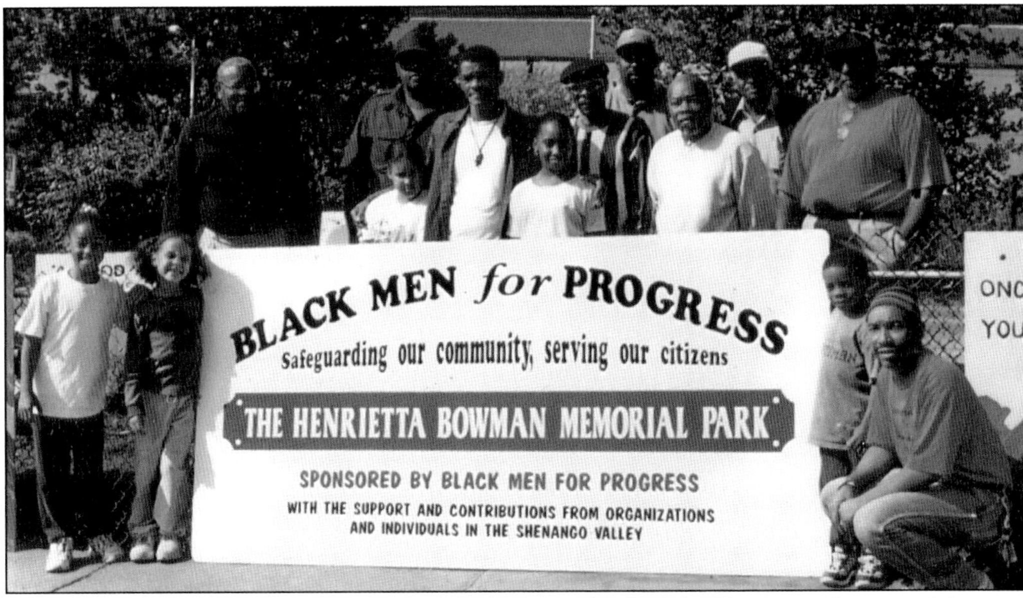

Black Men for Progress (BMP), an advocacy group, established the Henrietta Bowman Memorial Park on Market Avenue in Farrell to promote literacy. Henrietta Bowman (1904–1970), a charter member of the Crowder-Stewart Blue Star Mothers, was a tireless youth advocate at the Carver Community Center. Pictured are, from left to right, Ron Weston, Juan Houston, Raymond Wilson, Billie Gunn, Michael Harris, Joe Moss, Elbert Otey, Forest Underwood, and BMP president Milton Wilson (front, kneeling). (Courtesy of Milton Wilson.)

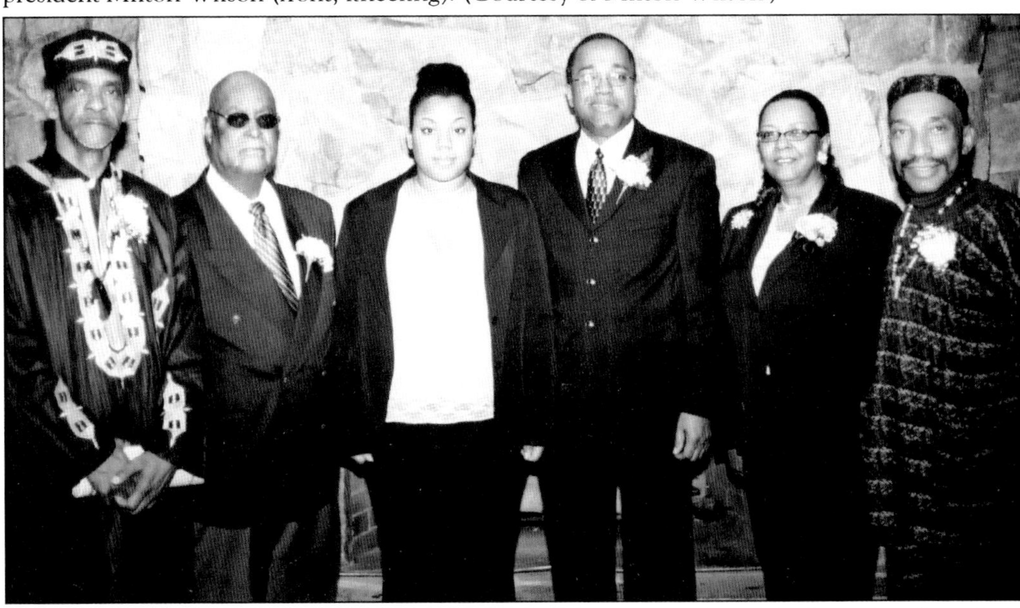

A section of the business corridor was renamed Martin Luther King Boulevard in Farrell due to Dea. Donald Wright of Bethlehem Baptist Church, although Hermitage and Sharon did not positively respond to requests. Mercer County Frontiers Club honorees are pictured at the Rosemont Banquet Center in Sharon in 2006. From left to right are Raymond E. Wilson, Wright, Lindsay Ellebie, Dale K. Adair, M.D., Jacqueline Gates, and Milton Wilson. (Courtesy of Mercer County Frontiers Club.)

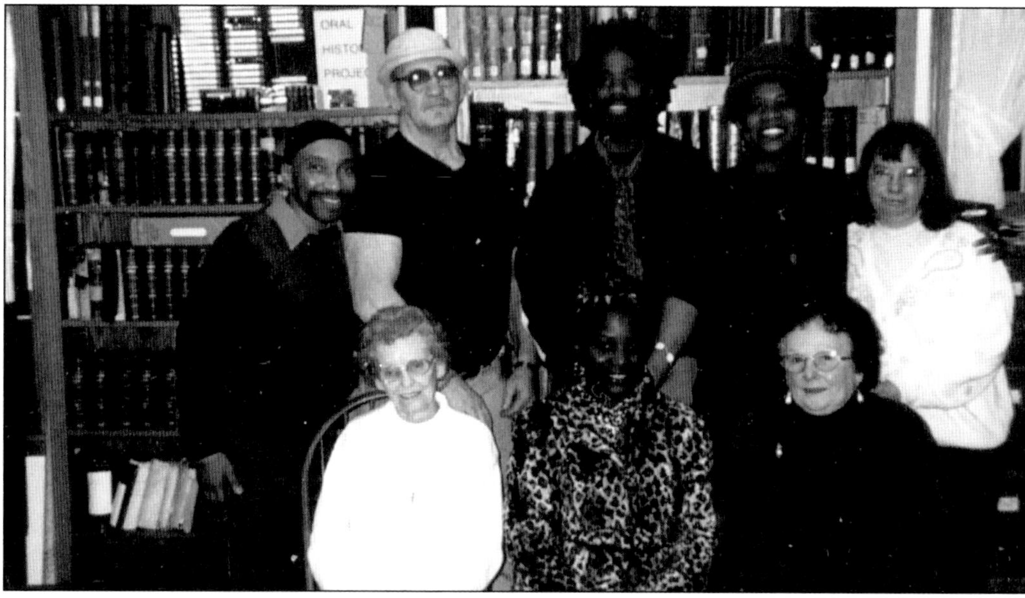

The preservation of the African American experience in Mercer County committee held a joint meeting with the Underground Railroad group in 2001. Mercer County Historical Society director William Philson displayed a black woolen shawl likely made by a runaway slave in Liberia that is part of the historical society's collection. Members are, from left to right, (first row) unidentified, Charlene Anderson, and unidentified; (second row) Milton Wilson, unidentified, Roland Barksdale-Hall (moderator), Dr. Kimberly Richards, and Gail Habbyshaw.

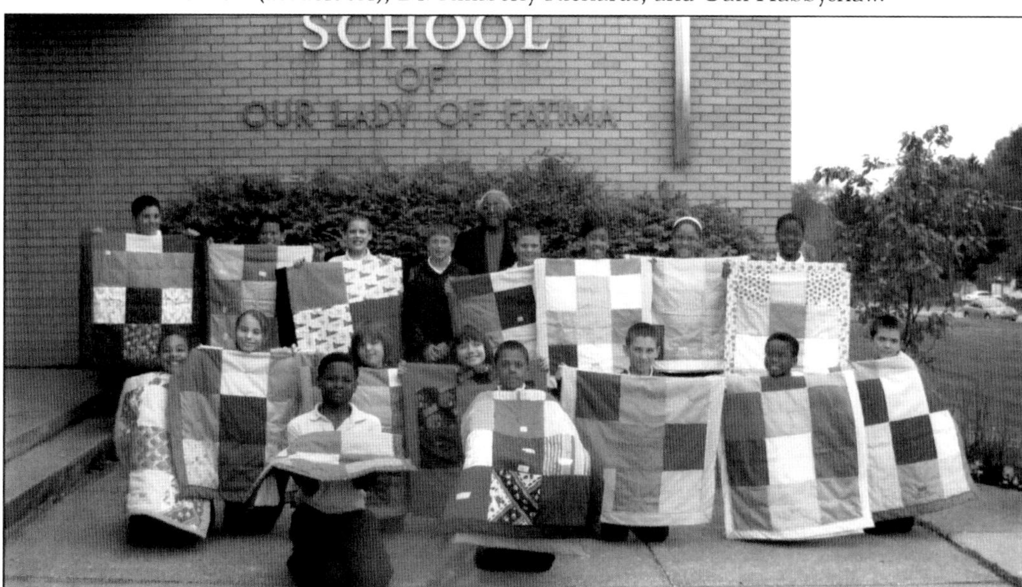

The 1994 Black History Month observance saw the first meeting about the preservation of the African American experience in Mercer County, convened by Roland Barksdale-Hall at the Henry W. Richards Southwest Gardens Center in Farrell. Pioneer Hermitage teacher Rev. Willie E. Peagler (back, center) exposed the next generation to traditional quilting. Hermitage educators included Joyce Barlow, Guy Gibbs, Leonard Hall, and Jeanette Whitehead. (Courtesy of Msgr. Geno Monti School of Our Lady of Fatima.)

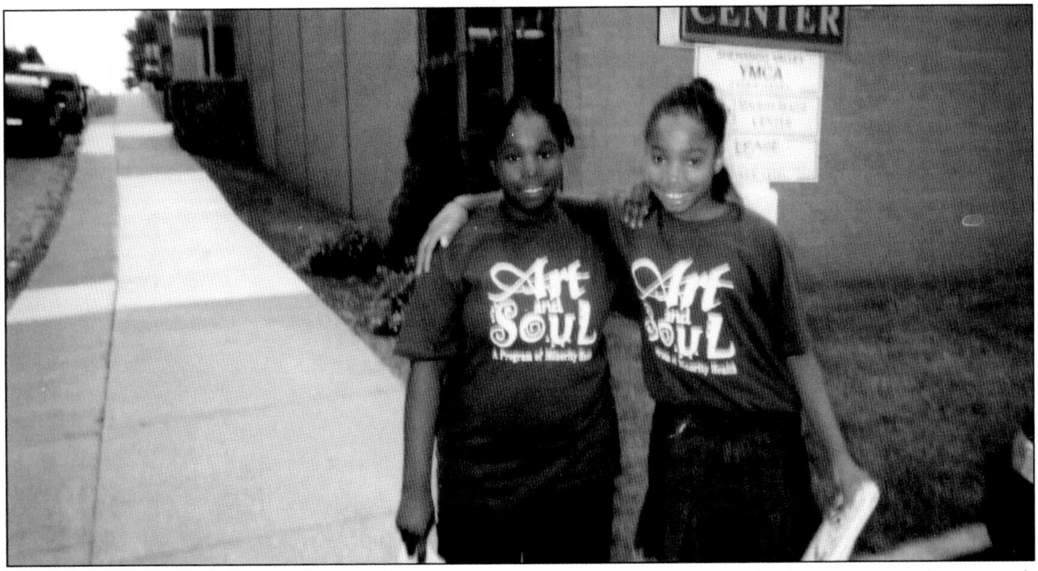

Youth enrichment is the focus of the Mercer County branch of the NAACP's youth council. Sponsored by the Mercer County branch of the NAACP, Roland Barksdale-Hall, Donna Marie Lee, and Charlotte Pegues previewed more than $1,000 worth of biographical works about famous African Americans that were distributed to children at Greater Mount Zion Church of God in Christ in Farrell during Kwanzaa in 1996. Youth participated in yearlong enrichment at the Robert Chavers Community Center, previously known as the F. H. Buhl Memorial Center, in Farrell.

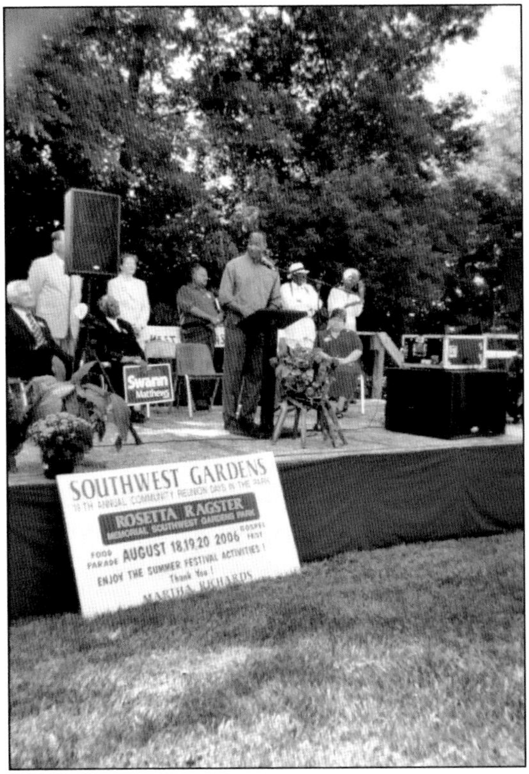

African American leadership created a safe environment for youth to grow and develop. The owners of Gibbs Demolition and Paving, Benjamin and Josephine Lawson Gibbs, and their family established a community in Hermitage. Lynn Swann stumps during his bid for governor at the Rosetta Satterwhite Ragster Park in Farrell in 2006.

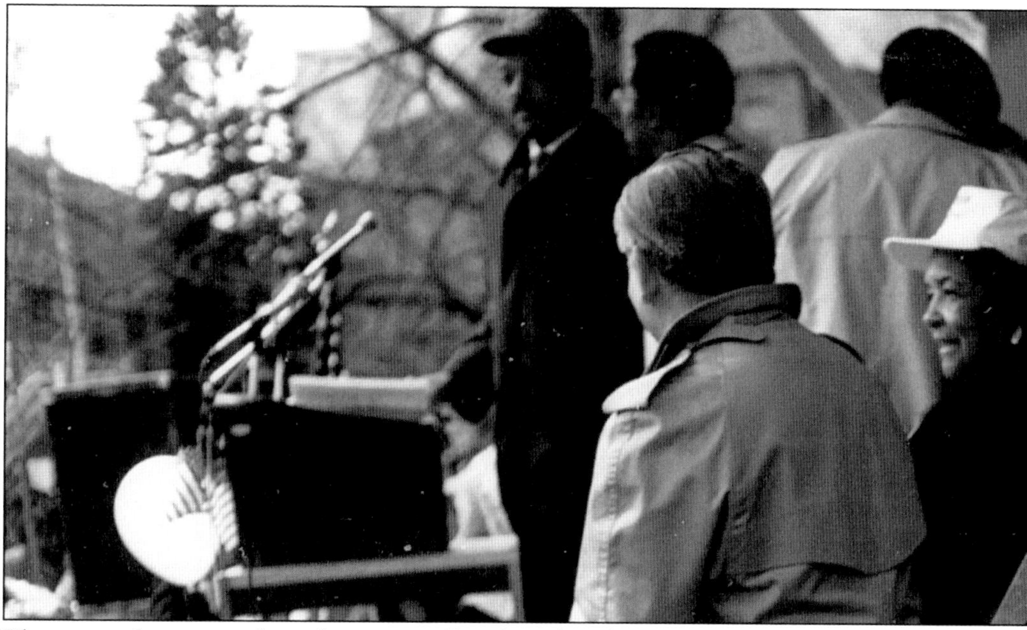

The atmosphere was electrifying as well-wishers lined Spearman Avenue during Rev. Jesse Jackson's run for president in 1983. Jackson prepares to address the audience at the Second Baptist Missionary Church in Farrell. Rev. Dr. Carroll M. Felton Jr., pastor of the Second Baptist Missionary Church, was instrumental in bringing Jackson and former U.S. congresswoman Shirley Chisholm to Farrell. (Courtesy of Toby and Dorothy Jackson.)

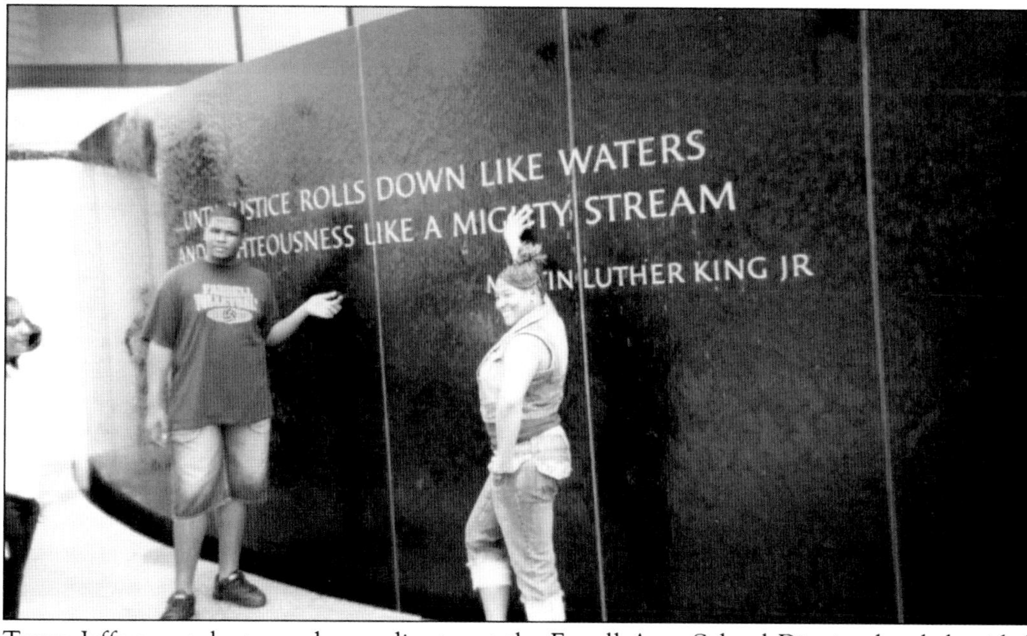

Teresa Jefferson, talent search coordinator at the Farrell Area School District, has led guided tours for Historically Black College and University (HBCU) and historic civil rights sites. Several Shenango Valley students have received exposure to their heritage and attended HBCU events. The Mercer County Frontiers Club cosponsored the HBCU bus tour. On the HBCU heritage tour, youth visit the King Center in Atlanta in 2007.

2005 SCHEDULE

Juneteenth - A Celebration of Freedom

Juneteenth is the oldest African American Holiday. June 19, 1865 is the date that that word of freedom finally reached the slaves in Texas, some two and a half years after slavery was abolished. Historians have written that slaves had a major role and took great risks in helping to bring about their own emancipation. As a result, many lives were sacrificed for the freedom that allows African Americans to be all they can be today. When word of freedom reached the slaves, there was great joy and many celebrations - the way Juneteenth and the celebration of freedom continues to be observed today.

On April 10, 1997, the United States adopted legislation officially recognizing June 19th as Juneteenth Independence Day and encouraging its observance. Passage of Juneteenth In-

9:00 a.m. Lineup of Parade Participants

10:30 a.m. Parade Procession Begins

<u>Mistress/Master of Ceremony:</u>

Tiffany Holden ~12:00 p.m.

Leon Harrison ~ 3:00 p.m.

12:00 Welcome:
Deputy Mayor Lou Falconi

12:15 Opening Prayer: Tiffany Holden

12:20 Negro National Anthem:
Billy Jean Jackson

12:30 Reading of Emancipation Proclamation:
Roland Barksdale-Hall

2 ~ 2:30 Presentation of Essay Awards
(1st, 2nd, & 3rd Prizes)

2:30 ~ 4:30 Gospel Groups:
(in no particular order)
Saint D
Judah
Charlene Johnson
Shenango Valley Praise Team
Mt. Olive Baptist Male Chorus
Greater Mt. Zion COGIC Kingdom Builder's Choir

4:30 ~ 5:30 Community Line Dancing:
Destiny International

5:30 ~ 6:30 Talent Showcase
Coordinated by:
Kavon Wright and Adrienne Gordon

The 2005 Juneteenth celebrated African American fathers. Juneteenth National Freedom Day is the oldest African American liberation emancipation celebration, which recalls the arrival of Maj. Gen. Gordon Granger and the Union soldiers who arrived in Galveston, Texas, with the announcement that the Civil War had concluded and all slaves were free on June 19, 1865. This event commenced the celebration of Juneteenth and led to the holiday's name.

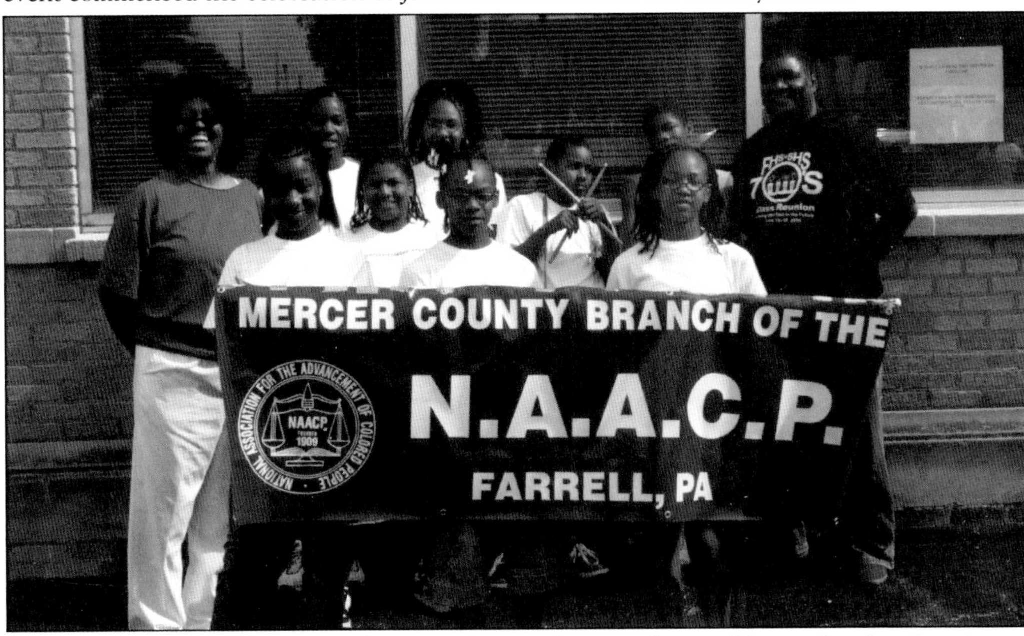

The Mercer County branch of the NAACP youth council assembles under the direction of Monica Williams and Alexander Robinson at the staging area in front of the SVUL on Indiana Avenue in Farrell. By 1931, the first Mercer County branch youth council was organized. The first president was William Houston, and the first secretary was Sara Dillard Austin. (Courtesy of Veral Adair.)

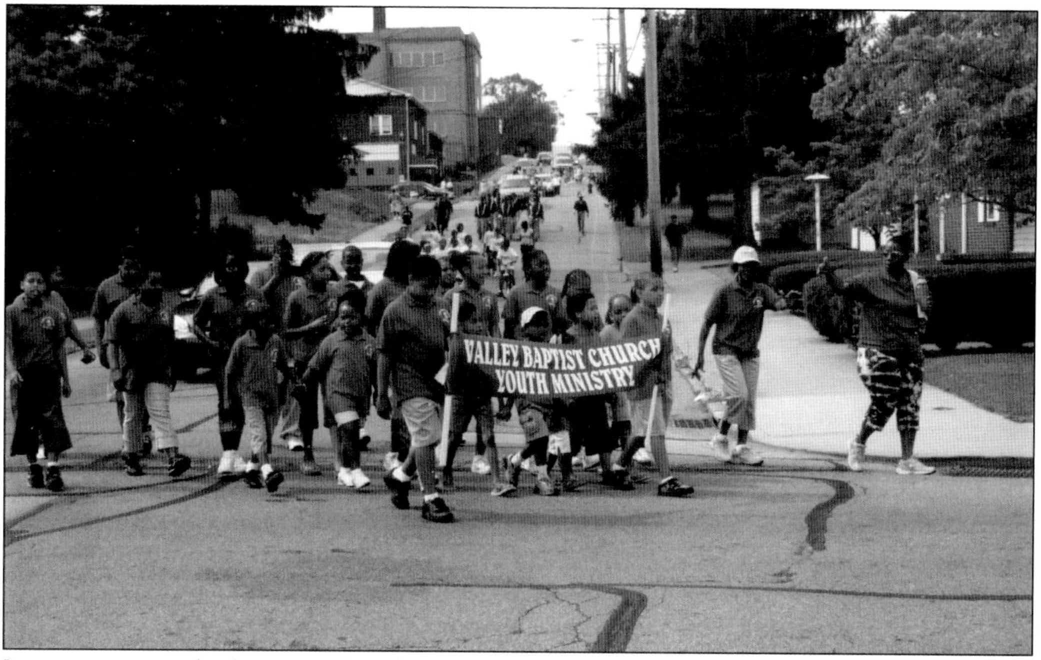

In recent times, both national and local Juneteenth organizations have contributed to an increase in cultural awareness. The parade heads down the hill from Indiana Avenue and turns onto Roemer Boulevard with rousing Valley Baptist Church Youth Ministry and Farrell/Sharon stomp teams stealing the show. (Courtesy of Veral Adair.)

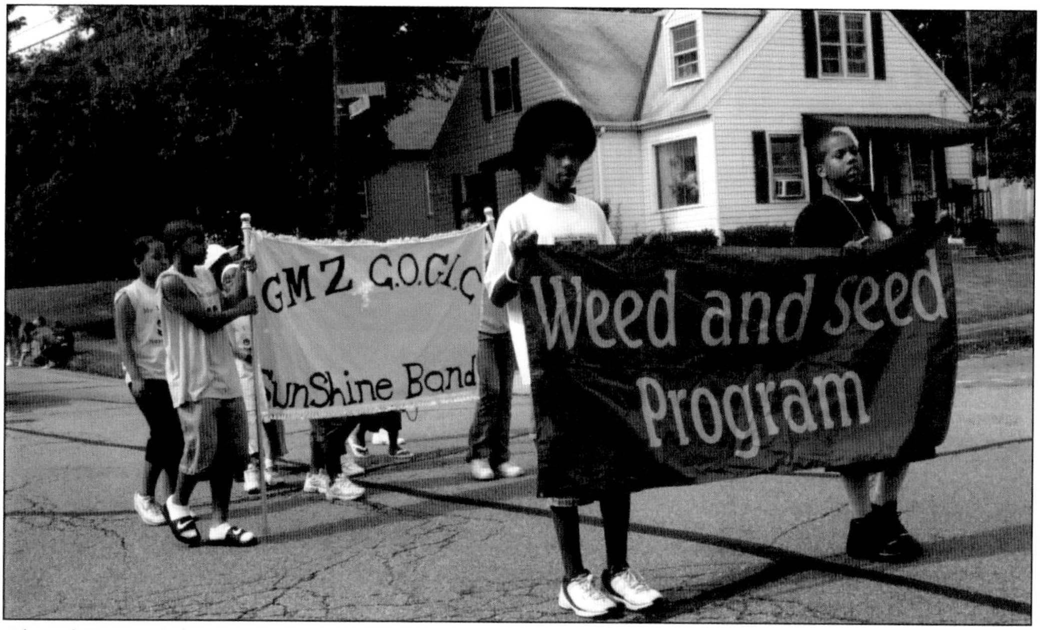

Cheryl King of the SVUL was instrumental in bringing the Juneteenth National Freedom Day celebration to the community. The holiday has taken on a variety of expressions from parades to commemoration programs. Youth groups from Weed and Seed and the Greater Mount Zion Sunshine Band march down Roemer Boulevard. The destination is Veteran's Square. (Courtesy of Veral Adair.)

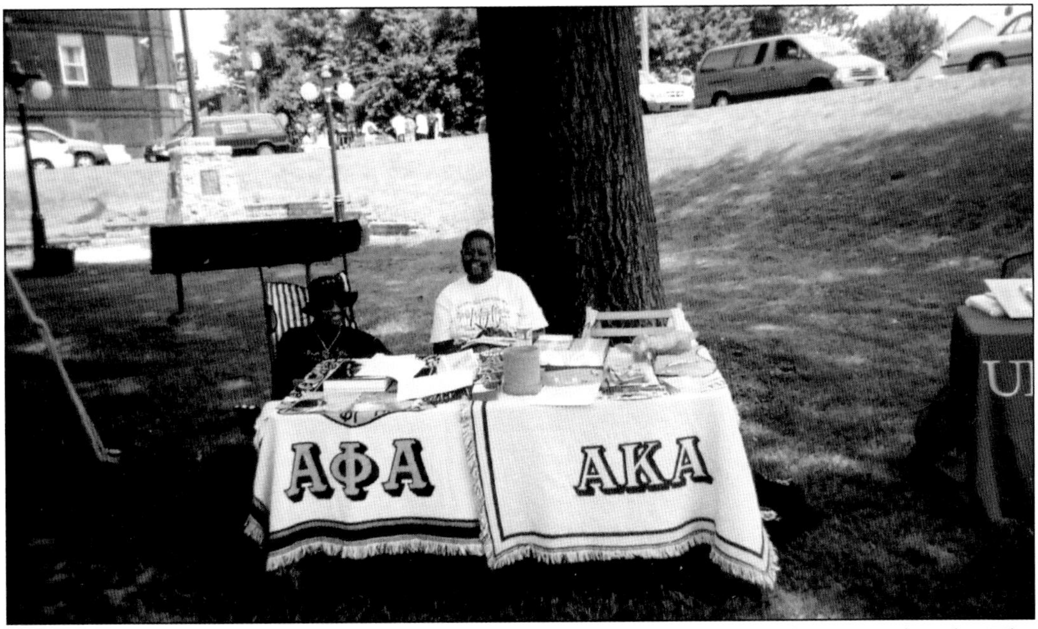

Alpha Phi Alpha fraternity and Alpha Kappa Alpha sorority man the information booths. The 2008–2010 president of the Epsilon Mu Omega chapter of Alpha Kappa Alpha in Youngstown, Ohio, is Theresa L. Yarboro. Her mother, Deanna M. R. Yarboro, is a former chapter president. Active members include Deanna (Dee-Dee) Yarboro Brown, Gloria Jefferson, and Danese Keller Wright.

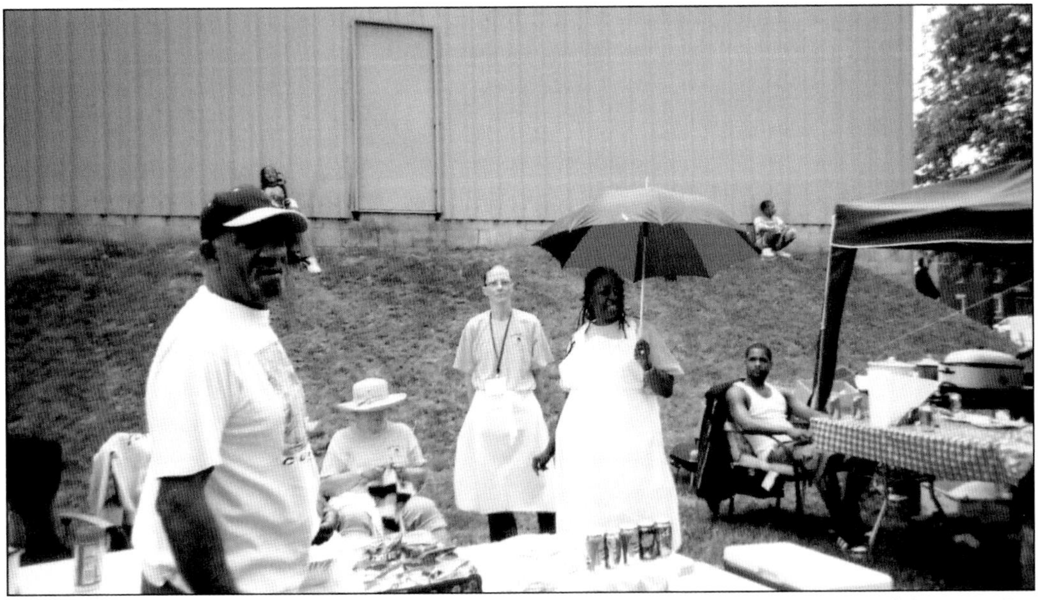

Farrell's Juneteenth National Freedom Day celebration was a cultural awareness celebration. Dr. Martha Bruce and Rev. Willie Eva Peagler exhibited on African dress and naming practices. Food vendors sponsored by Valley Baptist Church, Bethlehem Baptist Church, and Ruth African Methodist Episcopal Zion Church youth ministries, Sankofa House, and Southwest Gardens Economic Development Center tried to beat the heat. Lynda Moss-McDougal, the executive director of the Sankofa House, holds an umbrella.

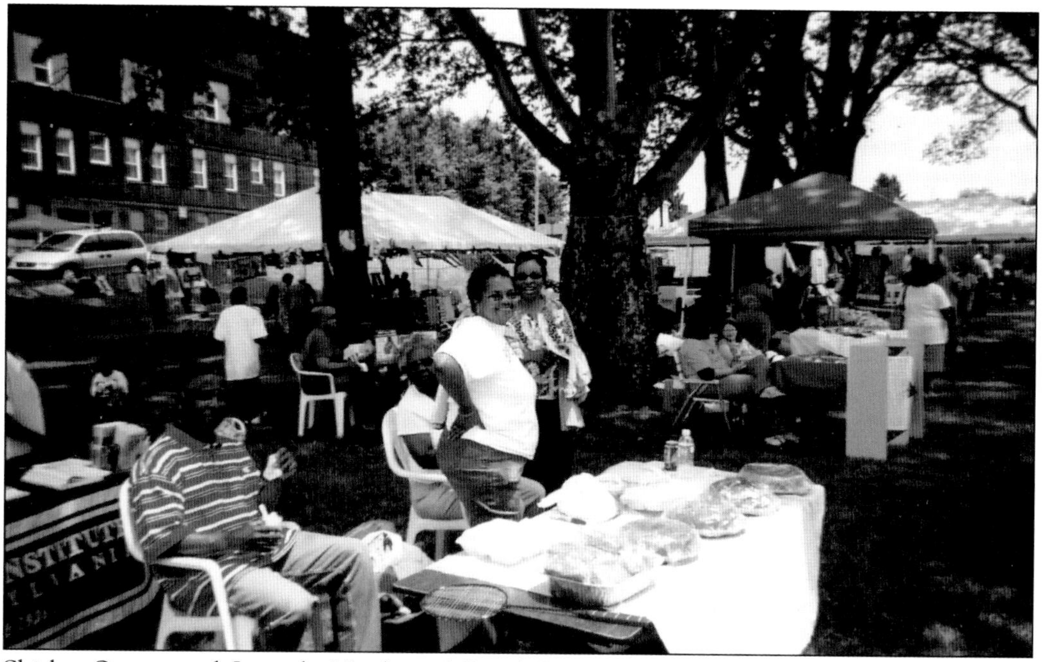

Shirley Owens and Javonda Harden of Royal Designs dressed in traditional African garb and talked about black hair. Families collectively worked booths with finger-licking ribs, mouthwatering sweet potato pie, and Italian ice. Rev. Jerry Graham, his wife, Lori, and his mother man the booth with homemade pies and cakes.

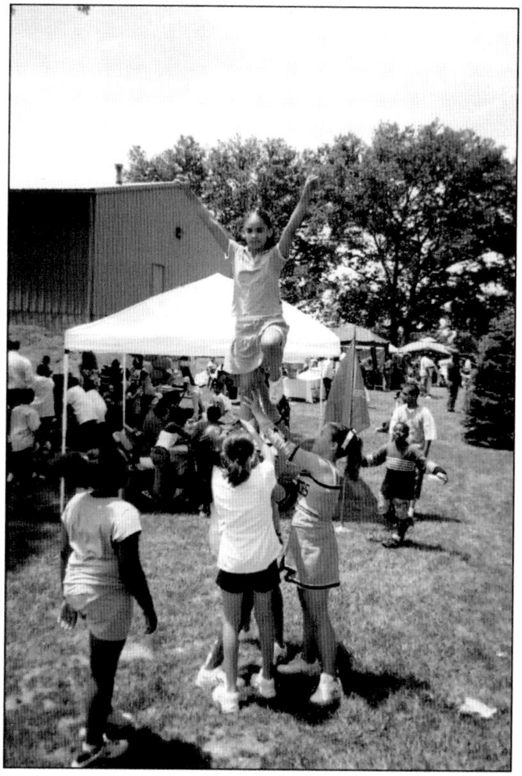

Youth laughed and danced the electric slide. Activities included the Greater Mount Zion Church of God in Christ youth bouncer, the LLP Graphics play station, and Party Zone youth games. The Panthers, a competitive cheerleading team, show off their talent at Veteran's Square in Farrell.

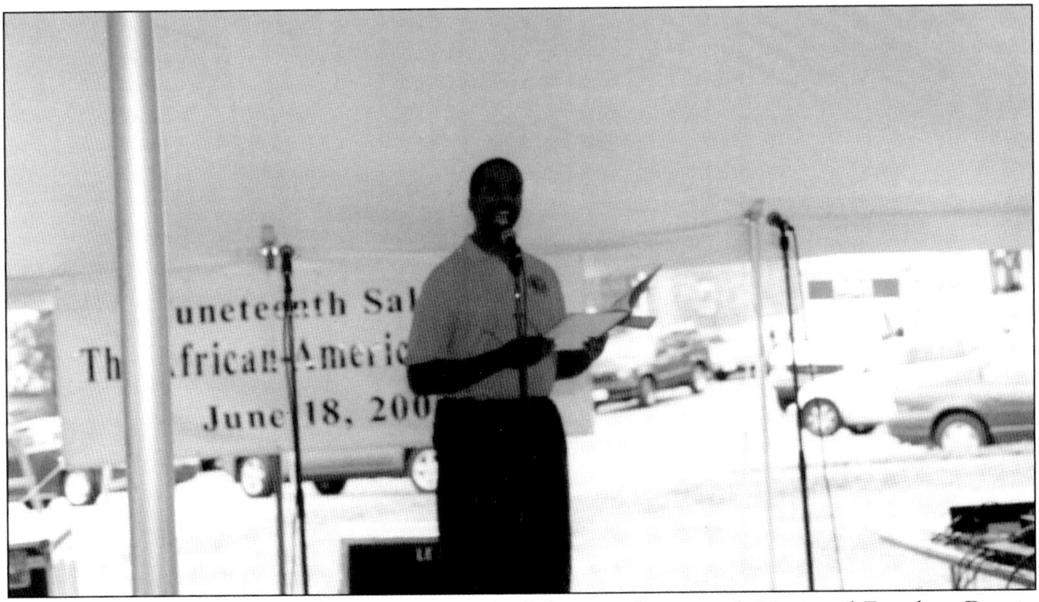

The year 2009 marks the 15th anniversary of celebrating Juneteenth National Freedom Day in the Shenango Valley. The Juneteenth National Freedom Day celebration has taken on a variety of expressions from parades and commemoration programs to cookouts and dances. Yet the prominent feature remains the reading of the Emancipation Proclamation and a reflection upon the significance of freedom. Roland Barksdale-Hall reads the Emancipation Proclamation under the pavilion.

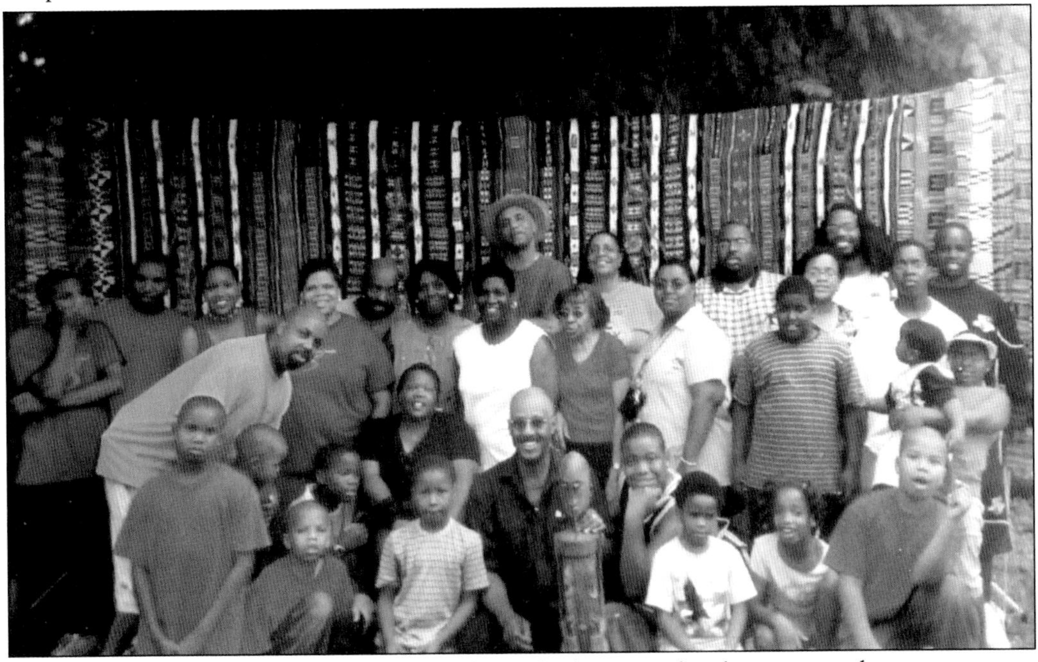

Farrell's celebration was much like a down-home barbecue or family reunion where guests were treated to a sweet atmosphere complete with tasty aromas, gospel music, and well-wishers, including Pennsylvania state representative Mark Longietti. Pictured are the descendants of Etania Steverson at a reunion in Farrell.

In inaugurating Barack Obama as the 44th president of the United States of America on January 20, 2009, "Free at last, free at last" rolled from the hilltops as descendants of slaves and slave owners joined hands, crossed over the Jordan River, and entered the promised land. Shown is the Obama campaign headquarters in Sharpsville.

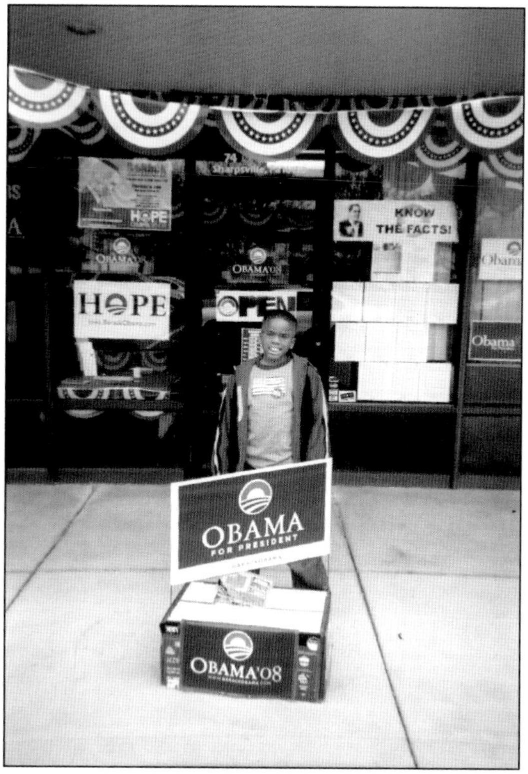

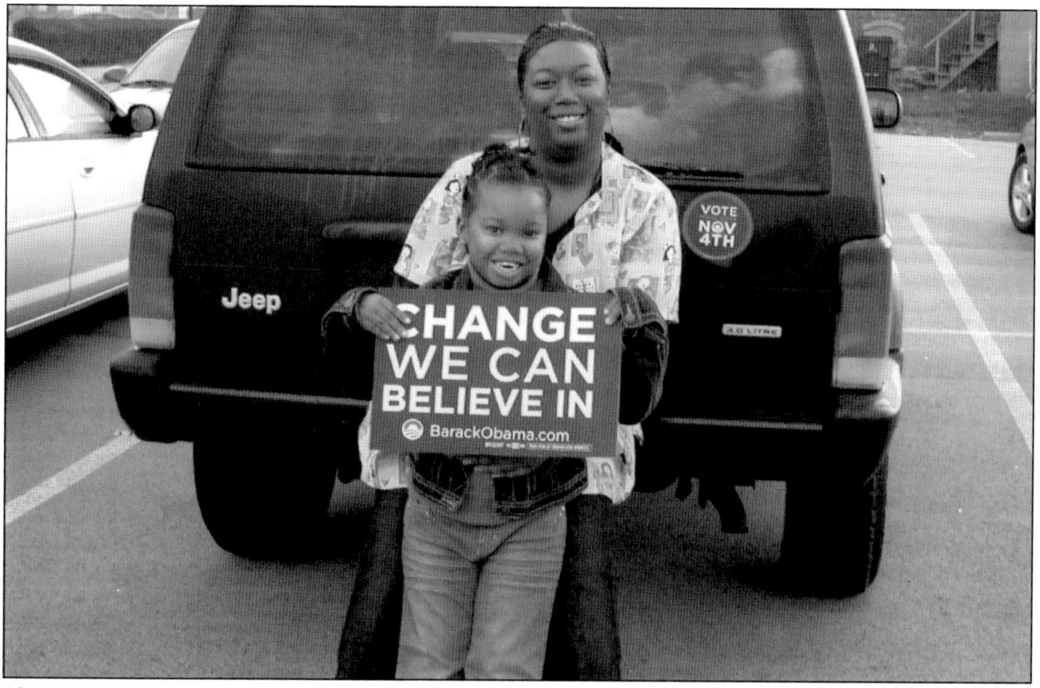

Shown outside the Second Baptist Missionary Church polling station, Americans express a revived hope in "truth, liberty and the pursuit of happiness." Let freedom ring. (Courtesy of Second Baptist Missionary Church.)